The Third Adam

JERZY PETERKIEWICZ

The Third Adam

LONDON

Oxford University Press

1975

Oxford University Press, Ely House, London W.1

GLASGOW NEW YORK TORONTO MELBOURNE WELLINGTON
CAPE TOWN IBADAN NAIROBI DAR ES SALAAM LUSAKA ADDIS ABABA
DELHI BOMBAY CALCUTTA MADRAS KARACHI LAHORE DACCA
KUALA LUMPUR SINGAPORE HONG KONG TOKYO

ISBN 0 19 212198 7

Printed in Great Britain
by W & J Mackay Limited, Chatham

To the children of
the mystical marriages
with great affection, and understanding

Contents

Plates

ILLUSTRATIONS IN THE TEXT

Acknowledgements

I wish to express my deepest gratitude to Archbishop Rafael (Wojciechowski) of Felicjanów and Bishop Innocenty (Gołębiowski) of Plock, to Sister Felicyta (Tułaba) of Plock and Sister Leonia of Warsaw for letting me use their collections of Mariavite publications, manuscripts, and photographs. Without their generous help and testimony a greater part of this book could not have been written. I am equally indebted to Mr. Filip Jerzy Feldman (now in Geneva) who offered me copies of his father's unpublished memoirs and notes. His kindness, patience, and willingness to provide me with information contributed much to my initial researches. The above-mentioned persons, however, are not responsible for my opinions or for any errors of fact.

I would have liked to record the full names of other people who have kindly allowed me to use their Mariavite material, in particular Sister Miłość and Brother Augustine, an English priest now in retirement, but both prefer to be known by their Mariavite names only. Alas, the help of many Mariavite or ex-Mariavite priests and priestesses cannot be acknowledged even in this way. When interviewed, they explicitly asked me to protect their anonymity. So did the children born of the mystical marriages, whose evidence was of primary importance to me. I agreed to change their Christian names in the book, but may I at least mention the admirable Maria whose character and integrity epitomize for me the spiritual qualities of Mariavitism.

Outside the Mariavite circles, I would like to thank Emeritus Archbishop Dr. A. Rinkel of Utrecht, Prelate A. Murat, Rector W. Gastpary of Chrześcijańska Akademia Teologiczna in Warsaw, Dr. Barbara Koc of Biblioteka Narodowa in Warsaw, Dr. K. Lewicki of Biblioteka Jagiellońska in Cracow, Mrs. Janina Cunnelly, and last but not least, Mr. Z. Deczyński and Mr. K. Askanas, both distinguished lawyers in Poland.

My very special thanks go to Catharine Carver and Jon Stallworthy whose encouragement and advice during the years of my work on this book meant so much to me as true signs of friendship.

J.P.

AUTHOR'S NOTE

I have used anglicized forms for all Christian names throughout the text; thus I speak of John Michael and not Jan Michał Kowalski, of Philip and not Filip Feldman. The name Maria, however, has been retained, whether it refers to priestesses or to priests as it does in Polish. Moreover, it helps to remind one of its connection with the word *Mariavite*.

The Little Mother's surname, Kozlowska, is spelt without the crossed 'l'. So is Plock, the cradle of the Mariavite movement, and the surnames of certain well-known historical figures, as Pilsudski and Slowacki. Towianski is spelt without a diacritical mark, as is Zebrowski. The better-known Polish towns, like Warsaw, Cracow, and Lodz, appear in their accepted English forms.

Translations of Polish sources quoted in the text are my own unless acknowledged otherwise. The place of publication, for English works mentioned in footnotes, is London unless otherwise indicated.

J.P.

Prologue

I WAS nearly ten when I heard about the abominable Mariavites, but children, it seems, take longer to be scandalized than their elders. It took me a week to convince myself that the Mariavites were real people and not goblins, a week more to grasp that they belonged to a sect, which was a bad thing, my mother said; and then through whispers behind the outspread newspapers I gathered that something awful was going on, which made the Mariavites more abominable than ever.

They worshipped their Little Mother, married one another, and there were babies born in their cloister—that much I learnt from overheard conversations. Puzzled though I was, I couldn't grasp why my aunt Casimira's nose should twitch so briskly and her face grow purple at the mere mention of those Mariavite babies. Her old voice rose to a shriek of denunciation: They should be put on trial, the whole filthy lot!

She was on one of her visits to us, and since my father always tried his best to speed up her departure, he disagreed with whatever she said. There won't be a trial. People can't be dragged into court for their religion. Religion, you say!—the shriek merged with the purple—it's filth, filth and blasphemy.

I was not yet sufficiently corrupted by the high-minded indignation of adults, so I was able to accept the Mariavites with all their wickedness. Once they had entered my own world, they were welcome there. A child's imagination is tolerant as long as his curiosity has no censor and is ready to admit anything: fact, fantasy, even fear.

One morning that memorable autumn, aunt Casimira forgot to hide from me the magazine she and my mother had been reading with visible relish. Both hurried out to rescue something burning in the kitchen. I snatched the paper and my eyes fell on the lines in the middle of the page: 'Suddenly he pulled me by the hand into the next room and said I must pray by the bed of the Little Mother. He knelt down with me and once more began to cover me with kisses.'[1] No time for what followed. I heard steps approaching from the kitchen. Yet the two sentences were enough to produce a lingering scent of erotic mystery and somehow I identified that scent with the juniper incense in our parish church.

Later came another identification: with my mother's piety. It was she who took me to church every Sunday, it was with her that I knelt before the statue of the Virgin Mary at home and prayed every evening. And now in my baffled innocence I saw that my mother responded to the same erotic mystery as I did. But she also wanted to be scandalized by the Mariavites. The disclosures printed in the press gave her a pleasurable excuse: whatever happened inside *their* cloister was outside the true religion she professed. A moral censor must have protected her from herself if only on the surface of piety. The same was probably true of thousands of women all over Poland who found in the case of Archbishop Kowalski, leader of the Mariavite church, a personified religious fantasy and let it grow to preposterous dimensions, especially when the rumours and vilifications were taken up by the law at the Archbishop's trial in 1928.

Until Mrs. Janina Tołpyhowa's disclosures entitled 'A Year's Stay at the Mariavite Convent' began to appear in a Plock periodical in 1926, the general public had associated the sect with the excessive cult of the Virgin Mary whose life, *Mariae vita*, provided the spiritual model for each *mariawita*.[2] The other model was the foundress of the sect, Feliksa Kozlowska, venerated as *Mateczka*, the Little Mother. She died in 1921, and Archbishop Kowalski became her successor. The cathedral-like Temple of the Mariavites, with its cloister, boarding school, garden, and workshops, formed a large enclosure at Plock, the old capital of Mazovia, about 120 km. north-west of Warsaw.

Plock was and still is a nice, sleepy town, picturesquely situated on the Vistula. It is a town in which everybody knows everybody. Kowalski and his suite of priests and young nuns in their silver-grey habits attracted visitors to the Temple, but the traffic of tourists fifty years ago was, after all, negligible. The community had to rely on the skills of individual members, and the results impressed even hostile observers. The Mariavites were admirably self-sufficient as a group, but this, of course, increased their sense of dependence on one another. This interdependence was breached when a member of the Mariavite community, a potential convert, published allegations concerning sexual offences committed by the Archbishop not only

---

[1] Sources of direct quotations not otherwise acknowledged in the text are given in the Reference Notes at p. 235.
[2] The plural of *mariawita*, a member of the sect, is *mariawici*. The movement is called *mariawityzm*. I have used the anglicized forms 'Mariavite' and 'Mariavites' throughout this book.

against herself but against girls who were under age; evidence subsequently submitted to the public prosecutor in Plock brought about the sensational trial of Kowalski, which turned a provincial rumour into a *cause célèbre* reported in the national press and also abroad.

I shall return to these allegations in the following chapters. No moral censor, however, will interfere with what I have to say in this book. I had no censor at the age of ten: there is no reason why I should compromise with one now. I want to establish the truth as far as it is still possible.

The death of both my parents at the time of the Mariavite troubles sealed in my memory a curious bond of sympathy for the much maligned sectarians. A few years later I discovered by chance that one of our cousins whom I remembered as a gentle creature, was in fact, a Mariavite, but after Kowalski's trial the jeers of his fellow farmers drove him out of his faith and then out of his native village. Nobody talked about him in our family, his name was taboo, and I couldn't understand why.

A month or so before my father's death, an incident occurred in our village which brought me even closer to the Mariavites. One of their priestesses happened to be passing through on her way to Plock. She was whistled at and abused until a boy of twelve, urged by a group of hysterical women, threw a stone at her. The blood began to trickle down over her eyelids. When at last she was able to move on, the priestess came up to the boy and touched his head, as if sensing his need of forgiveness.[1]

The trial of 1928 damaged the self-confidence of the Mariavites and they never recovered from this public exposure and the split within their church which followed. The war and the German occupation maimed their human and material resources still further. Now there are no more than 30,000 of them, only a small fraction of their number at the height of the sect's popularity when Mother Kozlowska was fully active. They have become a rare religious species faced with total extinction. Their fate appeals to one's protective instinct. *Non omnis moriar*, a good last cry to utter.

My reason for writing a book about them is rooted in childhood recollections, but this alone would not have sustained the effort demanded by such an undertaking. Finding primary sources was, to start with, difficult and sometimes impossible. Many documents had vanished during the last war. I was lucky enough to trace some of the oldest members of the Mariavite movement who helped me to understand the moods of their youthful enthusiasm.

But the more I thought about the strange events in the Mariavite story, the more I was aware of a pattern emerging from that strangeness. The

[1] I described this incident in my novel, *The Knotted Cord* (1953).

pattern began to resemble other religious patterns, and far beyond them I perceived a blurred outline of a very old matrix. This is perhaps how the mind gropes with the fingertips of intuition.

Here we have a modern phenomenon that came to life in the first decade of this century and may disappear altogether before the century is out. It is in a sense a fully observable phenomenon. Yet there is something elusive about such observability. The Mariavites may have quite a few skeletons hidden in their old cupboards. But even if there were none, the secretive aura around them would remain, impenetrable as ever. Is this then a condition necessary for the preservation of mystery in any religion?

Without secrets there is no mystery. Archbishop Kowalski baffled his enemies because sometimes he appeared to be so indiscreet about the mysteries he was supposed to guard. Was it spiritual ebullience or authoritarian arrogance, or both? Whether or not Kowalski was guilty of the sexual offences imputed to him, his own pronouncements make it sufficiently clear that his church was Love Incarnate in all its manifestations. The children born of the mystical marriages he established were to come into the world without original sin, a new beginning for mankind. If Christ was the second Adam, was he then to be the third, the father of the sinless? How deep in the dark of the psyche lay this redemptive mystery?

To many Poles Kowalski is still a ridiculous if not embarrassing figure from the past, an oddity which they cannot quite accept as legitimately belonging to their past. The Roman Catholics, despite their spirit of reconciliation towards the different churches of Christ, find the Mariavites an offence to their theological good taste. They wish they had never existed. They will be glad when they cease to exist.

Poland, unlike Russia, had produced remarkably few heresies. This almost clean historical record was spoilt for some patriotic interpreters of the past by a most extravagant heresy which, being modern, is difficult to erase from the annals of their nation. I am therefore prepared for reprimands rather than approval when and if this book is read by Poles. But I find some encouragement in my memory of aunt Casimira. Her twitch and purple salute me across the years, no longer indignant but mischievously forbearing.

And there is another reminiscence, still fresh in my mind. At the end of August 1971, I paid my first visit to the Mariavites at Felicjanów, a community of sixty people, mainly women, who live and work on the land that once belonged to their foundress.[1] This is the place, too, where Archbishop Kowalski resided after the split in his church, until his arrest by the Germans.

---

[1] The estate, only 22 km. from Plock, was purchased in 1910 and some of its land was distributed among Mariavite peasants. This created a friendly environment for the community.

When I was near the gate I saw a few women and a man who were moving about in a field nearby. The man looked at me, shading his eyes. I nodded to him, but I don't think he noticed the movement of my head. Very likely, he was not looking at me but far beyond me.

Later the same afternoon I heard that Kowalski's only son was one of the six men living in the religious commune at Felicjanów. And I believe he was working in the fields that day. Without knowing it I had greeted the son of the third Adam, who like the children of the first, was still tilling the soil in the sweat of his brow.

1

The Little Mother

AMONG the devotional pictures representing the Little Mother I have found a card covered with silk, on which dainty flowers are embroidered round her portrait. The effect is quaintly tender and begs for an epithet. How should one invoke you, my fair lady? Our Lady of the Embroidery, perhaps? A symbol in this case also happens to be a fact, for it was the art of embroidery that the Little Mother taught her fellow sisters to master from the very beginnings of her religious movement. Later the Mariavite convent became renowned for the workmanship of church vestments which were produced there.

The feminine touch is needed in all manner of worship. The patient needlework of prayer. Little flowers and little words strewn at the feet of the Little Mother. But in the language of adoration a diminutive of this type easily transforms itself into a mystical augmentative and behold! the Little Mother appears in the moment of awe as the woman of the Apocalypse, a big cosmic Matron clothed with the sun. This is how the Mariavites came to see their foundress.

The real person, however, born at a certain point in time, intrudes, demanding dispassionate attention. The Little Mother was much vilified by those who feared her power over the priests and ordinary people. In their eyes she was a devil-sent witch whose origins were as dubious as her ascent to notoriety was mysterious.

But the biographical facts are much on the side of respectability. Her family background was impeccable. Born Kozlowska of noble but impoverished parents, on 27 May 1862, in the Russian part of Poland,[1] she was christened Feliksa Magdalena. When a patriotic rising broke out in January 1863, her father Jakub joined a group of partisans and was killed in battle only eight months after her birth. The widow and the baby came under the care of the grandmother, whose second husband was named Pulaski, another link with the heroic past. A Pulaski, Casimir, fought as a general in

---

[1] In the village of Wieliczna near Węgrów in Podlasie, where her father was chief forester on a large estate. Kozlowski's heraldic cognomen was Nałęcz, as was that of Joseph Conrad.

the American War of Independence and was mortally wounded in the defence of Savannah (1779).

Feliksa ('a happy one' in Latin) had no choice: she belonged to the deprived and vulnerable generation growing up after the abortive rising, under the dominance of strong-willed women who often took charge of family affairs when their husbands and sons were killed or deported to Siberia. Their idealism—and there was no shortage of it among those lonely women—had to be tempered with a strong practical sense. The positivist exaltation of work appealed to the first Polish feminists, including the novelist Eliza Orzeszkowa.[1] Women, she preached, had to learn how to look after themselves; husbands were not their only *raison d'être*. Kozlowska as the Little Mother taught the Mariavites how to fend for themselves. The will of God and the will to work must go together. Her organizational abilities, exceptional by any standards, were forged in the mood of the post-1863 generation. In a photograph taken when she was twenty-one she looks both forceful and attractive, her body well shaped with a trim waist emphasized by a belt which is wide after the fashion of the day. The lips are generous, unafraid to speak up, but sensitive as those of an orphan child. The eyes have a visionary far-away look.

From the day of her first communion at the age of ten, Feliksa Kozlowska dedicated herself to Christ; she was to work for Him and not for herself, and she would never marry.[2] The expression of her face altered dramatically when she was still in her early twenties: the light of her right eye was extinguished, as she put it, so that she could see more deeply into human souls with one eye only. From now on her photographs, especially those taken when she was leader of her church, do not show her full face. Out of consideration, no doubt, they give prominence to the left side of her face, slanting her features and giving them a withdrawn appearance. The penetrating power of the Little Mother's eye was often described to me by the oldest among the Mariavite nuns who had a clear memory of their spiritual leader. Her eye knew all my answers before they reached my lips, one of them said.

Whether it was this power gained through physical affliction or simply the experience of yet another deprivation, the effect on the young girl was the same: it confirmed her in her renunciation of worldly success. Yet, in a paradoxical way, she had in her a will to succeed, and would have succeeded in any career of her choice.

---

[1] Orzeszkowa (1841–1910) as a young woman had worked for the partisans in 1863. Her feminist novel *Marta* (1872) created a stir in Germany and Russia.
[2] So Kozlowska told the Mariavite bishops, as reported later by Philip Feldman.

Her secondary education led to private coaching—a typical occupation of unmarried women—but the inner voice persisted. She was soon in touch with a nun who practised her vocation in secret, for since the rising the Russian authorities in the part of Poland under the Tsar did not allow religious orders to accept novices. As a result a number of secret religious associations sprang up, and their Rule was Franciscan. St. Francis, according to the encyclical pronouncement of Pope Leo XIII, was the reformer of the Church for all times. A Capuchin priest who sponsored these clandestine novitiates, Father Honorat Koźmiński (1829–1916),[1] had the reputation of a soul-finder and in his confessional one day he found Kozlowska. He directed her to work for the sick in Warsaw. She obeyed, joined a community of sisters, was sent to look after some rich invalids in their homes, but this, of course, did not meet her spiritual needs.

In September 1887 at the age of twenty-five she embarked on a project whose consequences she could not possibly foresee. Kozlowska moved to the cathedral city of Plock and with five other women established the nucleus of a religious community. To the outside world, which included the Russians, they were a group of young ladies earning their keep by sewing linen and embroidering vestments; to themselves they were nuns following the strict rule of Poor Clares. Poverty was certainly their mistress. They had one warm coat and one pair of adequate shoes among them, so in winter they went to church by turns. They had little food and were often cold. But they were guided by a resolute ascetic who mortified her body by wearing a sharp iron belt and who in secret flogged herself with a spiky cat-o'-nine-tails. One of the nuns heard the scourging through the wall when Kozlowska thought she was alone in the house. Both objects of her mortification have survived.[2] Later, however, she abandoned this morbid practice and did not permit the Mariavite nuns to inflict pain on their bodies.

The seal of secrecy imposed on her first community did in my opinion influence the development of the Mariavite system. The clandestine aura remained with her and even more so with her successors. In 1887, for better and, as it turned out, also for worse, a great adventure had begun for her. Young Feliksa had to mature within herself, and in a hurry. The awkward chrysalis was shed, the extinguished eye put out much vanity, on the right side of the face at least, and a Mother emerged, bearing two names: that of the Virgin and that of the saint of Assisi. Maria Frances (Maria Franciszka) was now ready to dispense authority. This was certainly felt by

[1] See Maria Werner, O. *Honorat Koźmiński* (Poznan, 1972).
[2] They are now at Felicjanów, where I was allowed to photograph them.

those novices who were much older than herself. One of them, meeting Maria Frances for the first time, was compelled to kneel down, and she called her 'my Mother'. No Little Mother as yet. The respectful diminutive came later, and it came from priests.

The adoration of the Eucharist was for Kozlowska and her small group the most important spiritual activity. Without it their small works and mortifications would have served little purpose. When years later the first Mariavites appeared in public as a separate group of priests and nuns, they wore the monstrance embroidered on their habits. By this sign they wished to be recognized. As for their name it was not man-made but, according to Kozlowska, given by the Maker himself in the first revelation of 1893, the year the Mariavites see as the spiritual birth of their church.

2

Like other founders of religious movements—Mary Baker Eddy, for instance, or Joseph Smith of the Mormons—Kozlowska claimed to have acted on divine orders. And since the orders were precise, she tried to record them with equal precision in her own handwriting.

> In the year 1893, on the second of August, after hearing Mass and receiving communion I was suddenly detached from my senses and placed before the Majesty of God. Inconceivable luminosity suffused my soul and I was then shown the universal corruption of the world and the finality of time—the laxity of morals among the clergy and the sins committed by priests. I saw God's Justice aiming at the world to punish it and also his Mercy giving the doomed world its last chance of rescue in the Veneration of the Most Holy Sacrament and in Mary's Help. After a moment of silence the Lord spoke: 'To spread this worship I want to see a congregation of priests under the name of the Mariavites. Their motto is: All for the greater glory of God and for the veneration of the Most Holy Virgin Mary. They will be under the protection of Our Lady of Perpetual Succour. For as endeavours against God and the Church are perpetuated, so Perpetual is the need of Mary's Help.'—I was greatly astonished and began to rejoice, but the Lord spoke again: 'For the present I give all this Work into your hands—you are to be its mistress [*mistrzyni*] and mother—and I entrust that Priest[1] to you; you will guide him according to my directives.' . . . I understood that he was to be the first Mariavite and immediately I uttered: 'Behold the handmaid of the Lord; be it unto me according to thy word.'

Like St. Francis she received her mission (the voice told Kozlowska) on the feast of Our Lady of the Angels. It was also the feast of St. Alphonsus

[1] The priest was Father F. Strumiłło, a teacher at the Plock seminary, who was Kozlowska's confessor and to whom she imparted her revelations. He accepted their validity and called her 'the Dove of Noah's Ark with an olive branch'.

Liguori, so she went to read his life, and during the reading the voice announced that St. Alphonsus would be the patron of the Mariavites. Kozlowska accepted the voices as coming from Christ and she was filled with joy, gratitude, and peace. She spent the rest of the day in prayer. Next morning, however, she started to question the whole experience: was it a dream? a delusion?—why should God speak to a sinner like herself? Perplexed she went to church and prayed to be released from the memory of the previous day. During Mass she heard the voice, stern in tone this time: 'Rise and listen!' She trembled with fear. The reading from the New Testament that morning was about Jesus chiding Jerusalem for killing her prophets. 'And you too must not kill God's voice within you,' she heard, 'for this is the day of God's visitation.' 'Lord, do anything you like with me,' she answered. 'I am ready for everything.'

Then during her further meditation she saw the congregation of the Mariavites and the entire world enfolded in the adoration of the Eucharist. She also saw persecutions and sufferings that would have to be accepted.

Without going into the meaning of an experience which is claimed to be supernatural, one has to comment on its pattern and the accompanying circumstances. After much inner struggle Kozlowska was obviously longing for a dramatic confirmation. The analogy with the Virgin Mary gives a typical symmetry to the pattern. The Work of Great Mercy—as her mission came to be called[1]—in the scheme of Kozlowska's revelation was to resemble the Work of Redemption in every detail,[2] and the linking of the two names, Mary and Frances, with the Virgin and St. Francis allowed for a symmetrical identification with the mediacy of the obedient handmaid and with the rescue operation of a holy enthusiast. The modern Church, too, must be rescued through a new religious organization.

Let us consider the immediate context. After the shock of her first revelation Kozlowska read the life of St. Alphonsus Liguori (1696–1787), the luckless founder of the Redemptorist congregation. The fact is significant in view of the cult of Our Lady of Perpetual Succour which the Redemptorists and the Mariavites had in common. This thirteenth- or fourteenth-century Byzantine picture, probably from Crete, was kept in Rome (now in the church of Sant' Alfonso). It shows the instruments of the Passion being presented to the Christ child by the Archangel Michael and Gabriel the Angel of

---

[1] Archbishop Kowalski used *The Work of Great Mercy* as the title for his Mariavite scriptures (1922–4), a big book with documents, memoirs, and letters, in which the 'Revelations' of the Little Mother occupy more than 80 pages.

[2] Like the previous Annunciation it demanded total obedience. In a few years the Voice would insist: 'My will must be done to the letter, to the letter, to the letter.' The thrice-repeated order was in psychological terms a warning.

the Annunciation. The Virgin in the picture is the Mother of Perpetual Succour (she is said to have revealed this name to a child in a vision). Her cult was revived early in the nineteenth century during the French occupation of Rome. St. Alphonsus' book, *The Glories of Mary*, ran into many editions.[1]

The second name of St. Alphonsus was Maria, a further analogy with the practice adopted by the Mariavite priests. Another book of his, *Visits to the Blessed Sacrament*, has many points of resemblance with the Mariavite devotion to the Eucharist. This, too, belongs to the contemporary context, in which one must include the work of Father Honorat, Kozlowska's spiritual adviser at the critical time of her life. Father Honorat advocated both frequent communion and devotion to the Virgin Mary. He published pamphlets proposing a Marian congregation of lay priests observing the third Franciscan Rule.[2] The priests were to add Mary's name to their Christian names on entering the congregation. Kozlowska found the means to put these ideas into practice once the divine intervention, in which she believed, had pushed her into action.

Another source of influence was St. Louis (Maria, his other name) Grignion de Montfort (1673–1716). Kozlowska tells how one of her visions was prompted by the reading of his text: 'Again in a clear light I saw the future congregation of the Mariavites, knowing that it was the same Congregation which the Blessed Louis de Montfort had foretold—and then said the Lord: "This is the army of Mary: place everything in her hands and be at peace: pray, have trust, and work. I shall be your support." Afterwards', she says, 'I was very happy and spent the whole night in prayer and thanksgiving.'

Why was Kozlowska reading Louis de Montfort at that time? He had left two spiritual legacies which must have appealed to her paradoxical search for authority in submission: one was a society of priests called the Company of Mary; the second was *The Secret of Mary*, his letter written to a nun, which is a treatise on the holy slavery of love. The French title makes it painfully plain: *Le Secret de Marie ou Lettre sur l'esclavage de la Sainte Vierge*. Rediscovered in 1842, the book became very popular and was translated into many languages, including Polish.[3] In 1888 Pope Leo XIII,

---

[1] Passages from his writings were used in the *Manual of Our Lady of Perpetual Succour*, by a Redemptorist father, published in England in 1900. 'Since devotion to Our Lady of Perpetual Succour is spreading on every side,' we read in the Preface, there is need of a devotional manual in English.

[2] The pamphlets were published anonymously in Cracow, outside the reach of the Russian censor.

[3] It is perhaps ironic that this treatise which so obviously influenced the Mariavite Little Mother, should still be read by Polish Catholics, even in exile. A new cheap reprint was published in London as recently as 1966 by the firm of Veritas.

whom Kozlowska and her followers always exempted from their attacks on the papacy, had pronounced Louis de Monfort Blessed.

Today St. Louis's language of holy slavery may be embarrassing to read, but considered in terms of Baroque concepts it has a certain evocative power. He speaks of 'the manacles of love', the rosary is for him 'a ring of betrothal to Mary'. All is through Mary, with Mary, in Mary, for Mary, because the Virgin 'received from God singular power to rule over the souls'. We should offer ourselves to her. A servant can ask for a reward, but not a slave. The final act of handing oneself over must mean unconditional surrender.[1] This slavery Louis Maria de Monfort accepted willingly; he was already branded with her name like the other Maria, Alphonsus Liguori.

The missionary methods of the adoring slave were unscrupulous, but they impressed the poor, among whom St. Louis worked, and intimidated the Jansenists. One passage in his tract on the Secret of Mary is applicable to the secret of Maria Frances Kozlowska: 'Accept the mystery: God himself has entrusted it to me. . . . Say piously *Ave Maris Stella* and *Veni Creator*, asking God for true understanding.' The hymns recommended here are one addressed to the Virgin and the other to the Holy Spirit. But most important of all is the word 'understanding', translated into Polish as *zrozumienie*. It is this *zrozumienie* which the Little Mother and her successor Archbishop Kowalski were to use again and again to describe the nature of their revelations. I had an understanding at prayer that night about this or that, the Archbishop would say, and no other explanation was expected from him, unless he chose to embroider a theological gloss for his own intellectual pleasure.[2]

But the Lord is a jealous God towards those he loves most. After a preparatory period he forbade Kozlowska to read ascetic books, as she was to forbid her nuns the ascetic addiction to self-flagellation.

3

A year after her revelation Kozlowska had but two Mariavites, both priests teaching at the Plock seminary. The first, Father Strumiłło, was to die in

---

[1] Father Honorat, too, wanted his lay priests to be 'the slaves of Mary'. The chains of that Baroque concept were much in fashion, spiritually speaking.

[2] Kowalski himself tried to elucidate the meaning of *zrozumienie*. The Little Mother, he argued, never claimed that she saw physical apparitions in the timeless moment of her visionary understanding, though it was nevertheless vision-like. What the Little Mother received from Christ was *visio intellectualis* as opposed to *visio sensitiva* or *imaginativa*. The value of the intellectual vision, which Kowalski compared to the bardic inspiration, mentioning the names of the Polish Romantics, is that it can never delude, for it is charged with its own spiritual meaning of which the visionary is instantaneously aware—hence the *zrozumienie* accompanying such a vision and binding the mind to the Giver of Grace (vision is grace).

1895; the second, Father John,[1] became the real fisher of priests for the Work of Great Mercy. He travelled from parish to parish, talked to priests who were often frustrated and disillusioned with the tepid religiosity of the Church. They waited for a sign, and the sign was now given, veiled in the secrecy which made it even more desirable to follow. One after another priests from distant parishes would travel to Plock, often by river boat, as the lower part of the Vistula was navigable. They would be taken to a pleasant house with a garden, no. 8 Dobrzynska Street, not far from the ancient cathedral, where Kozlowska lived and ran her workshop.[2] Once the visitor met Maria Frances face to face, or rather eye to eye, the inevitable would happen: he would 'open his soul to her' (this phrase recurs in various accounts), feel waves of strength and peace radiating from her—at once all was understood, forgiven, and transformed. The act of submission that resulted from such a meeting had every appearance of a voluntary decision. Thy will be done; if you want my soul, take it now. Bending his knee, the priest would kiss Kozlowska's hand: this was apparently the ceremony of acceptance.

What worried the first priests who in this manner became enslaved to the Virgin Mary—to use the masochistic expression of St. Louis—was not the mystical manacles, but the feminine hand of Kozlowska, which held the key to them on earth. Could and should a priest obey a woman in religious matters? Kozlowska, too, had qualms about this at the beginning. The Capuchin, Father Honorat, was consulted in the confessional and by post, and this wise keeper of many secrets quoted examples from the history of religious orders in which women exercised spiritual power over men: St. Colette, St. Catherine of Siena, St. Teresa of Avila, St. Jane Frances de Chantal. And didn't the great seraphic saint seek St. Clare's advice on many occasions? That side of Kozlowska's work then could do no spiritual harm. But sensing possible trouble, Father Honorat had reservations about her likeness to the Virgin Mary and about the idea of putting all clandestine congregations under one Mariavite roof.[3] After all, those organizations had been formed by him, and he did not wish to see them vanish in a semi-mystical merger.

However, the state of the Catholic Church in its visible form was beyond

---

[1] K. Przyjemski, regarded as the first active Mariavite. He later published his memoirs of those early days.

[2] The property was bought by Kozlowska's mother Anna, who after initial doubts became convinced that her daughter had a great mission to fulfil. Like St. Clare's mother, Ortulana, she joined the community, accepting a mother in her child. The original house still stands.

[3] Kozlowsak did not hide Father Honorat's objections; she listed them all in her account of the revelations. She had respect for documents.

Father Honorat's pastoral influence. In the Russian part of Poland at the beginning of the twentieth century, the situation was aggravated by both political and social conditions, which the rulers used to their advantage, curbing the mutinous gentry and keeping the peasants uneducated. The Catholic priests found themselves in a class dilemma. Many of them came from peasant families, understood the village and its needs, but with their own social advancement they tended to side with local squires. Squire and parish priest were supposed to protect the Polishness of those small, often backward communities, and the abuse of their joint authority was inevitable.[1] No farmer, however prosperous, yet had sufficient confidence to challenge that paternalistic state of affairs.

As for the Catholic hierarchy, it performed a balancing act between the national interests and the politics of an international organization. Although certain poets in exile had once denounced the Pope as an ally of the Tsar for his condemnation of the 1830 November rising,[2] the cautious Poles at home, practising a kind of moral statesmanship, knew that their country could not afford to alienate the Vatican. The Catholic Church in Poland was, after all, a semi-independent institution which for a people with no diplomatic representation abroad was a channel of influence outside and a check to the Russian administration. The Russians tried their best to undermine the semi-state within the empire. Their restrictive policy towards the religious orders, for instance, was one such attempt—there were many others—and the rise of the Mariavite movement owed much to the uneasy relations between the Catholic Church and the Tsarist empire, as well as to the crisis of confidence among the parish priests.

Did the priests care enough about the welfare, let alone the souls of their parishioners? In her mental 'understandings' Kozlowska heard bitter words spoken about the moral laxity and laziness of the clergy. They abused their sacramental immunity and did not guard their flocks. Practically every priest visiting Kozlowska in Plock was a man dissatisfied with himself, a once-dedicated soul plunged into a crisis. Without exaggerating the claims of the Mariavites, the evidence shows that in the beginning of their movement some of the best priests of the new generation accepted Kozlowska's guidance simply because they could not find it elsewhere. The crisis lay deeper than the bishops realized. Spiritual longings apart, the young were attracted to the social conscience of Kozlowska, perhaps her most admirable quality as one surveys the whole of her life. No edict at home or from the

---

[1] This theme is frequently explored by late nineteenth-century novelists, e.g. Sienkiewicz, Reymont, and Żeromski.

[2] Gregory XVI is cleverly caricatured by Slowacki in his play *Kordian* (1834).

Vatican was capable of preventing the storm that gathered in the hearts of the truly religious.

How did it finally break into the open? After four years, in 1897, Kozlowska had several Mariavites under her wing. They observed the first Franciscan rule of *Fratres Minores* and propagated the cult of the Eucharist in accordance with the revealed Work of Mercy. But they continued their separate lives, each guarding the Mariavite secret. As a mark of distinction they wore black cuffs instead of white, hence the nickname of 'cuff-buddies' (*mankietnicy*) by which they were called later. The only outward signs of their allegiance to Kozlowska were visits to the house in Dobrzynska Street, which for a time passed unnoticed. Officially, it was a place where priests would come to order vestments or to collect them.

Like a mystical radar, Kozlowska kept picking up her 'understandings', but towards the end of 1897 she had a vision with a difference. She saw three legions of devils in combat array, sneering at her: What can you, a weak female, do before such power as ours? 'I felt abandoned', she writes, 'even by the Lord Jesus; sadness and fear seized my soul; only when I invoked Our Lady of Perpetual Succour, the vision vanished.'

A few months later the priest in her parish attacked her by name from the pulpit as a woman scandalizing the town, and the town began to take a closer look at the house which the priests frequented. The 'cuff-buddies' were also denounced. Gossip did the rest. However, it was still a local affair, but when other priests joined in the attack to stamp out the influence of 'that satanic woman', jeers and nicknames poured on to the Mariavites. They were bleating goats led by a lecherous she-goat (an allusion to her surname, *koziol* meaning 'goat'). Kozlowska admitted she suffered greatly at the time: she heard no voices of consolation and her body was afflicted with severe sickness. Like other visionaries, whether true or false, she was prone to suffer physical breakdowns. This was her first trial of strength and fortunately, the hostilities subsided within a year. The Mariavite priests were left in peace and their number increased.

Kozlowska heard Christ's voice again. He said he was now her only teacher—enough of the lives of the saints, listen to me, 'I alone want to be your Master.' And it was at this spiritual juncture that he revealed her own mystery: 'Of all the graces I bestow upon you, the greatest is this: the Most Holy Virgin was exempted from sin, likewise you are exempted from passion [*namiętność*, which has an erotic connotation]; the way along which I lead you I have led no other soul. Seek your likeness in the Holy Virgin. As I offered myself to the Heavenly Father through Mary's hands, so I want to offer My Mercy to the world through your hands.'

The mystical progress of Kozlowska reads impressively in her own account of it. Her heart underwent fifteen stages of purification, and then her soul was purified 'through a mystical death linked with the Mysteries of His life'. She was also freed from pride and sensuality.[1]

There were many more counsels given to her by her Teacher. Once during Elevation she was ordered to offer the host as a rogation for the sins of the whole world. Whenever you do this, the Teacher said, the wrath of God will be averted. The God of her mental 'understandings' is a judge angry with the transgressions of his servants the priests. 'I shall stir the people against the Priests and they will throw them out as I once threw out the tradesmen from the Temple of Jerusalem, because they [i.e. priests] serve me for money and honours [*zaszczyty*].'

The revealed 'understandings' had now a number of points touching upon a highly inflammable *materia theologica*. Sooner or later, an explosion was certain to occur and shake the rock of dogma on which Peter and his successors had built their church. Who then was this woman upholding the Work of Mercy in her hands which were used to needlework and gentle gestures of piety? The question to be answered had far to travel: through the admiration and curiosity of men, through hatred, persecution, and the martyrdom of an incurable illness. Its progress notched the growth of a new church with a very brave woman at its head. And only the apocalyptic halo would show whether she was the long-awaited third Eve.

[1] 'Your pride was in this,' the Voice told her, 'that you wanted to be wise and to be regarded as such; your sensuality—that you wanted to love and be loved.'

2

Born on the Day of Christ-Adam

IF to part is to die a little each time, then to meet is to be born each time in another person. John Kowalski experienced this when he met the Little Mother on 28 September 1900.

You meet to be born again: he never tired of the idea. On the contrary, he managed to transform it repeatedly into a spiritual reality, in which he was the Little Mother's son, therefore her inheritor, and later based most of his religious innovations on the concept of rebirth. He kept returning, so to speak, to the womb of the Apocalyptic Mother. Back to chapter 12 of St. John's Revelation, back to the same mystical intersection in outer time.

Down in Plock, by the river Vistula, their calendar meeting of 28 September was well timed for him. Kowalski was nearly twenty-nine, she thirty-eight. His first three years of priesthood had brought him to a crisis. He could not find any solution or remedy until a colleague turned up at his lodgings in Warsaw and told him of a secret congregation of priests, without however revealing its name. Then he put him in touch with Father John, the first Mariavite apostle, who told Kowalski more of the congregation and suggested a three-day retreat, after which he would be accepted into the Mariavite novitiate. And so Kowalski the priest became a clandestine monk without a habit. He also gave up cigarettes, though he had been addicted to them since childhood. 'The desire left me as if I had never smoked in my life.' Anxious to have instant signs he got one straightaway. His will stubbed out the last cigarette. Ashes to ashes.

The next day Father John proposed that they should travel by a river boat to Plock. 'You must see the lady who had the revelation.' They arrived in Plock in the afternoon, and went straight to no. 8 Dobrzynska Street. Kowalski imagined he would find a saint from a holy picture, deep in ecstasy, her pose perhaps theatrical, with eyes uplifted and hands crossed over her breasts. Instead, he saw a middle-aged woman wearing secular clothes, modest yet fully at ease, her whole face aglow with welcoming smiles. He addressed her as 'Madam' (*pani*) thinking that 'Little Mother' which Father John was using would sound too familiar in his mouth. He was at first tongue-tied, then asked her to say a word, any word she heard from Christ. The Little Mother replied that her soul was now passing through a dark night. 'It is a state in which everything is erased from memory', unless Christ himself chooses to bring it back. Suddenly a smile appeared on her face. 'Yes, now I remember,' she said. 'A light has just flashed in my mind.' And Kozlowska quoted the words of Christ about his punishing the world for the sins of priests. Kowalski wanted to jot the words down at once, but the pen he was given would not write. The lady graciously explained that Christ's words were so deeply engraved in her heart that she would be able at any time in the future to reproduce them in the same order as she had heard them. This pacified the zealous listener. However, he was still anxious to know all her revelations. Meanwhile the sisters began to lay the table.

After supper the Little Mother offered Kowalski some fruit from her garden, like a new Eve enacting the symbolic sequence. She was careful, though. No apple this time. And he took the fruit and ate it. He ate, in fact, more than he wanted. Here are his words:

> . . . with her little hand she gave me a large pear (of the Duchesse type) and when I ate it, she gave me another, much the same. And though I was full and one pear was enough, I didn't dare refuse the Little Mother and took the second and ate it. The stems of both pears which the Little Mother gave me, I hid discreetly in my pocket, happy that I would have for ever as a keepsake some object a saint so great had touched. For I didn't think that I would see the Little Mother ever again or communicate with her.

The tone of this passage is characteristic of Kowalski's devotion to the Little Mother. He dresses his memories with tender diminutives and omits no detail, however trivial. How could anything be trivial while his true self was being born? He wanted to record it all faithfully.

The following day they met again in a different house. It was St. Michael's day. This had great significance for the future Archbishop because as a Mariavite he assumed, besides the customary name of Maria, that of the Archangel. Later he would sign his pastoral letters and documents: John Maria Michael (Jan Maria Michał).

The Little Mother greeted him with an encouraging smile. Surprise! She had a message to pass on to him. The Lord Jesus told her to be sincere and hide nothing from Kowalski. The message itself concerned his future mission: 'As St. Michael fought defending God so he will fight in defence of the Mariavite congregation, but he needs great humility and willingness to destroy himself for the glory of God.' The words apparently came from the Lord Jesus.

Kowalski was taken aback. 'Would God have deigned to say anything about such a sinner as myself?' He immediately expressed his doubt but the persuasive lady reassured him and the message was accepted 'under a certain pressure', to use his own words.

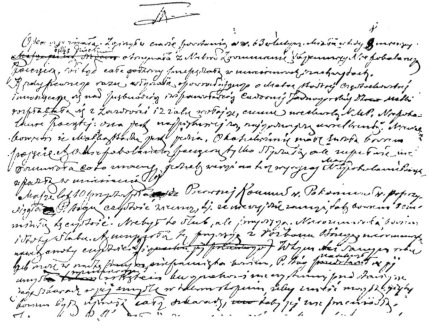

Kowalski's notes on the Little Mother's life (1900)

Now Kowalski asked the Little Mother to answer a few questions and tell him briefly her own life. She agreed, Kowalski knelt by a little table (another affectionate diminutive) and began his respectful enquiry, taking notes from time to time.[1]

As the life story was being unfolded, Kowalski learnt about an 'understanding' which the Little Mother had received in her childhood. It concerned the mystery of the immaculate conception. Apparently the phrase

[1] He entered them in the same exercise book he had been using for his translation of Huysmans' *En route* (see p. 25); they come suddenly after chapter X. Looking through the manuscript at Felicjanów in December 1973, I stumbled on these notes—beyond doubt the earliest Mariavite record by Kowalski. On them he later based his account of Kozlowska's early years in his 'Brief Life of the Little Mother'. (Its brevity, however, is on the generous side; the account fills 235 pages of *The Work of Great Mercy*.)

Maria Frances Kozlowska, the Little Mother
Embroidered card with Kowalski's portrait of her, painted before 1906.

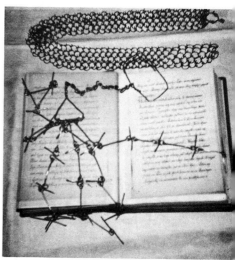

(*Above*) Manuscript of the Little Mother's Revelations, with the iron belt she wore and her cat-o'-nine-tails.
(*Left*) The Temple of Mercy and Love at Plock.
(*Below*) Mariavite band in the parish of Leszno, with three of the early Fathers, *c.* 1907.

itself used to make her fall into ecstasy although like St. Bernadette of Lourdes she had no idea what it really meant. ('Understanding' then should not be confused with meaning—a point worth remembering.)

In the first encounter between the Little Mother and Michael the defender there is already an intimate give-and-take relation, and the desire to keep it so. He opens his soul and she hers, widely. They must hide nothing from each other—such is the Lord's order. Blessed be the Lord. The Little Mother tells Kowalski her life so that he can be enfolded by it like a child in a womb.

This also sets a pattern for future communication between the Mariavites. They readily bare their souls to one another. Facing a crisis—and there were many crises in the Mariavite congregation—a priest would go over his whole life in a general confession just to make sure he had not mislaid any of his previous sins. Self-accusation (*oskarżenie*) became a moral pastime, as it were, in this repeated game of introspection.

The Little Mother was certainly good at persuading each newcomer that whatever crisis he brought with him would not escape her thorough scrutiny. With one eyelid lowered, she concentrated the other eye on the soul struggling to reach her. Unless you become as little children, you will never enter the queendom of the Mother.[1] She flattered the doubting spirit in Kowalski and the doubt dissolved. Your spirit, she said, is that of Archangel Michael reborn on the Archangel's day. Rise and defend your God against the wickedness of priests. Persuasion and mystery were the Little Mother's strength. She recognized the pride in Kowalski and put a secret into it. Then she exchanged a secret for a secret: their common destiny was now under an apocalyptic seal.

Like other priests who made a pilgrimage to Plock, Kowalski wanted to believe in God's plan of Great Mercy and in the mediator who was once more a woman. Hence the immediate rapport between him and the Little Mother. From that crucial St. Michael's eve 1900, his mind was attuned to hidden messages in dates, anniversaries, names, dreams and premonitions. If you are born to be re-born, your life must have a double, triple, or a quadruple meaning.

2

The significance of Kowalski's birthday is certainly twofold. He was born in Latowicz near Minsk Mazowiecki on Christmas eve 1871. His followers

---

1 Philip Feldman in his unpublished memoir tells of his child-like reaction when he first met the Little Mother on Christmas Eve 1906 (he was then twenty-one). He knelt and kissed her hand, she bent down and laid a kiss on his head. Afterwards he felt 'joyfully at ease in her company'.

today attach much importance to the date of his birth. They see in it a Eucharistic link with Christ and, I would add, a link with the first Adam whose name is by tradition celebrated in the Christian calendar on the same day. The analogy here is self-evident. According to legend, St. Francis was born in the *stalletta*, a stable, just like Christ: a symmetry of this kind appeals to the popular imagination. The point at which you enter life is umbilically connected with your predecessors in the chain of rebirths. In this respect 25 December seems more reassuring that either 26 or 27 December (both given in biographical articles on Kowalski).[1] In my opinion, 27 December could well have been the day of John Kowalski's birth, since it is the feast of John the Evangelist. Peasants usually chose the name they found in the calendar when a birth occurred. The child brought the name with him, they believed, and the tradition was rigorously observed until the last war.

Did Kowalski shift the date to suit his parallelistic mind? Certainly, by the time he was Archbishop, he had made it a cornerstone of his personal myth and helped to propagate it. For instance, his own poem in *terza rima* was quoted in a Mariavite periodical on the occasion of his sixty-fifth birthday:

> On the sweet night of Christ's Nativity
> a twin I was born of my mother[2]
> so that I could find a still sweeter Mother.

It is an atrocious piece of verse, far below the standard of his translations, yet the sentiment expressed between the rickety rhymes in Polish has some interest. The real mother is spelt with a small *m*, the other (i.e. the Little Mother) with a capital letter. The title of the poem, 'Who is like God', glorifies Kowalski after the Mariavite vows because it alludes to the Hebrew etymology of the name Michael. In other words, what matters is the rebirth.

> The parental house where I was born,
> stood in the street of the Holy Ghost near the cross,
> and forty-four was its number.

A good omen for the future interpreter of the Apocalypse that his street was named after the Holy Ghost. As for the number of the house, it happens to be the same as the Messianic 44 of Mickiewicz's *The Ancestors* (1832), which has mystified far too many earnest scholars. The Kowalski of his commemorative plaque in verse is a prophet laden with significances. It is

[1] The Warsaw *Illustrated Weekly* for 10 March 1906 (see p. 34) gives Kowalski's birth date as 26 December; *Słownik biograficzny* has 27 December. As for the veracity of birth certificates in Russian Poland, they were often copied by half-literate clerks.

[2] His twin sister was very weak and needed all the attention. 'I sucked my mother's breasts for only three days,' Kowalski says in his unpublished memoir. The twin sister died when she was not yet three.

hard to imagine him as a little boy going to school in Latowicz; it is even harder to imagine his family background.

However, an unpublished memoir of his early years, dictated in 1928 to his wife Isabel, supplies many facts.[1] Kowalski's father, also John, was a farmer, though socially he had more in common with the lower middle class. Latowicz was a small town into which newcomers from nearby villages were moving, and this created a tension between the old town and the new. Kowalski senior sat on the local council, employed servants on his land, and entrusted the running of the farm to his wife, a pious and practical woman who was much older than he. She made the children say their prayers together and aloud, so that she could correct them; she took the future Archbishop to church.

The boy was put in charge of a few oxen and cows that grazed on pastures six km. outside the town. Waked by his father at four in the morning, he was given food for the whole day and didn't return home before nine in the evening. 'But I had a loathing for all things connected with husbandry,' he says, and he told his father that he would much prefer to study. The local parson noticed his piety as well as his respect for priests. This didn't prevent the boy from displaying his physical prowess whenever he could. Latowicz was surrounded by ponds. 'I loved swimming. I would swim eight or ten times a day. . . . I covered such long distances in the water that people would stop and watch my performance.' At school they nick-named him Samson.

Kowalski senior got into bad company, took to drink, and the farm was soon in debt. Now there was no guarantee that he would be able to support his son during his studies. But he agreed to have him trained for the priest-hood. 'As I was leaving for Warsaw', we read in the memoir, 'my mother cried, yet I felt no sorrow that I was parting from her, none at all. On the contrary, I was glad to be going away, though I dearly loved my mother.'

At first he didn't do well at the secondary school in Warsaw, was too fond of pranks and jokes, threw stones at the door of a brothel to upset the clients, went to swim in the Vistula and liked showing off his strength. Yes, he committed 'sins of impurity, though not with a woman'. Was it masturbation or merely erotic thoughts? The memoir is not clear. After finishing the seminary, he was helped to get a state scholarship to study at the Catholic Academy in St. Petersburg, the only school of this kind open to candidates from the Russian part of Poland. Later Kowalski expressed

---

[1] Preserved at the Felicjanów commune, the memoir (*Pamiętnik*) is 76 pages written in pencil in an ordinary school exercise book. It ends abruptly with an incident at the St. Petersburg Academy before Kowalski's ordination (see p. 24).

reservations about its method of teaching theology,[1] but in my opinion the Academy was responsible for developing his intellect which his enemies always tried to minimize.

Kowalski himself saw other powers hovering over him. He believed that in St. Petersburg the Holy Ghost began to work on him through a series of crises. The vice-rector who must have been aware of these struggles said to him one day: 'Obviously, God has some design for you.' On another occasion he made a further pronouncement in front of the pupils gathered in the refectory. His voice was solemn as he placed his hand on Kowalski's arm: 'You'll see, all of you, he will be a great man.' And Kowalski adds this comment in *The Work of Great Mercy*: 'Everybody was amazed at what the vice-rector had said because I neither excelled in academic studies nor distinguished myself in any particular way.' The vice-rector knew of his talent for drawing, that's all, but the Holy Spirit breathed hard. In 1897 he was ordained priest at the age of twenty-six.

Kowalski remained on friendly terms with some colleagues from the Academy. Like a prophet of old, however, he felt he was indebted to no one, least of all his parents, and in his book reprimanded his father for constant demands for cash. Such expectations were quite usual. Educating a son to be a priest was a sound family investment. Young Kowalski rebelled against this money interest which drew priests away from their vocation.

He begins his own story in *The Work of Great Mercy* with a description of his way of living before the crisis in which he found himself in 1900. He wasted God's time; he played cards, smoked, over-ate, and, like other clergymen, feathered his own nest. In his account of the crisis itself there is a conscious echo of St. Augustine's manner which he adopted probably while translating the *Confessions*. Something else was forcing a change within him and he ascribed this to Our Lady of Perpetual Succour whose picture he received from a woman penitent. At that time, of course, he didn't know of Kozlowska's devotion to the same icon. He hung the reproduction above his bed and 'soon', he writes,

> without any reason that I could understand, the world grew unpleasant to me and I unpleasant to the world. . . . Now that I had paid the debts of my parents I decided to begin a spiritual work on myself, I paid no visits and received no guests. For the time being I embarked on the translation of quite a beautiful novel by Huysmans, *En route*, and then tackled the *Confessions* of

[1] In his correspondence with the Catholic bishops (1929), Kowalski criticized the syllabus of the Academy, e.g. the Scriptures were taught badly, and the students crammed in too many facts. Nevertheless, the Academy had a brilliant rector in Bishop F. Symon, himself a notable theologian.

St. Augustine. In my spare moments I would say the rosary, holding it inside my pocket.

He couldn't give up smoking, but at least he gave up playing cards with his friends.

Huysmans' novel fits the situation: Kowalski was himself *en route*, anxious to arrive somewhere. The novel describes Durtal's return to faith and much of it is thinking aloud before the final commitment. Durtal (the same character as the hero of *Là-bas*) has turned his back on arid speculation. His sins were the sins of the flesh: debauchery and sacrilegious acts like defiling the host after a black mass with a demonized woman. The *fin-de-siècle* satanism of Huysmans had an additional attraction: it suggested a possibility of freeing oneself from the clutches of evil through the appreciation of art. Hence Durtal's musing on medieval hymns, hence the aesthetic pleasure of his visits to various churches.[1]

When, finally, Durtal decides to confess his sins, the priest explains to him the importance of the Eucharist for his spiritual regeneration. He has more need of it than others. And since he will be tortured by his imagination, he must fight the temptations with an effective weapon. Have you got a rosary? the priest asks. And the words of St. Bernard are quoted: *Totum nos habere voluit per Mariam*. We are back on the familiar track with St. Bernard at one end and St. Alphonsus at the other, like two watchmen shouting across the ages: All through Mary, with Mary, for Mary. Durtal's state of mind after absolution and communion reminds one of the Mariavite adoration of Christ in the host ('the Sacrament anaesthetized his mind,' Huysmans says of his alter ego).

No wonder that Kowalski found in *En route* a juxtaposition of ideas that haunted him before his re-conversion at the feet of the Little Mother. The hero of *Là-bas* and *En route* regains his peace of mind after going through the ordeals of temptation, his fantasies oscillating between licentiousness and asceticism. Hence Durtal's interest in the Gnostics who were supposed to 'render homage to God by the foulest uncleanness'. Also the concept of expiatory suffering which Huysmans thought necessary to balance the weight of evil resembled in essence the teaching of the Little Mother: the Mariavite should be prepared to accept the will of God in all its consequences and pay the ransom of pain for the sins of mankind. Suffering from cancer of the mouth Huysmans accepted it as his share in the work of expiation. Thy will be done.

---

[1] One of them is St. Severin in Paris where he sees 'the chapel dedicated to Our Lady'—the very chapel used by the Polish and French mystics in the 1840s when Towianski was preaching his gospel of spiritual rebirth (see p. 63).

In his crisis Kowalski took to the road as if to act out Durtal's *en route*.
Five weeks before meeting the Little Mother, in August 1900, he travelled
to the holy city of Czestochowa where he hoped to rekindle his faith. But
the Pauline Fathers at the cloister excused themselves one after another when
asked to hear his 'general confession'. Many pilgrims were arriving, so he
heard confessions himself, still in doubt whether his doing so was valid in
his state of suspended belief. And he prayed before the miraculous icon of
the 'black Virgin', but something within his conscience said that it was no
use praying to a picture. He should instead speak to Christ present in the
sacrament, and his prayer would be answered. 'I didn't know', he writes,
'what I had asked for and what was answered, though I felt a great joy and
peace in my soul.' Again he spent a whole day in prayer, slept little and at
four o'clock in the morning woke up sick with dysentery. His illness lasted
three days, he could not eat, felt no hunger, and continued reading books.
Kowalski's illness, it would seem, was an archetypal shamanistic experience.
In his initiatory illness the shaman recognizes that he is chosen and his body
is subjected to the experience of the mystical death.[1] The demons of illness
cut him to pieces and he sees his own dismemberment in a dream.

Kowalski began to loathe the Pauline cloister, as he saw dirt and disorder
around him, so he decided to go back to Warsaw. He managed to tuck in a
good dinner on the train, went to a doctor straight from the station, was
thoroughly examined, but the doctor could not diagnose his illness. At
home Kowalski found a colleague from the seminary waiting for him. A
coincidence or an intervention of destiny? It was this unexpected visitor
who put him in touch with the Mariavites.

And thus the man who was born on the day of Christ–Adam reached the
road which was to lead him to a new paradise on the banks of the Vistula,
the mother river of his land.

3

'True enough, I thought, if every man needs humility, I need it most of all,
for I never had it and never recognized anybody above myself, no authority
whatsoever, only God; and if ever before I submitted to some man, it was
more out of human prudence than out of any feeling of right or duty'.

This is Kowalski confessing in St. Augustine's manner soon after his
encounter with the Little Mother. He knows he has to humble himself, but
he also knows that his pride has always been at God's disposal. People who
later met him commented on this paradoxical trait in his character: he was

---

[1] See Mircea Eliade, *Le Chamanisme et les techniques archaïques de l'extase* (Paris, 1951).

an authoritarian, even a bully, who could suddenly forget about his authority and meekly accommodate those who served him. His behaviour in 1900 is full of such contradictions. He has to observe secrecy, do nothing that could point to his Mariavite vows, but in fact he longs to manifest his faith in public ('I wanted the whole world to learn of my happiness'). Soon he tries to impose the message of the Little Mother on two fellow priests. One of them reacts violently, travels to Kowalski's native town and spreads the news there that Father Kowalski has gone mad. The Lord, however, in his infinite justice marks the spiteful priest for punishment in a few years' time.[1]

Kowalski's own father had a simple proof of his son's madness. When he arrived as usual to ask for money, the pious son told him he was now a monk and therefore possessed nothing. So he gave his father only a few roubles and a picture of Our Lady of Perpetual Succour, saying: 'The Most Holy Mother herself will lead you out of your debts.'

The father took the picture and the roubles, but a few days later wrote a bitter letter accusing Kowalski of ingratitude. Nevertheless, all turned out well on the paternal front. The succour emanating from the holy picture stopped his perpetual getting into debt, and, having increased his property, Kowalski senior sold it at the end of his life. He died a Mariavite on the Little Mother's country estate.

John Maria Michael went on working sudden changes in people, often by handing them a small medallion with a representation of the Mother of Perpetual Succour. In *The Work of Great Mercy* Kowalski describes some of his early successes and attributes miraculous powers to the Work of Mercy revealed to the Little Mother.

Soon he received the first letter from her and although she did not say much, observing the code of secrecy, Kowalski felt that each of her words touched his spirit. From that day on, like a lover he eagerly waited every morning for a letter from Plock. And strange things began to happen to Kowalski. In his book he claims to have experienced the presence of the Virgin Mother ('I spiritually kissed her from head to foot').[2] Later, however, the Little Mother told him that this vision was not of the Virgin but of herself (and Christ, she said, called her 'My Beloved the Sealed Fortress'). One evening, lying in bed, Kowalski claims to have witnessed the visitation

---

[1] This priest, according to Kowalski, was so hostile when preaching against the Mariavites in 1906 that during one of his sermons he went off his head, had to be taken down from the pulpit and carried straight to a madhouse, where he died eight months later.

[2] In Kowalski's autobiographical novel, *My Ideal* (1932), the hero, who is a priest, after praying to the Virgin Mary senses her presence, and with great passion begins to kiss her blue eyes, her cheeks and lips, then her neck, shoulders, and breasts. He adores her whole body. And the Most Holy Virgin, he writes, did not forbid him to do this.

of Satan. The invisible fire was hissing as the evil spirit approached him from behind and only a cry to the Virgin of Perpetual Succour saved him in time. Another day, while he was drying himself with a towel, his soul sensed the approach of Christ. He was much afraid and with his heart pounding he shouted: 'No, no, no!' as if to push back the visiting Majesty. When he later described this to the Little Mother, she explained that such awe within the heart was 'a sure sign preceding a true revelation of the Lord Jesus'.

Whatever one thinks of supernatural claims of this kind, they can be related to the shamanistic phenomena in which celestial or infernal powers are supposed to act on a possessed mind, testing its resilience. Possession and spiritual initiation are complementary states, madness—a divinizing experience.

About eight months after their first meeting, the Little Mother visited Kowalski in Warsaw. When she entered, he prostrated himself before her, kissing the ground on which she was standing and also her feet—he already regarded her as equal to the Virgin Mary—and had she not lifted him up, he would not have dared to rise. She said she had attended his Mass that morning and after communion experienced a spiritual union with him which, she added, frightened her at first. She also told him there would be a separate heaven for the Mariavites and that he, Kowalski, would be near her in that heaven. Kowalski writes that he did not grasp the full implications of her promise, he only experienced supreme joy. He had a sudden urge to confess all the sins of his life to her, but was afraid that they might offend her purity.

The Little Mother behaved like a holy oracle: she neither forbade nor allowed him to confess, leaving the decision to his free will. And Kowalski's will gave him a push: he briskly made a sign of the cross and began to accuse himself, opening the secrets of his conscience. Half-way through he burst into tears and sobbed. It was 'as if he had torn off all his skin', the Little Mother told him later, and she felt great love for him during his self-accusation.

With all this commotion going on, he forgot to give her food during the whole day—then apologized for the omission, but the Little Mother smiled graciously and said she felt only thirst, but no hunger. No hunger at all.

The psychological ups and downs continued for Kowalski and each in some way deepened his relationship with the Little Mother. Passing through Warsaw in July 1901, she had one of her collapses, due either to excessive fasting or worry, was taken ill at a hotel, and at Kowalski's request agreed to be moved to a guest room at his home. He looked after his Little Mother and on 19 July, kneeling at her bedside, asked whether he could kiss her feet. She said nothing, which he took for permission and 'with great reverence, love, and peace of the soul' he kissed her legs covered with stockings, then her hands and head. At first the Little Mother was quiet, but soon she became apprehensive and finally disturbed. She wept and Kowalski tried to console her as best he could. It was then, he writes,

> that the Little Mother saw me as a small baby, given to her by the Lord Jesus. Holding my head in her little hands she herself told me that a few times with great love, and I was very surprised for I could not then understand the meaning of her vision. Only later on, the Lord Jesus explained to me that it was the fulfilment of the words from chapter 12 of the Apocalypse about the Woman in great pain giving birth to a grown-up son. . . . From that time my love for the Little Mother and for Christ entered a completely different state, and it was not seemly then to talk about it to people and to our priests because they were not yet capable of understanding such things.

The date of his spiritual rebirth, 19 July 1901, Kowalski guarded as a precious anniversary and often alluded to it in his writings after the Little Mother's death. It is difficult to say to what extent his acceptance of the event was due to the recurrent crises which culminated in an emotional fever shared with the woman whom he adored as the second Virgin Mary. Once she made a remark about his state of exaltation, which upset him. He could not pray afterwards, was unable to utter even a simple *Ave Maria*. But when she pronounced that there was no hysteria in him, this satisfied him at once and he felt at peace. The mood for prayer returned.

Whichever interpretation one applies to this incident, one thing is clear: Kowalski's emotional dependence on the Little Mother. In those critical shamanistic months of 1900 and 1901 she was his mediatrix, his hope and comfort, and a source of relief through tears. There were, indeed, many tears shed in the history of the Mariavites. The admiring nuns saw Kowalski weep during Mass or during adoration at night. The Little Mother sobbed as she reported Christ's message to the chapter of her priests assembled in Plock. Other leaders of the movement, too, preferred on occasion to argue with tears rather than with words. The emotional intensity of the Mariavites was their psychological strength and also their weakness, and who knew it better than Kowalski himself who had gone through the nine months of spiritual pangs in the Little Mother's womb?

There is a mysterious piece of information in his 'Brief Life' of Kozlowska:

> In January 1902 when I was at the Little Mother's in Plock the Lord Jesus brought me closer and united me with her, not only as the son but also as the Beloved, in the likeness of our first parents. A year earlier the Lord Jesus in

the same way brought together and united Father Jacob with the Little
Mother, and in the later years Father Bartholomew and Father Philip.[1] In
the morning of the same day on which the Lord Jesus bestowed upon me this
inexpressible Grace of His, the Sisters brought from the Little Mother's
garden a beautiful red flower which had opened under the snow, and they
also brought a few daisies in bloom from under the snow. This phenomenon,
most unusual in so severe a winter, attracted the attention of all the Sisters.
For fulfilled were the words from the Song of Songs: 'Rise up, my love, my
fair one, and come away. For, lo, the winter is past . . . the flowers appear
on the earth' [2. 11–12].

Apart from Solomon's Song there is another analogy among the legends
woven round the life of St. Clare of Assisi. She, too, made the roses bloom
in winter when St. Francis was departing from her. The Little Mother took
St. Clare as her model, and in a number of instances tried to emulate her.
She would, for example, like St. Clare, mark the sign of the cross on the
forehead of a person who came to her for spiritual advice.

The facts and the emotional tone of the passage which I have quoted seem
to point to the same conclusion: the mystical union which bound Kowalski
to the Little Mother could well have been a physical act. Moreover, the
repetition of it with the other three priests suggests some kind of pattern in
which an equilibrium between the soul and the body is sought for a mystical
purpose. If the snow symbolizes virginity as it surely must, then the symbol
of the opened bud is obvious, especially since its colour is red. The concept
of rebirth, too, seems relevant to Kowalski's acceptance of the Little
Mother's gift. She is for him the Beloved of Solomon, born again in their
union. Whatever the will of God has decreed for them, they must joyfully
obey. The Bible is a book of promises, both open and secret, and every one
of them has to be fulfilled.

The language of adoration which Kowalski lavishes on his Beloved
betrays his anxieties as well, and it is to his credit that in *The Work of Great
Mercy*, published three years after the Little Mother's death, he tries to keep
faithful to the moods of 1901, recording them all with a lover's care. For
him they have become relics enshrined in his heart and protected by his
memory.

> Whenever the Little Mother noticed some bad habit or imperfection in
> me, which I failed to see myself, she at once rebuked me, causing a great
> suffering in my soul, because I would then imagine that the Little Mother
> had no true love for me and could not have it for a sinner as great as myself,
> and only forced herself to show it, so that I would not be hurt. . . . One

[1] The three Fathers are the future Mariavite bishops: Jacob Próchniewski, Bartholomew
Przysiecki, and Philip Feldman.

day I decided to note her every word and her every act towards me to see whether any lack of love on her part would show. And I thought to myself: should this lack reveal itself, I would withdraw from the Little Mother and treat her only as my Superior. For two weeks I observed her every word, every gesture, looking for some flaw and imperfection, however small, and could find none, only love and goodness.

This is a lover testing his beloved, a psychological device often adopted in pastoral romances and romantic novelettes. In his ardour Kowalski doesn't see the silly side of his reminiscences.

At that time, too, because of my clumsiness I cut the Little Mother's little finger while shutting her travelling bag so that she cried aloud like a child. I had then a foreknowledge that it would be through me that the Lord Jesus would pass the greatest torments to the Little Mother. Yet I didn't feel her sufferings, I only felt them in the last year of her Passion.

Kowalski visited Kozlowska in Lublin. She was writing down her Revelations at a house of her nuns, and he suffered a great deal being separated from his Little Mother. 'For eight days and nights,' he writes, 'I couldn't sleep, waiting for God's mercy and listening through the wall for the Little Mother's call to me.' But she was too busy writing and, as Kowalski puts it, felt no will of God to summon him. 'At last on the eighth day she came to me of her own free will, and it was then that the Lord Jesus told the Little Mother: "To me give your soul, to him your body."' At that time, too, she experienced 'my being torn out of her entrails and for a few days felt a wound in her heart'.

Reading this account served up in Biblical dressing one cannot help arriving at the conclusion that a deep intimacy had occurred between the Little Mother and her Beloved Son, a sort of mystical incest, if one takes Kowalski's phraseology literally. Yet even today the critically minded Mariavites who reject Kowalski's later teaching are most reluctant to throw any suspicion on his relationship with their foundress. They want at all costs to preserve her image as that of a saint, although they have themselves abandoned the Catholic worship of saints. In any church tradition, however, there must be at least one person wholly exempt from the faults of ordinary mortals. What, to my mind, has to be considered is the use of language. Kowalski had a certain flair for Biblical travesty and left his mark on the style of other Mariavites, even those who later wanted to have nothing to do with him. The records of the mystical marriages, for instance, which were written by the participants, reveal much affinity with Kowalski's erotic symbolism. Some echo his phrases addressed to the Little Mother, and since there is no doubt whatsoever about the sexual nature of the mystical unions after 1924, one has to place Kowalski's union with his spiritual mother in the same context. It was Kowalski who instituted these marriages and linked them with the concept of the new heaven which the Little Mother had opened to him.

4

I don't intend to elaborate on the early squabbles between Kowalski and his superiors while he was still nominally a Catholic priest. What concerns me here is the development of his Mariavite identity. Kowalski tells us about the long queues outside his confessional and about his sermons in praise of the Virgin, which irritated the suspicious authorities. He was summoned before the Archbishop of Warsaw, reprimanded, and moved to a suburb, then to a provincial parish.

For a time at least the medallions representing Our Lady of Perpetual Succour seemed to be the chief worry of the hierarchy. They were freely distributed by the followers of Kozlowska, usually after confession. Although they didn't differ much from other devotional objects worn round the neck, suspicion fell on their purpose. Some priests, Kowalski among them, were accused of treating the medallions as obligatory aid to the sacrament of penance. Ironically enough, the Redemptorist Fathers, whose founder St. Alphonsus had inspired Kozlowska, used their missionary zeal in rousing the faithful against the medallions. They are contaminated with heresy, so bury them deep in the ground. The peasants did that, and more. They crushed the metal with stones or hung the medallions on the horns and tails of their cattle for mock display. The idea was to turn the visible signs of a new cult into ridiculous objects and thus render them harmless. But the revivalist mood held.

In 1903, ten years after the first revelation, Kozlowska was told by the Voice to write down everything that had been revealed to her, and to present the whole text to the Polish bishops (she was given the names of three), and afterwards to the Pope himself. Kozlowska obeyed, and the Mariavite Rules and the text of the Revelations were submitted to the Bishop of Plock, Szembek, who appointed two priests to investigate the affair. To forestall Bishop Szembek's action, sixteen Mariavite priests went, with Kozlowska, to Rome. There, on 6 August 1903, they elected Kowalski leader of the Mariavite congregation.[1] Then on 23 August they had an audience with Pope Pius X in a corridor leading to the Vatican gardens. It

---

[1] This election was confirmed in 1907 by the first General Chapter of the Mariavite priests and the delegates from all the parishes, which met at Kozlowska's order in Praga, a suburb of Warsaw.

was indeed a passing encounter: the summary of Kozlowska's Revelations, a rug embroidered by her nuns, and other gifts were presented, the Pope handed the papers to the attendant prelate, thanked them for the gifts, and departed. In her humility Kozlowska did not look up to see the Pope's face.

A year later, on 31 August 1904, the Congregation of the Holy Inquisition in Rome handed down its verdict: Kozlowska's messages, which she attributed to Christ, were mere hallucinations. The Mariavite congregation was to be disbanded, the priests were forbidden to communicate with Kozlowska and were released from their Mariavite vows. At first the Mariavites obeyed the edict of Rome, and Kozlowska was summoned by the Bishop of Plock to sign the document condemning their whole congregation. In March 1905, Kowalski was once more removed by his bishop, to the parish of Sobótka, a village of 700 inhabitants, and other Mariavite priests were sent to remote parishes in the hope that they would be isolated from one another.

An Inquisitional hunt after Kozlowska's sympathizers was on. Poor Father Honorat had to explain his past associations with her. When the Mariavites produced the letters of support he had written Kozlowska, they were said to be forgeries—a charge echoed by Honorat in a pamphlet he published in which he denounced the Mariavites, and thus cleared his name of any suspicion of heresy. Others did more and, out of fear, joined the hunters.

At the beginning of 1906, however, both the Catholic majority in Poland and the Mariavite rebels were still hoping for some kind of reconciliation, for a *deus ex machina* to be conjured up by the Vatican. The Roman Catholic Church could not afford to lose thousands of followers in a class which was traditionally loyal to the Pope. And there was also the historic sense of the Catholic mission in eastern Europe, with Poland as its strongest outpost. The mood therefore wavered from week to week.

In February 1906, seven Mariavite priests were suspended by their bishops for persisting in their zealous cult of the Eucharist.[1] They in turn challenged the authority of the bishops, and two of them, Kowalski and Father Jacob (Próchniewski), went to Rome to appeal. There they presented a memorial to the Curia, accusing six bishops and 1200 priests of immoral acts. Kozlowska's Voices had urged her to counter-attack: 'A judgement for a judgement.' The dossier had been compiled with a view to proving the truth of her Revelations. The Pope granted the two priests an audience on 20 February 1906.

---

[1] Although the Eucharistic fervour of the Mariavites was held suspect, both Pope Leo XIII and Pius X in their encyclicals advocated frequent communion.

In the turbulent month of February 1906, the Warsaw *Illustrated Weekly* sent a journalist and a photographer to report on the Mariavite dissension in the rural communities. Three articles appeared in the magazine, from 3 to 17 March.[1] The second describes a visit to Sobótka, where Kowalski had been parish priest before his suspension. All the peasants were full of praise for their priest and expected great things from his visit to Rome. The journalist attempted a character sketch of Kowalski:

> An artist by nature, he paints well and likes music.[2] But his is a proud character, craving for power. Among the Mariavites he wants to be regarded as their bishop and always shows his hierarchical supremacy to all the priests who come for sectarian instruction to his parish as if it were an academy. Priests kiss the hand of their General disregarding his young age. . . . He is a sociable man, sometimes even friendly and gay. With the village people he is particularly gentle, his manner winsome. He has no deep education.

This is Kowalski seen by others at the age of thirty-five. The photograph reproduced in the weekly shows a handsome face with bold eyes, full of innocence and charm, in contrast to the later portraits where a heaviness of features betrays the inner pride and the sense of power.

But the Demon of Noon (a spirit of darkness disguised as an angel of light)[3] began to manifest his power over Kowalski through a series of temptations. From now on this luminous spirit would lay traps for John Maria Michael who dared to be born on the symbolic day of the Nativity. Which the great Tempter considered an unpardonable offence and a challenge to a duel of souls.

[1] Though their tone is often patronizing, the information in these articles is of considerable value. In the first of them (3 March 1906) we find this conjecture: 'As for Kozlowska and some other priests, a medical scrutiny would undoubtedly reveal in them psychopathic perversions of sexual origin. . . . The whole affair will have a sad end.'

[2] Kowalski painted an early portrait of the Little Mother which has survived and is preserved at Felicjanów. He also made a drawing of her and hung it in his parish church, but she ordered him to destroy it.

[3] Kowalski identified the Demon (*duch południowy*) with 'the destruction that wasteth at noonday' in Psalm 91. This *demonium meridianum* (*démon de midi* in French) is associated with Pan, the god who creates fear (panic). He strikes at noon when we are vulnerable, because we cast no shadow.

3

The Temple of Love

WHERE there is no love, there is no God. In every parish, in December 1906, the Mariavites formed processions and, singing hymns to the Sacred Heart, took with them the hidden God and forsook the Roman churches, 'leaving their House empty'. And the Lord went with them because they loved him. Kowalski describing the Mariavite exodus uses a Biblical parallel: 'As the Israelites in the desert after departing from Egypt praised God in the Tabernacle, that is in the tent, so we too prepared humble tabernacles in peasant huts among poor people who were pure in spirit, and it was from them that God began to receive a true glorification after having been expelled from the hearts and from the churches of the Roman Catholics.'

The December exodus took place after weeks of bitter fighting over the churches, and followed a period of great confusion after the failure of Kowalski's appeal to the Pope in February. On 5 April Pius X published the encyclical, *Tribus circiter abhinc annis*, condemning the Mariavites once again; whereupon violence broke out. Some parishioners followed their Mariavite priests and removed by force the priests who were sent to replace them. Others opposed the Mariavites, and in the struggle there were dead and wounded on both sides. On 22 April, for instance, a crowd of 3,000 Catholics, led by a few priests, marched on Leszno, near Warsaw, to take the parish church away from the Mariavites. The two groups, armed with clubs, guns, and scythes, clashed. Six people were killed, twenty-seven wounded.[1] Near Lodz, at Stryków, five people were killed. In Sobótka the Mariavites fought over the church, but had to abandon it and build a new one. In some villages the Russian police and the Cossacks had to intervene, and they acted with their customary indifference. This created a bitter mood: some Polish leaders feared a religious civil war, a thing unheard of in their country.

In the first week of troubles nineteen large parishes declared their allegiance to the Mariavite priests, then the number rose to seventy parishes with nearly 100,000 faithful. Polish peasants whose docility was taken for

[1] A Warsaw paper, *Warszawiak*, published a special issue on this incident with illustrations—blaming the Mariavites, of course, for the whole affair.

granted by the intelligentsia and the gentry now found new leaders in priests who would not take money for their services and who practised religious democracy in everyday life. And the peasants stood up for freedom of conscience. The subjugated nation was shaken in its patriotic complacency.

Mateczka Płocka w objeździe swojej dyecezji i w drodze z wizytą do Mateczki Lubelskiej

1906 cartoon of the Little Mother with the devil

There could not have been a more propitious year for a radical movement than 1906. The revolution of 1905 had forced the Russian government to liberalize its internal policy and to relax censorship. In the Russian part of Poland some national issues could at last be discussed in the open, even if allusions had still to be veiled, a stratagem to which Polish writers were accustomed.

The series of articles on the Mariavites in the Warsaw *Illustrated Weekly* in March 1906 had been followed, significantly, by a report on the low state of education among the peasants. The practical needs of the people were ignored, the report says, not enough attention was given to their language and religion; since 1870 when the teaching of Russian was introduced in village schools, the number of pupils had declined steadily. One of the conditions for autonomy was the use of the national language in schools and offices, and the Mariavites' introduction two years later of a Polish liturgy was to become an important attraction, and a weapon against counter-attacks from Rome.[1]

The first *Illustrated Weekly* article on the Mariavites had ended with a reference to Russian policy: 'It is not yet known whether they [i.e. the Mariavites] will get support from the influential quarters who want to push them into the creation of a separate "national" church. Politics, too, here come into play.' Some nine months later, on 28 November 1906, the Russian government legalized the Mariavites as a sect. They had to give back the Catholic churches in their possession, but could now build their own. The legal status of each of their new parishes would be confirmed locally.

On 31 December 1906 the Inquisitional axe fell on the heads of Mother Kozlowska and Kowalski: they were both excommunicated. The breach with Rome was final. Bells were rung in all the Mariavite churches, and the people, relieved of the tension, kissed one another and sang a hymn of thanksgiving. The children of the Little Mother were now on their own.

Within one year of the exodus, practically all Mariavite parishes had their own churches and parish houses which were to be used as kindergartens and schools. The priests themselves lived humbly in one or two cells over the sacristy. To the Mariavites the house of worship meant a place from which brotherly and sisterly love should extend in social work as, for instance, caring for the children, the old and the sick. No doubt, the Franciscan spirit of worshipping God through all his creatures merged here with the positivist ideal of work and service to the community.

Brought up on these ideals, Maria Frances Kozlowska had a true feeling for the needs of the poor; her example and her great organizational ability succeeded in producing within a remarkably short time many thriving communities, in which layman and priest worked together. They built churches literally with their own hands, a priest laying bricks next to a peasant. Several families handed over their entire property and with their children moved to the religious communes. In the parish of Leszno, an enthusiastic priest called Furmanik introduced common ownership in 1908. All earnings were paid in and the money distributed according to particular needs. Savings were communal, too, though the scheme didn't last long.

To one another the Mariavites were simply 'Brother' and 'Sister', equal under the Brother Sun. The Biblical term for priest, *kapłan*, replaced *ksiądz*

---

1 The Polish liturgy was introduced first in Plock on Christmas day 1907, and during the following year in all Mariavite parishes. Though it appealed to the masses, it was also regarded with suspicion, because dispensing with Latin brought the Mariavites closer to the Russian Orthodox Church.

whose connotation was originally 'prince'.[1] The same happened with the word for church (*kościół*, from the Latin *castellum*). The Mariavites preferred the Biblical *świątynia* (temple) which had a sonorous native sound. After the introduction of Polish liturgy in 1907 the Mariavites became even more language-conscious, and Kowalski, whose interest in translation was to develop into an obsession, had a hand in every experiment in the vernacular.

Both he and the Little Mother dreamt of building a temple in the city of Plock which the Lord had chosen for his Work of Mercy. A new temple of Solomon, a new Song of Songs composed in stone and brick, in prayer and in vision. The Biblical concept of fulfilment informed most of the Little Mother's projects, but her spiritual son had an inventive mind, ready to pounce on each of her angelic pronouncements. At this time Kowalski formed the habit of drawing parallels between the now which they were both creating and the ancient prophetic map of the future unfolding before their eyes. And we shall build Jerusalem in Poland's green and pleasant land.

The sinister Demon of Noon, however, didn't like that at all and interfered by whispering his own parallelism. You may feel safe with Solomon cooing his Song of Songs, but have you forgotten the monsters breathing evil from the dark corners of the Apocalypse? Like St. John, the Little Mother experienced (according to her claim) the glory and the terror of a divine revelation, so she did remember how infernally clever and sudden were the Beast's interventions. If she was a mediatrix between the heavenly designs and the earthly paradise to be recreated on the banks of the Vistula, then Kowalski, too, was a go-between used by the crafty Demon of Noon. Later he freely admitted to being a conveyor of grief and pain to the woman who made his rebirth possible, but his frankness in no way excused his conscience. The guilt between mother and son was building up and could only be resolved by her death, provided he would share her agony.

It is worth observing in passing that Kowalski's real mother is conspicuously absent from the autobiographical pages of *The Work of Great Mercy*. At the time he was writing these—the Little Mother already dead—he had no room in his heart for the mere physical mediatrix whose womb he used as a means to an ordinary birth so that he could be reborn fully at the age of thirty. Perhaps St. Francis, the Mariavite hero, felt the same when he discarded his terrestrial father Pietro Bernardone like the robes made up of his cloth, which the saint threw off in honour of Lady Poverty. John Maria Michael with the triple seal of names on his vocation aspired to the saint's purity in his archetypal dreams, but the vigorous body with which he was

---

[1] In common parlance, however, this meaning was no longer felt, and the diminutive, *książę* was used.

endowed by the forgotten mother in Latowicz had no urge to receive any stigmata, painfully real or superficial. And who knew that better than the prompter of unfulfilled desires, the Demon of Noon, hot as the flame of his angelic ancestry?

Kowalski's personal triumph came after the breach with Rome when the Mariavites succeeded in being recognized as a religious body outside Poland. At the suggestion of a Russian friend, General Kireyev, Kowalski went to Vienna to attend a congress of the Old Catholics who had split from Rome after defying the Vatican over the dogma of Papal infallibility.[1] When the congress ended, he followed the Dutch Old Catholic bishops to Holland. There, on 5 October 1909, Kowalski was consecrated bishop by Gerard Gul, Archbishop of Utrecht, and three other bishops.

Soon after the consecration, with the Little Mother's approval Kowalski issued his first pastoral letter. He now had sacral authority, for in terms of the apostolic succession his title of bishop was valid. This alone gave the Mariavite dissidents a new confidence *vis-à-vis* the Catholic Church.[2]

For Kowalski it became a source of pride which, as he later admitted, made him think he was at last somebody in the presence of the Little Mother. Against her wishes he began to wear a bishop's cross to distinguish himself from other priests. He soon recognized this act of disobedience as a sin, but she in her maternal understanding of grown-up children, allowed him to wear a cross, a modest ivory one, unlike the previous one which was plated with silver.

The Demon of Noon worked through Kowalski's pride pulling him down to the level of sensuality. And though the newly-baked bishop did not (according to his testimony) fall into a grave sin, he nevertheless had his soul nibbled at. Soon his second-in-command, Father Jacob, succumbed to the temptation of pride so that the eleventh chapter of the Apocalypse could make sense: 'These are the two olive trees, and the two candlesticks standing before the God of the earth . . . and the beast shall make war against them.' The passage referred to the two of them, said Kowalski. He had this information from the Little Mother who had it from the Lord Jesus and the Lord, of course, remembered the chapter and the relevant verses from his own book. Moreover, he told the Little Mother at the beginning of 1910 to warn all the Fathers and Sisters about the pending campaign of the Demon of Noon who—to quote the supreme authority—'tempts man to evil under

[1] The dogma, defined by the Vatican Council in 1870, confirmed in psychological terms the supreme authority of the father.
[2] Though the Russians had recognized the Mariavites as a sect, and pamphlets had been printed in Russia to inform the public about them, to be fully recognized as a church they needed consecrated bishops.

the guise of good, therefore nobody can resist him, save him who is enlightened by God himself and thus delivered from temptation'. Maria Frances Kozlowska was such a person, an *illuminata*.

Already some Mariavite priests had fallen from their previous angelic heights. *Nomen et omen*, Father Gabriel was one: he fornicated with the fair daughters of man and celebrated Mass without confessing his sins. Other priests committed similar transgressions. Kowalski gives seven names, a symbolic number under the apocalyptic sky, and among them there is, curiously enough, a Father Marx (spelt Marks in Polish). Again a few ominous words of St. John were fulfilled, for the Beast was permitted to overpower saints and to kill them. Since the passionate Demon of Noon had no access to the elect such as the Little Mother (fifteen degrees of purification, according to her testimony), the next best evil he could do was to tempt her through her spiritual son Bishop John Maria Michael. And he certainly tried.

First came the way of greed. Kowalski suggested a financial scheme: 60,000 roubles to be invested at a high rate of interest to safeguard the security of their congregation. Kozlowska rejected it outright.

The second was the way of pride. Kowalski publicized the holiness of the Little Mother and compared her to the Virgin Mother which caused her great sorrow.[1]

Third came the way of sensuality. The Little Mother was the target of Kowalski's passion. This last temptation created much emotional turmoil. Kowalski persisted, she cried, they parted, a few days later Kowalski went away, then he sent her a letter asking to be called back. She called him back, and again there were temptations and abundant tears, until the Little Mother refused to receive communion from Kowalski's hands. Soon afterwards, she fainted in the chapel at Felicjanów. 'Just like the Lord Jesus on the Mount of Olives', comments Kowalski. And so on and on. To gain strength against the demon of passion, the bishop castigated himself with work, translating the Psalms of David; their content, he says, 'expressed the state of his own soul'.

He thought he had lost the love of the Little Mother, his guilt tormented him and there were angry scenes. His ebullient temperament swayed his moods. One day he rebelled against the mother image, the next day he begged her forgiveness. This son-and-mother conflict was to go on for ten years until the beginning of Kozlowska's serious illness in 1920.

Impressed though one is by Kowalski's naked exposure of his sins against the Holy Spirit (incarnated in the Little Mother), one is still uncertain as to the exact meaning of these frontal attacks on her purity. There is a cryptic

[1] When pressed to explain whether this was against the will of God, Maria Frances Kozlowska was, as usual, noncommittal.

hint at one point in *The Work of Great Mercy*, concerning his need of comfort in sensuality: '. . . This search was not evil in itself, but as the time had not yet come for God's Will to be fulfilled in this respect, so it wasn't the Will of God then but rather the pull of sensuality and Satan's temptation.'

What is he alluding to in this passage? To the fulfilment which obviously came with the mystical marriages which he was introducing while the book was in progress? This, of course, reads like hindsight. The question is still open. What made him act the way he did? Would he so persistently have tried to tempt the Little Mother, had there not been a previous relation entitling him to such a behaviour? Why then did she refuse to give him what he wanted? Did she see a danger in a continued intimacy? Was the example of the fallen priests, her angels, a clear warning to her?

How far was the proximity of illness responsible for her strict adherence to the ascetic rule she had imposed on herself? She ate little, fasted often, and was altogether abstemious in her daily habits. She spared no energy, however, when matters of the church required her attention: she gave counsel to her nuns, received priests who reported once a month, interviewed candidates for the novitiate, visited the parishes, wrote letters, and during all these activities rigidly observed the hours of adoration before the Sacrament.

The old nuns who remember her always speak with tender reverence about the stillness of her body in prayer. The act of adoration seemed to consume her whole being. Something was obviously happening within her which excluded the possessive love of others, Kowalski's especially. He wanted to possess his mother like a greedy child still unweaned from her breast, spiritually or otherwise. He did, more than once, admit to being hurt whenever she showed more affection to the other priests.[1]

There was enough of the writer in Kowalski to observe himself from a distance with fascination and disgust. Spiritual self-accusation became a spiritual hobby with him and he indulged in it, as witness many pages in *The Work of Great Mercy*, his gargantuan scripture.

2

The activities of the Demon of Noon were temporarily checked by the Magi from the north, the Old Catholic bishops from Holland who came at Kowalski's invitation to take part in the consecration of two more Mariavite bishops, auxiliary this time.[2] The group included a few senior priests, one

[1] His emotional rival was the future bishop, Philip Feldman, who seemed to have won the Little Mother's affection. Their brotherly love was to end in hatred.
[2] Jacob (Próchniewski) and Andrew (Gołębiowski) were consecrated bishops at this time.

of whom, Kenninck, the future Archbishop of Utrecht, was to be instrumental in ousting the Mariavites from their Union of churches (1924).

During their visit the Little Mother revealed all her social graces and charmed the solid worthies from the north. They were under her spell and visibly impressed by what they saw of the development of the movement. It was 1910, less than four years after the separation from Rome, and everywhere the Dutch went they could witness the Little Mother's achievement. After so much abuse in the past[1] her personal triumph dazzled not only her followers and the foreign visitors, but also many Catholics. The consecration took place on 4 September and in the course of the arranged tour the Little Mother went with her guests to the industrial city of Lodz, one of the Mariavite strongholds. They drove through the town in an open landau, and the faithful and the curious lined the streets in their thousands. Needless to say, Kowalski described the scene as the entry into the New Jerusalem. 'Blessed be the King that cometh in the name of the Lord. Hosanna in the highest!'[2]

In Warsaw, too, they met with an enthusiastic welcome. Crowds gathered in the square outside the Mariavite church and they shouted for their Little Mother. When she appeared with the Dutch guests on the balcony, van Thiel, Bishop of Haarlem, kissed her hands—'little hands', of course, in Kowalski's scripture. This homage by a distinguished foreigner— Poles are susceptible to foreign praise—delighted the people and made them feel proud. Kowalski's comment at this parallelistic juncture is a bit odd: he thought of Christ being shown to the people with Pilate uttering his *Ecce homo*. Whether he told this to the Bishop of Haarlem we do not know. One wonders how the serious Dutchman would have reacted. We know, however, what Gul, Archbishop of Utrecht, said on their departure. As the river boat was passing the Mariavite property he raised his hat and exclaimed in a hieratic manner which must have thrilled the spiritual son of Maria Frances:

'Farewell to thee, seat of saints! May God bless thee and guide the work of the elect.'

It appears that neither the natives nor the foreigners could remain indifferent to the Little Mother's charisma. This was a propitious omen for the possible spread of the Mariavite gospel abroad. The Old Catholic bishops

[1] The hatred of her was indeed paranoiac. A woman who happened to have the same name as hers was attacked by a mob and nearly killed. They spat on her, threw mud and horse dung in her face until someone who knew the victim pointed out their mistake.

[2] A curious incident occurred during a later visit of Kowalski to Lodz, in January 1912. A demented Mariavite woman urged a hysterical crowd to crucify him, and the police had to intervene. One female zealot even brought a crown of thorns for Kowalski. It was a mystical compliment in a way. They were sure he would rise from the dead on the third day.

did, in fact, lecture on the Polish movement after returning home. And though the Little Mother seemed at first reluctant to have consecrated bishops in her church,[1] she now saw the effect which the Union had produced, and declared that their name should be: 'The Old Catholic Church of the Mariavites'. So be it. *Nihil obstat* for the excommunicated.

One can also understand why the Dutch bishops were genuinely keen on being affiliated with the Mariavites. Their own parishes were small and dwindling away. The same was true of the Old Catholics in Germany, not a great prospect for the future.[2] To see a vigorous new movement in eastern Europe, now 100,000 strong, attracting not only peasants but also industrial workers (as in Lodz and in Silesia) was for the westerners an answer to their prayers. Van Thiel did not only kiss Kozlowska's hands in gratitude; he also wrote her a solemn letter (dated 10 October 1910), in which he recognized her spiritual leadership over the Mariavites and, what was more important from a theological point of view, the divine origin of her mission ('we see in it not the work of man but of God'). Bishop van Thiel probably hesitated over what form of address was appropriate for him to use. He combined respect with affection and called Kozlowska 'Most Reverend Mother and Dear Little Mother'. The Slavonic diminutive was catching on.

One would think that with all these signs of acknowledgement around, Bishop Kowalski should have been in high spirits. Quite the contrary: in a group photograph taken with the foreign guests he looks glum, and in his memoir he admits that he was not as cheerful and helpful during the whole visit as he would have wished, because his estrangement from the Little Mother weighed heavily on his mind. With customary breast-beating he confesses:

> So often spurred by pride and the desire to show my superiority, by jealousy and self-love, I caused the Little Mother a great deal of distress (*przykrość*] because of my unjustified grievances and sulks.[3] With the greatest humility and love she softened my anger and for a long time yet she had to suffer it patiently. . . .

The Demon of Noon was blowing hard and in all directions at once. Feeling the heat on his own bovine neck, Bishop Kowalski had little patience with the fallen apostles in his own ranks. Like Dante whose *Divina Com-*

1 She had an 'understanding' that the new priesthood should come from Kowalski as it had once come from Aaron.
2 Before the war, in 1937, there were 30,000 of them in Germany. Today there are only 10,000 Old Catholics in Holland.
3 We must, of course, bear in mind that this and other self-deprecatory remarks were written shortly after the Little Mother's death.

media he was to translate, Kowalski applied the master's strictures to each Judas and sent him tumbling down into the Mariavite hell. *The Work of Great Mercy* is merciless in this respect: the traitors are named with their relevant and irrelevant particulars, the vocabulary of indignation spits venom and fire; Kowalski is at his apocalyptic best. He knows what the sly tempter can do. No mercy in hell, therefore no mercy for hell.

There was a certain angelic priest called Zebrowski, much beloved in the Mariavite congregation, and he turned Judas while the Demon of Noon was blowing hot and hard. The Demon, it seemed, revealed his sinister sense of humour when he produced an anti-Revelation through a woman whom the priest Zebrowski recognized as a successor to the Little Mother. And he wrote down the messages received by her from above.

There is a scene described by Kowalski which one would have loved to watch: the face-to-face meeting between the Judas priest and the Little Mother, he clutching the new postscript to the Apocalypse in his pocket, while kissing (hypocritically of course, says Kowalski) the little hand of the holy foundress. And the cheek of it all!—Zebrowski fished out the piece of paper and gave it to her. Whereupon the Little Mother learnt from the rival Revelation that she had fallen out of the divine grace and was no longer a Mariavite. Moreover, God, eternally efficient as ever, had already transferred the whole Work of Mercy to Zebrowski and his woman visionary.[1] Both were to reform Mariavitism and introduce public confession: the cult of the Sacred Host was not enough.

Then the Judas departed, absentmindedly leaving his notebook on the Little Mother's little table. The notebook revealed more Revelations, this time his own. Now Kowalski had no doubt that the shadow-devouring Demon of Noon was behind them. Soon afterwards a band of Zebrowski's followers turned up and abused the Little Mother when she tried to explain the unpleasant business. Zebrowski appropriated a Mariavite church in Warsaw, refused to obey orders from Plock, and when Kowalski came to assert his authority, the rebels attacked him with the intention of trampling him to death. But the Will of God willed otherwise, and the Russian commissar backed up Kowalski. Zebrowski was removed by force from his parish church, but his influence continued: he urged the dissenting Mariavites to demand the return of money which they had lent to the congregation. Many financial complications resulted, some parishes fell into heavy debt, and only during the First World War was the situation stabilized.

Apart from the Demon of Noon it was, according to Kowalski, the desire

---

[1] Her name was Cychlarzowa. Kowalski was relieved when the civil authorities deported her as an Austrian subject.

to become bishop that drove the deluded man to such wickedness. But the interesting thing about Zebrowski and his new 'Little Mother' is precisely the free-for-all repetition of the divine scheme. Let's have another revelation and another holy mother. Who is to tell which one is false? When Kowalski reminded him of the vow of obedience, the rebel priest replied that he vowed to obey the Will of God, nothing else. Will *v.* Will, and may the best will win. Rumours said that his woman visionary celebrated Mass, which shocked Kowalski. At that time he considered it sacrilegious. Things would look quite different after 1929.

3

The whole Zebrowski incident left a scar on the moral edifice of the movement. A stronger building was needed that could withstand the forces so visibly unleashed—as Kowalski believed—by the demon of discord.

The wise King Solomon built the Temple.

We don't know whether King Solomon designed the Temple in Jerusalem himself, but we know that Bishop Kowalski drew the plans of the Mariavite temple in Plock. He had artistic inclinations, was good at drawing, but the sense of structure which he revealed in so complex an undertaking is truly impressive. Anxious to give the Little Mother every credit he tells of her initiative (prompted, as usual, by the Lord) and attributes to her the choice of the actual site, which was on her property in Dobrzynska Street, adjoining the small houses where her nuns lived. The position itself would have inspired any architect: it was close to the left bank of the Vistula, elevated at Plock, and giving a magnificent view on to the curve of the river and the flat fields on the other side. Not the paradise of Adam and Eve perhaps, but a good substitute for it in the northern hemisphere.

Kowalski racked his brains how to fit the buildings into the shape of the all-embracing M: M for Maria, *Mateczka* (the Little Mother), Mariavites, Michael, Misericordia, and *Miłość*, of course, which is 'Love' in Polish. The slant of the street seemed to be in the way so he asked Maria Frances for advice, and 'Ah, never mind,' said she; 'if this cannot be, let's do it in accordance with our necessity and poverty.' This sounded like Solomon's answer, and the spiritual son got busy. For economic reasons he had to use the existing walls of the houses, for aesthetic reasons he had to run the front buildings (i.e. the cloister) parallel with the street. Somehow he solved the problem of the temple (with three towers on top) by proposing that the whole edifice should be shifted back. Thus it could be constructed as a rectangle without upsetting the line of the street.

When the plans were accepted by the authorities, one of the Mariavite Fathers looked at them and noticed that they formed the letter F, the initial of the Little Mother's Christian name, Feliksa. She in turn discovered that together with F there was also E. Kowalski was quick to grasp the double significance. E for the Eucharist with which the Little Mother was so closely united. And later, when it came to counting the number of tiles needed for the building, another discovery was made. The whole structure, seen as a straight line, measured three hundred cubits in length, the same as the Ark of Noah.

What a joyful surprise for Kowalski! He was building a new Jerusalem and a new ark at the same time. The ark in the Work of Mercy would protect the new species of man and the new creatures. And wasn't he triply endowed for this rescue operation? Archangel Michael, Adam, and Noah in one. He soon began to think in threes, his parallelism couldn't be satisfied otherwise. The ark symbol appealed to the punishing urge in him. We'll drown them all with God's help, all the renegade Zebrowskis and the papal Babylonia as well. A three-day retreat then as penance for the people: this was the Little Mother's wish, for the wrath of the Lord would manifest itself before long. When a few years later the war broke out, peasants saw she was right and many became Mariavites overnight.

The foundations of the temple were consecrated on 27 May 1911, the forty-ninth anniversary of the Little Mother's birth. No doubt, the bishop architect worked out the combined significance of all those numbers. A few thousand of the faithful turned up to see the ceremony. And for as long as the work continued, each parish promised to send volunteers to help the professional builders. Willingly they came, a new batch every fortnight. One wonders what pious rules applied to the workers of Solomon. In Plock they were simple: Mass at five o'clock in the morning, all volunteers received communion, then they had breakfast and at six punctually they were on the site, working. Silence and prayer dominated the scene. 'One could never hear a single bad word uttered', writes Kowalski, 'although there were more Roman Catholics among the masons than Mariavites.' The local people, surprised by the size of the building, would ask the workers what it was going to be. Half-jokingly they would answer: 'The New Jerusalem'. No doubt they heard the phrase bandied about by the volunteers. 'And what happened to the previous one?' the locals asked. 'It's got old and it's falling to pieces,' they replied without realizing, writes Kowalski, that it was the Holy Ghost speaking through them.

Although the total costs had been estimated by experts at half a million roubles in gold—a considerable sum in 1911—less than a quarter of a million was, in fact, spent. Volunteer labour contributed to this reduction. The money came from the dowries of Sisters, offerings and free contributions from the Mariavite people. Like their charitable institutions they knew that generosity expressed love. It is in giving that we receive, a Franciscan motto. The Little Mother insisted that nothing dishonestly earned should pollute the Temple fund. Not a single coin.

The walls were finished within six months, record time, and in December the masons came down from the scaffolding. Some citizens of Plock complained about a prolonged drought, for no rain fell while the work was in progress, but the local wits would reply: 'Not a drop will fall, for Kozlowska is building.'

It was certainly her dream and it was realized without any major mishap. Kowalski supervised everything, but he had among his priests some technicians whom he could consult at will. Father Matthew, one of the Szymanowski brothers (both remarkable men in the movement), was a trained engineer. Like other young enthusiasts he joined the congregation with the full knowledge that he was giving up a brilliant career in his profession. What, in fact, made the Mariavites such an interesting community in those early years of expansion was the mixture of people from all walks of life. If it had been only a protest group of discontented priests, it would have fizzled out between the edicts of excommunication, followed by mob violence and the persistent attempts from every quarter to undermine their faith in the Little Mother. Ridicule was and still is a powerful social weapon. The Mariavites were for years clubbed with this weapon and to their own surprise they grew tougher.

The Temple was their communal act of faith. In much the same spirit cathedrals were raised in the Middle Ages, each involving the population of a whole city. The work in Plock, however, didn't go on for long. By a propitious coincidence—Kowalski seemed to summon coincidences from the air he breathed—the Temple was finished when the World War began, almost on the very day it broke out. The consecration ceremony on 15 August 1914 coincided with the entry of the first German units into Plock. Next day they marched out of the town, and the Mariavites who had gathered in their thousands could leave for their parishes undisturbed.

To mark the great occasion Bishop Kowalski ordained six priests in the new Temple, two of whom—Philip Feldman and Bartholomew Przysiecki —were to become bishops. It was also an important move in the direction of sacerdotal independence: he was creating his own clergy, including deacons, the latter at the command of the Little Mother who wanted to revive the spirit of early Christianity. By orthodox standards their training for priesthood was neither long nor thorough. In his later years Kowalski would now and again ordain a person with hardly any education, but 'such was the Will of', etc. After all, one could argue that St. Peter wasn't exactly a Latin scholar, and since the Little Mother believed that the Lord himself would through her mediation appoint new apostles, it was not proper to question the Lord on this issue.

The names of the apostles (each reinforced by Maria) were distributed according to the virtues each of the elect possessed. Jacob, Philip, Thaddeus, Jacob the Elder, Matthew—in time the Mariavites acquired them all. A full set of apostolic copies. The choice of the name, however, came from the superiors and was kept secret till the last moment. Sometimes a prospective apostle sensed what was coming. The breath of the spirit was upon him. This happened to Przysiecki on being admitted to the congregation.

Przysiecki, like Feldman, had studied at a Polytechnic abroad,[1] and if asked, would have described himself then as an atheist. After a few weeks in Plock, talking leisurely with Kozlowska and others, he suddenly felt an urge to receive communion. With the Little Mother's permission he took it and behold! a great transformation occurred. Put down your nets and follow me—he had no wish to resume his engineering studies in France. In the period before the vows he couldn't, understandably, settle down. One day he took a walk in town, picked up a book which he didn't really want and bought it. When he showed the title to the Mariavites at the cloister, some of them laughed. The title read: *Father Bartholomew's Goat.* 'It's the name that has been chosen for you,' said those in the know.

Judging by the number of such incidents, telepathic communication of this kind was frequent at the cloister. Which is not surprising to me. The Mariavites in Plock formed a closely-knit community, and, though the nuns were kept *in clausura* and the Fathers had their separate cells, the Temple with the attached cloister buildings embraced them all with the arms of the letter E. They were one family under one big roof, with the monstrance shining at the top of the cupola.

The monstrance, which they also wore on their habits (grey for men and beige, at that time, for women) as the embroidered sign of their worship,[2] distinguished them easily from the Roman Catholic religious. When did they start wearing it? The young Feldman who was sent with a letter to Kowalski in early March 1906, saw him already in the Mariavite habit.

---

[1] Przysiecki in Nancy; Feldman in Riga where he belonged to the influential students' association, Arconia.
[2] The congregation called itself 'The Mariavites of the Perpetual Adoration for Beseeching God' (*Związek Mariawitów nieustającej adoracji ubłagania*).

('The others still walked in their black soutanes.') Yet they were not the only order that displayed the monstrance in this fashion, as many Mariavites tend to believe. The Blessed Sacrament Fathers, for example, a society founded in France in 1856, have it embroidered on their habits.[1] There is also a lay Confraternity of the Blessed Sacrament, established by a Dominican in 1539, and a contemplative congregation of women religious called the Servants of the Blessed Sacrament. Cervantes belonged to the brotherhood of the Esclavos del Santísimo Sacramento, that servile concept again.

In her Rules of the Mariavite congregation, which Pius X rejected in 1904, Maria Frances Kozlowska includes among the patrons of the congregation a forgotten saint, the Spanish Franciscan Paschalis Baylon (d. 1592) who had a particular devotion to the host. However, it seems to me that there was a more obvious influence at work. St. Clare is often represented with a monstrance which she held to protect Assisi from the attack of the Saracens in the service of Frederick II. And they apparently turned away. How could the Little Mother possibly have overlooked that miracle of the host? Like all skilful adaptors, she borrowed whatever suited her purpose. The pattern of the Rules which she wrote down was that of the three Franciscan orders. Both St. Francis and St. Clare of Assisi figured in the Rules as examples of perfection. She added a fourth vow: the Veneration of the Holy Eucharist (the other three were, of course, Obedience, Poverty, and Chastity).

As the movement grew and altered, the Franciscan origin of the Mariavite congregation eluded the sympathizers and annoyed the enemies of Mother Kozlowska. What were those heretics supposed to be—priests? monks? or some dressed-up mongrels? Bishop Kowalski explained it all very simply: 'The Mariavites differ from other churches in that they constitute an order on the model of the Apostles and have the organization of an order based on the Rules of St. Francis of Assisi.'

When he wrote this, Kowalski was already the architect of the Temple of Love. He added things and changed rules. With the introduction of marriages between the priests and the nuns, the Franciscan lineage of the Mariavites branched off into a dark corner of mystical heraldry.

4

The founder of a new religion, big or small, successful or ephemeral, must think hard how to make the most memorable exit from life. By this exit he

---

[1] The founder of the society, Pierre Julien Eymard, was canonized quite recently, in 1962. His feast day in the calendar, 2 August, coincides strangely enough with the day and the month of Kozlowska's first Revelation.

or she will be judged. A sacrificial end is undoubtedly the one which the majority of believers favour. A young god must be slain; long live the resurrected god!

During the first two years after the dissension and double anathema, the Little Mother never left her home. Had she ventured into the streets of Plock at that turbulent time, she would have been killed by a mob or a single fanatic. Her martyrdom would have resembled the martyrdom of many a saint, or to use more recent examples, that of Malcolm X or Martin Luther King. Would Mariavitism have survived without her at such an early date? I doubt it. Martyrdom, if it has to come, must come after organization; an obscure candidate for a halo of sainthood needs a strong team of professional canonizers. Since the undocumented saints are now chucked out of the calendar—St. George with his dragon, St. Christopher with his gigantic pole—the power over the glory rests with the devil's advocates. And Maria Frances Kozlowska wasn't the type of woman who would get a halo from them. She had much more chance by breaking a few seals in the book of the Apocalypse. This she did with Bishop Kowalski's help.[1]

Her way to death was not spectacular; it was a quiet acceptance of pain in a long illness. In January 1920 after Spanish influenza she did not fully recover and it became obvious that her illness was incurable. The analysis showed cancer of the liver. There was not much that could be done about it, but she, distrustful of doctors, refused their care and all remedies except herbs. That was her vow. The Little Mother wanted to experience the full impact of suffering, month by month, day by day.[2] Thy Will be done, to the last drop in the cup.

Her cell, with an antechamber for receiving guests, was on the level of the choir, near the altar, and she had a praying desk there, at which she knelt contemplating the Eucharist. She herself chose the spiritually advanced nuns for the choir of the 'God-minded'[3] whose primary task was to attend to the adoration. They were excused most other duties in the cloister.[4] The Little Mother's praying desk was white, and white was the interior of the Temple. She loved the airy luminosity of the place, uncluttered by statues and pious adornments, with a prominent crucifix over the altar and a monstrance, like the sun, shining in the centre. The eyes were drawn to it. 'Let the whole

[1] He published in 1923 a lengthy commentary on the Apocalypse in which Kozlowska is extolled.

[2] Freud too refused to be deprived of the dignity of pain.

[3] This, I think, is the best rendering of *bogomyślne*, an awkward compound sounding Russian to Poles.

[4] There were three choirs in the Mariavite cloister. The nuns doing menial tasks were often overworked, but they received training in special workshops.

world adore you and implore you,' said the Mariavite motto,[1] imprinted on all their medallions, publications, and pictures.

The illness would nail the Little Mother to her sofa for days, and she found it difficult to get up and reach her place of adoration by the altar. Her absence in the choir made everyone in the cloister aware of the seriousness of her condition. Their Mother Superior used to be so meticulous in the observance of her devotions. Suddenly the Mariavite family felt a threat far more dangerous than the papal excommunications and the hatred of their own countrymen. What is to become of us when she is gone?

Kowalski conveys this mood well in a long chapter in *The Work of Great Mercy* describing 'The Last Moments [*Chwile*] of the Little Mother's Life and Her Most Holy Sacrifice'. The chapter occupies forty pages and the use of the word 'sacrifice' in the title clearly marks the scriptural character of his record. I have been referring to Kowalski's book on the Work of Great Mercy now as a memoir (which it is), now as a scripture (which it aspires to be), but the chapter on the agony and death of Maria Frances is, indeed, witnessing in a religious sense. This is the Passion of our Holy Mother, every word here is true, so help me God and Mother of Perpetual Succour.

One feels Kowalski's guilt, love, and sorrow—all shot through with the light of compassion. He has confessed earlier in the book how often he was the instrument of her pain, but only during her agony did he participate in her suffering, or so he thought. This was *Compassio* with a difference. The Mother was on the cross and the Son stood under it, watching the approach of death. One day he uttered: 'Happy are the eyes which have seen you, Mother, but nothing can be more painful than parting with you.' She replied with tears and said: 'God is all, I am nothing.' And she scolded him for exaggerating everything about her.[2] 'He causes the greatest pain to me who takes me for a saint, because I am a sinner and beg God to forgive my sins. . . . You know how you should live. The Lord Jesus will strengthen you and direct you. He gave you the Temple; that should be enough.' 'The four of you', she said later, addressing her chief apostles, Michael, Jacob, Philip, and Bartholomew, 'you are the four pillars.'

On 10 April 1920 Kozlowska asked for a lawyer and made her last will which she signed in the presence of witnesses. She expected to die that night, and instructed Kowalski about the order in which the next three bishops should be consecrated. She also appointed a senior Sister to be in charge of

---

[1] Cf. Psalm 66. The motto appears in the emblem reproduced at p. 222.
[2] Philip Feldman recorded that a few days before her death she implored him to protect her from any attempts at turning her into a cult. But judging by other evidence, she was strangely ambiguous when allusions were made to her mystical rank.

the nuns' cloister until the election of a new Mother Superior,[1] and she nominated other officers of the cloister.

However, she survived the night and the follwoing day, which was a Sunday, made a general confession before Kowalski. This was for him an act of pardon, for she had not used him as a confessor for a long time. After the confession, Kowalski writes, 'my soul was completely welded with the Little Mother's soul'. The spiritual son returned to the womb once again. He felt so confident that he now tempted the Lord to alter his Will and prolong her life by five years—and when he thought he was heard, he plucked up his courage and asked for more: twenty-five years or so, he said. He was convinced all would be well and told her about it, and then told the priests. Father Philip, whom the Little Mother loved much, didn't share his conviction and was reprimanded for being a man of little faith.

Kowalski celebrated a Mass, sang a hymn of thanksgiving, and she woke from her sleep, recited the same hymn, and had an 'understanding' about heaven and earth fighting over her. 'Your love won and tore me away from Heaven's hands.' Joy returned to the cloister and the Temple. But something went awry with the prediction, the illness came back, this time with a vengeance. So far she had not felt physical pain, only a death-like tiredness; now her belly began to be filled with bile, and a burning sensation was in her entrails. She had many sleepless nights.

By day priests and Sisters from outside parishes as well as ordinary Mariavites came to see her, and she received every one of them. She could hardly eat and her thirst became unbearable. Nevertheless she held her conferences with the Sisters and continued all the devotions prescribed by the Rule. She talked to her leading priests and they took notes, being aware of the significance of her final counsels. To Kowalski she explained the mystical meaning of the six days of Creation. Speaking of the fourth day she told him that the sun was the Most Holy Sacrament, the moon and the stars the Virgin and the saints. At the very end she confided that there was no man as yet. She repeated this a few days before her death. What did she mean by it: the process of evolution? the unrealized nature of man? the lost identity after the Fall? Kowalski must often have pondered on her cryptic remark when he began to write about the Kingdom of God on earth.

She talked about the unification of all the churches, but did not change her view on the papacy. New dogmas were a cause of further divisions among people. She could never forgive the Vatican for rejecting the Work of Mercy. Yet her advice to the Mariavite priest was: 'Don't speak about the papacy from the pulpit. You should ignore the Pope as if he didn't exist

[1] She suggested Sister Isabel (Wiłucka) as her possible successor.

The 1910 visit of the Old Catholic bishops from Holland (in black); the Little Mother between Kowalski and Father John (extreme right).

(*Above*) The Little Mother with Philip Feldman in the Mariavite cloister at Plock, the Vistula in the background.
(*Left*) The Little Mother's cell in the Temple at Plock, with her praying desk.
(*Below*) The Little Mother on her death-bed, 1921. The photograph is still used on Mariavite altars.

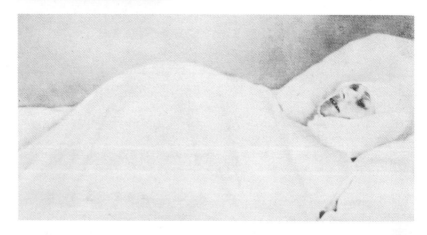

at all.' Perhaps there was a touch of charity in her instruction. Why go on castigating others? Enough of those superior attitudes.

The Little Mother was adamant in her pessimistic assessment of human nature. 'There is no perfection and there cannot be any perfection either in man or through man.' The sacrament of the Eucharist offered the only source of perfection and the means of attaining it. Early Christianity was Eucharistic in essence, one should humbly go back to the beginnings. The dogmatic edifice is crumbling just as the basilica of St. John Lateran was tilting in the dream of Pope Innocent III who took the hint and approved the Franciscan Rule.

There were troubles coming to the surface within the Mariavite communities: priests living in sin with nuns, fraudulent transactions over parish property, petty treacheries and open denials of the Mariavite cause. The Little Mother wanted to know all the news, good and bad, nothing was to be hidden from her, and this, of course, added mental pain to her physical suffering. Her pulse grew weaker and she fainted frequently. Fainting spells she had had before, but now the bile was a vicious new factor. The liquid gathering inside her belly made it bulge like a balloon and with it the burning increased. As she could drink little, thirst was her agony.

In June 1920, Father John, the first Mariavite apostle, died in his parish and Bishop Kowalski understood it as a sign. A chapter in the history of their church was drawing to a close. The war with Communist Russia was on and going badly for the Poles. The Red Army advanced on Warsaw and one of its units, composed mainly of Cossacks, broke into Plock. The Polish artillery was shelling the town from across the river and the Temple lay within range of their fire. The Cossacks ran amok; they killed the soldiers they had taken prisoner, robbed houses and raped women. The Little Mother told the Sisters to gather in the choir and pray. When a band of Russians entered the Temple, they did not for some inexplicable reason go up to the choir, but during the night a few drunks broke in again looking for women. Father Philip Feldman used a stratagem to get them out, then barred the gate from inside.

With great difficulty the Little Mother dragged herself out of bed and spent the night in the corridor behind the altar praying for the nuns' safety. Did she remember St. Clare and her prayers when the Saracens of Frederick II were approaching Assisi? It was on 19 August that she offered her life for the peace of the cloister, for Plock and the country. 'And the Lord Jesus accepted the offering.'[1] The enemy left Plock the same day. From a military

---

[1] Kowalski makes a great deal out of this. The Polish victory in the battle of Warsaw was popularly known as 'the Miracle on the Vistula', so he probably wanted to counteract Catholic

point of view they had no reason to stay there: the battle of Warsaw was over and the Russians were in full retreat.

After all those ordeals the Little Mother's health deteriorated further. The swelling continued. On Christmas eve she told the four priests with whom she was spiritually united, that it would be her last Christmas with them. Saying this she could no longer control herself and began to sob. However, when she saw that the four were weeping with her she reprimanded herself for this display of self-pity.

Lent came. She insisted on observing, as every year, the full forty days of strict devotions. During that time she spoke to nobody and when she wanted something, a few written words were dispatched from her cell. That was retreat all right, but not for a sick woman. As the weeks passed with no improvement—the same symptoms, the same burning pain—she would now and again tell her priests, as if to apologize for her lingering agony: 'Father Michael is holding me back.' She meant Kowalski, and he prayed on: a persistent knocking on the door of heaven while the door nearby was kept ajar and he heard her groans by day and by night.

During the last six months of her life the Little Mother couldn't even lie in her bed, she had to sit up, because of the enormous size of her belly. Down to her waist she was withered, the face and the hands seemed transparent, while the mound of liquid grew in the middle, pressing at the expanded skin, and the legs, too, kept swelling. Whatever she ate and drank felt like molten lead being poured into a pool of pain in the entrails. Every day she took communion in two forms. This was the only nourishment that mattered to her. Finally, she couldn't even be shifted on her sofa, so great was the weight of her belly. Once she fell over and like a huge beetle lay unable to raise herself until Father Philip came in and lifted her up.

On Monday, 22 August, she vomited bile mixed with blood, throwing up bits of the diseased liver. This was the end. 'Nothing purifies the soul as much as suffering.' She had lived through one of her own sayings. The four priests ('the pillars of the Temple') kept vigil by turns. About three o'clock in the morning Kowalski entered her room just as she was trying to pour water into a glass. He helped her kneeling by the sofa, then sat by her side in semi-darkness. The light was in the next room. She asked:

'Who is that?'

'Michael,' he answered.

'My little Michael.'

---

propaganda. The Russian retreat began on 16 August whereas Kozlowska's offering was made on the 19th. Mysticism is above dates.

The sound of her voice: a mother, close to death, caressing the name of her child. All was forgiven in that moment. At four o'clock Bishop Jacob entered, they both knelt, and Kowalski placed her hand first on his own head then on Jacob's. 'Bless us, Mother.' Cold, the hand was cold, and the breathing became faint. The other two, Philip and Bartholomew, were summoned and again Kowalski placed her hand on their heads as they were kneeling by the sofa. She was still alive. United with her, the four confirmed the mystical bond: until death us do part.

Two Sisters witnessed the scene: Honorata who had been with her from the beginning, and Raphaela. The Little Mother breathed three times very slowly and the bile mixed with lymph came out with her last breath. Philip's arm was holding her back to ease the agony. Her eyes closed, but the mouth remained wide open. Maria Frances Kozlowska was dead. Kowalski looked at his watch. It was four-thirty in the morning of 23 August 1921 and the light of dawn flowed through the window.

The Sisters managed to lay the corpse flat on its back. She had specifically asked that they should not wash her entire body, only the face and the legs. The four went to a side chapel in the sacristy and confessed to one another the wrongs they had done to the Little Mother. Then they celebrated Mass together, offering their oneness with her.

A doctor was called to remove the liquid from the swollen belly. Otherwise it would have been impossible to put her body in even a large coffin. The doctor made an opening in her side and drained the mixture of blood, bile, and water. He filled two big buckets with it and still there was as much liquid left in the body, which could only be removed by cutting the belly across. Kowalski didn't allow this to be done. Nor was the water drained from the legs. They poured the foul liquid into a hole dug out below her window. Now it is covered with a cement surface.

The Little Mother was buried in the cellar under the main altar. Some people in Plock, writes Kowalski, said of her that she must have been a saint since she had to suffer so much. Others sneered and said: 'If she is such a saint, let her perform a miracle and rise from the dead.' Someone pinned a card on the cloister wall with these words: 'Kozlowska is at the very bottom of Hell, damned.' All this, writes Kowalski, happened so that the Little Mother's likeness to Christ should be fully revealed. But, he comments further, 'there is no need to pray at her grave or to her body', because her presence now is on the altar with Christ; 'her Passion opened the Third Heaven in the Most Holy Sacrament.'

This Bishop Kowalski announced to his priests and the Sisters assembled in the refectory. And they all remembered her words, 'I will be with you always.' At the Temple of Mercy and Love a new theology was being groped for.

In her testament Kozlowska guaranteed the maintenance of the Temple and the cloister together with the boarding school and the kindergarten. This also applied to the medical unit and the free kitchen for the poor which, as during her life time, was to provide at least a hundred meals a day. Similar guarantees covered the property at Felicjanów and the institutions established there.[1]

According to the national statistics compiled in March 1923, the Mariavites had 67 parishes (and a number of affiliations), 77 churches, 15 chapels in private homes, 44 cloisters for women, 25 primary schools, 1 secondary school (*progimnazjum*), 4 boarding schools for orphans, 45 kindergartens, 13 homes for old people and invalids, 4 medical units, 10 kitchens for the poor, 32 workshops, 7 bakeries, 3 savings-and-loan associations, 3 fire brigades, 22 farms, 25 vegetable and fruit gardens.

On the day of Kozlowska's death there were over 42,000 Mariavites (their number having dropped after the war), including 3 bishops, 30 priests, 244 convent sisters, and 57 convent brothers. All this was achieved within fifteen years by one determined woman who inspired and guided thousands of people in fulfilment of the Work of Great Mercy.

A photograph taken soon after her death shows the pitiful misery of her distorted body. It looks like some prodigious pregnancy, the belly of the Earth Mother herself. The followers of Kowalski today have this photograph on their altars behind the monstrance. The connection is clear for those who know. She is the big Little Mother, giving a continuous birth to the children of her Queendom.

---

[1] The testament named Bishop Kowalski as beneficiary. In the event of his death, Bishop Jacob (Próchniewski) would nominally inherit everything. Since all Mariavite properties in the parishes were in the name of the priests, in accordance with Russian law, individuals and not congregations figured in the testament. This led to abuses. After the split within the church the whole problem of who owned what became a puzzle. Kowalski complicated matters further by passing on Felicjanów to his son. The legal entanglement was sorted out only a few years ago at the initiative of Bishop Innocenty (Gołębiowski) and with the help of a Plock lawyer, K. Askanas, with whom I talked in January 1973.

4

The Diviners of the Three

S HAME is a veil. It is cast over the sexes, hiding the Face of God. Thus
Dmitry Merezhkovsky whose work, *The Secret of the Three* (*Tayna
Tryokh*) (1925), Archbishop Kowalski quotes with approval.[1] Through
Merezhkovsky Kowalski also quotes Rozanov, another Russian, who suits
his own ideas even better: 'Why must the Christians perform the physical
act in marriage excluding from it prayer and the illumination of grace, as if
it were a sacrifice in honour of Belial?' The married couple should place the
picture of the Virgin Mary over their bed and keep the lamp alight. Such
advice was, no doubt, to Kowalski's liking. The body should be sanctified
in copulation instead of being demonized. Both Rozanov and Merezhkovsky
are relevant to his preoccupation with sexual matters after 1921.

That he should have read the two Russians is not surprising. During his
studies in St. Petersburg he improved his knowledge of Russian and later,
when the legal status of the Mariavites was being considered by the Tsarist
government, in 1909 and 1912, he had travelled to Moscow and met
influential Russians, one of whom, General Kireyev, was responsible for
putting him in touch with the Old Catholics.

By that time Vasily Rozanov (1856–1919) had acquired some notoriety
as a journalist working for the *Novoye Vremya*, and the author of impassionate books, in which he attacked Christianity and Christ himself.[2] His
subsequent return to the Church was reminiscent of Durtal in Huysmans'
En route. Back to the beauty of liturgy! 'The Church is the only poetic, the
only profound thing on earth.' He accepted the necessity of pain as well,
and in his agony kept repeating: 'Christ is risen.' With these words on his

---

[1] He translated *Tayna Tryokh* in 1938 for his periodical *The Kingdom of God on Earth*. Unlike
Merezhkovsky's other studies the work has not been translated in the west.
[2] His book on the Russian Church appeared in 1906, the year of the Mariavite dissension; his
Dark Face (*Tyomny lik*) in 1911. 'God, what madness it was,' he wrote later, 'that for eleven
years I made every possible effort to destroy the Church.'

lips he died in January 1919. Such an end was what Kowalski would have called a spiritual confirmation of rebirth.

Significantly enough, the book which Rozanov was writing on his death-bed bears the title, *The Apocalypse of Our Times*.[1] In it Rozanov tried to reconcile his ideas on sex with the Orthodox faith he was embracing again like a prodigal lover. This is how he sees nature expressing its sexual joy: '. . . it is obvious that in insects, cows, everywhere in the animal and vegetable world, and not only in man, this is a mystery, heavenly and sacred. And, indeed, it is so, in its central point, *in copulation*. . . .' It is amazing, he says, how 'insects (not butterflies only, but scarabs, beetles, ladybirds, etc.) rummage in the huge—as compared with their own size—sexual organs of trees and particularly of bushes, roses, etc. oleanders, orchids and such like. How do flowers appear to the *butterflies*?' A garden and flowers are imagined as Paradise. The very bigness of the flowers, Rozanov argues, is so designed as 'to allow the insect to enter *entire*. Then we can accept the idea that plants hear and think (as in the tales of antiquity) and that they have a soul. Oh, what a soul!'

Until his re-conversion Rozanov proclaimed the gospel of the sanctified body, unconditionally. For 'sex is holy'. During intercourse man is in direct contact with God. Moreover, 'the tie of sex with God is stronger than the tie of intellect or even conscience.'

Through aphorisms, twists of colloquial phrases, and exasperating cries, Rozanov probed the hypocrisy of accepted morals ('I don't even know how to spell morality—with one "l" or two'). His mediator between heaven and earth was Dostoevsky, and so much he wished to feel the body-soul of the dead man that he entered into a disastrous and masochistic marriage with Suslova, Dostoevsky's mistress. Rozanov must have imagined, to paraphrase his own dictum, that copulation with Suslova would put him in direct contact with his literary god.

His first book, published in 1891, was in fact a study of Dostoevsky's 'Legend of the Grand Inquisitor' in *The Brothers Karamazov*, in which he argued that Christ denied earth for heaven and consequently turned against the obvious needs of the body. But the body, Rozanov would say, is my body, and 'on myself even mud is good because it's me', he wrote in one of his exclamatory notes.

Wavering between self-assertion and self-disgust, he never doubted the holiness of life which the pagans knew how to celebrate in their worship of

---

[1] Translated by S. S. Koteliansky in the volume *Solitaria*, a collection of Rozanov's notes (1927). I have adapted slightly quotations from Koteliansky's version, and have also used renderings from Renato Poggioli's essay, *Rozanov* (1962).

animals and the cult of fecundity. The tree of life and the pregnant woman symbolized for him love, the continuous metabolism of the soul-body. For 'Love is renewal', and 'inasmuch as we have failed to achieve love', he jotted down in July 1912, 'we shall be punished in the other world'. But the human soul has the capacity to contain opposites at one and the same time. Dostoevsky, he said, was the first man to understand that the human soul can simultaneously yearn for Sodom and the Madonna, and even in the very midst of Sodom it does not forget the Madonna.

This observation goes beyond any iconoclastic urge. He who defiles the object of worship usually defiles his own religious desire. Archbishop Kowalski prayed to be guided by 'understandings' in matters which contained opposites such as virginity *v.* sexual union, celibacy *v.* marriage. Was it true that 'everything was permissible to a praying man', as Rozanov implied after his rediscovery of Christ? 'Prayer—or nothing,' he insisted; the answering God is within us. Kowalski certainly acted on that premise. And he did not stop at making pronouncements. The polygamy he began to practise was for him a sort of communal prayer, enacted in the flesh. He would have applauded Rozanov for the remark, 'The atheist is a sexless being'.[1]

Apart from *The Secret of the Three*, which Kowalski admired, Dmitry Merezhkovsky (1865–1941) wrote several books on religious subjects, comparative in their use of material and poetic in presentation. Two of them, *The Secret of the West* (1930) and *Jesus the Unknown* (1931), with *The Secret of the Three* form a trilogy and are, in my opinion, relevant to Kowalski's ideas. Each is a daring assault on the fortress of dogmatic theology. Like Rozanov whom he disliked and respected (the sentiment was mutual), Merezhovsky understood the erotic force in all religions. He also wrote in a style that lent itself to parables, oracular incantations, and sudden leaps into metaphor. *Jesus the Unknown*, in particular, reads like a scripture according to Saint Dmitry. With its apocryphal aura, the book appeals to one's fancy.

Now what Merezhkovsky wanted to retrieve from his probing into the cross-currents of religion over the ages was the lost total image of the Deity, which was hidden under the veil of shame and precariously poised—in our understanding of it—over the dark chasm between the opposites. His obsessive theme was that of Christ and Antichrist as revealed within a perpetual conflict between the Father and the Son, the religion of the flesh in disharmony with the religion of the spirit.

[1] In contrast to the Archbishop, Rozanov was a passive intellectual, a spectator rather than a man of action. 'The only masculine thing about you is your trousers', said his seventeen-year-old cousin, but this would not offend a masochist.

Since the Trinity comprised the mystery of their reconciliation, Merezhkovsky honoured the sacred number by planning and writing his works in
sets of three. *The Secret of the Three* is in a way his own mystical secret. And
the October Revolution in Russia convinced him that the Antichrist had
revealed himself.

Earlier the Mariavites had been scared by the imminent arrival of the
Antichrist. Their Little Mother was to accommodate him with a virgin
birth, but a change of plans occurred in the realm of Providence, and the
obedient handmaid of the Lord was saved from this ordeal. The Mariavites
in the villages accepted the divine cancellation with gratitude. But the whole
incident foreshadowed other warnings of apocalyptic character, which
Kowalski would now and again insert into the commentary on his version
of the Old Testament. He had to keep abreast of the prophets, Isaiah and
Daniel in particular.[1]

But once the Little Mother became the Bride of Christ after her death
and started summoning the virgins of the convent to 'the nuptials of the
Lamb',[2] the concept of the Trinity had to be re-examined by Archbishop
Kowalski to justify the presence of the Little Mother in the Eucharist, a
dogma he quickly produced out of his infallible 'understanding'. For there
wasn't much time to lose. Like Merezhkovsky, he heard the hooves of the
apocalyptic horses coming nearer and nearer. At this mystical juncture his
expectations coincide with those of Merezhkovsky. If only one could find
the secret combination to open the divine safe with the treasures locked up
inside it for all eternity!

Three was the only code number available. So they both tried to break
the code. Too respectful of liturgy to become mere iconoclasts, the Russian
and the Pole behaved like two holy thieves in the vaults of the Bank of the
Holy Spirit (not the Vatican one, the one above). *The Secret of the Three*
turned out to be the secret of the Mother, the Little Mother for the Pole.
Through comparative research into the rites of Egypt, Crete, and Babylon
Merezhkovsky reached the conclusion he had intuitively expected to reach:
namely, that the Trinity binds the mysteries in every religious pattern and
that the Eternal Mother-Spirit will resolve the struggle of the opposites
within the pattern.

Accordingly, he shows parallels: the Babylonian trinity of Ea–Ishtar–
Tammuz corresponds to the Egyptian trinity of Osiris–Isis–Gor. In the
Eleusinian mysteries Demeter is the mother, Dionysus the father, and

---

[1] In his commentary on the Book of Isaiah Kowalski predicts a gigantic world disaster (ch. 2),
God's punishment that is to come from Soviet Russia (ch. 10), and the destruction of America,
Italy, and England (ch. 23).
[2] See p. 90.

Iacchus the son, and so on. Merezhkovsky exemplifies the continuity of the Mother-Spirit in the Babylonian goddess Ishtar (Inanna is her ancient Sumerian name),[1] in the Graeco-Roman Aphrodite–Venus, and in the Christian Virgin Mother who is also *Ma-donna*, the Mistress. The sacred number again in the three manifestations of womanhood: the maid equals the mistress, and both are fulfilled in the mother. In the process of spiritual reconciliation therefore marriage is a necessary stage of completion. Kowalski would have added that it must be a mystical marriage or nothing. He, in fact, said so in his commentary on the Song of Songs.

But the continuous revolution of the code number three fascinates Merezhkovsky as if the sacred number itself wished to be unlocked by him alone.[2] In a poetic chapter in *The Secret of the West*, on the three colours of the Mother, blue, black, and white, Merezhkovsky unlocks the triple secret:

> The Trinity in God begins and is completed by the Mother-Spirit; that is why the shadow of the Mother in the world is triple: in the Kingdom of the Father, Atlantis (prehistory)—the Blue Mother Water; in the kingdom of the Son (history)—the Black Mother Earth; in the kingdom of the Spirit (the Apocalypse)—the White Mother Fire. All three in the world as in God are One.

The Eternal Woman-Mother then is the Holy Spirit manifesting *itself* in different rites over the ages according to the Russian mystic, and in one human incarnation according to the practical Mariavite leader—that is in Maria Frances Kozlowska (she was, of course, presaged by prophecies, from the Song of Songs onwards). She came as the Third Law and in her the First Law of the Father and the Second Law of the Son will be reconciled. She is the Secret of the Three: Kowalski uses Merezhkovsky to the greater glory of the Little Mother. That's all he is after.

But behind the mystery of this revelation there lies the mystery of the sexual division—the female and the male, which the pagans sanctified in their myth of fecundity and resurrection. The phallic cult, detached from the religious context, loses its purpose. 'The truth of the myth is in the mystery; its secret is the sacrament.' Sexual love, Merezhkovsky explains in *The Secret of the Three*, is 'the unended and unending path to resurrection. Vain is the striving of the two halves to the whole: they unite and once

---

[1] 'There is no God except thee', Ishtar was addressed in a prayer.

[2] 'He stated that man thinks threefold . . . that space and time are threefold. . . . He found the Trinity in physics and chemistry and cited the law of chemical reaction as an example.' Thus C. H. Bedford, in 'Dmitry Merezhkovsky, the Third Testament and the Third Humanity', *Slavonic Review*, no. 98 (December 1963), a clear exposition of Merezhkovsky's religious thought. (The quotations that follow are in Bedford's translation.)

more fall apart; they wish to, but cannot rise from the dead—they always give birth and always are.'

The division in sex must be understood as part of the primordial mystery. What was the human being intended for? And the total creature in Adam: what was his personality like? Merezhkovsky accepts one of Rozanov's definitions: 'Personality is the equinox of the sexes.' He goes on to argue that man was conceived as a Trinity, 'a perfectly whole personality: masculine and feminine joined into one'. Christ to him is neither male nor female. The love of Christ cannot be detached from the love of his Mother (i.e. the Mother-Spirit). 'He is in Her—She is in Him. . . . Little wonder that human beings love them together.' This is exactly what Jung thought when he came to see the necessity of a maternal deity for our psychic health.[1] All the unknown Jesus, according to Merezhkovsky, is in the Mother, and he wrote a separate study to prove it.

Imperceptibly, the broken code of the Three becomes for Merezhkovsky the dogma of divine bisexuality. If the image of God in man is two sexes in one creature (seen from above as the embodied mystery of the Trinity), then in another spiritual dimension Sex (i.e. two in one) 'is the Four joining in love two bisexual personalities'. Merezhkovsky devotes a long chapter in *The Secret of the Three* to this mystical speculation on the Androgyne,[2] and leaves the readers somewhat lost between the elusive halves of his personality.

Now Kowalski could have taken a few hints from Merezhkovsky, had he possessed sufficient courage to defend polygamy in public. There were some numerical possibilities in the dogma of divine bisexuality: husbands and wives could be halved, permutated, and joined together *ad infinitum*. Neither Merezhkovsky nor Kowalski seemed keen on exploiting the Trinity solely as the dimension of Eternity. That would have been a calculated profanation of the mystery. They preferred to sneak in and out, after the fashion of holy thieves.

2

Dmitry Merezhkovsky published a pamphlet, *Joseph Pilsudski* (1921), about a conversation he had with Marshal Pilsudski in 1920, the year of the Polish

[1] Jung speaks of 'the Freudian myth of the primal father and the gloomy superego deriving from that father' and observes that 'in the realm of Catholic thought the Mother of God and the Bride of Christ has been received into the divine thalamus (bridal chamber) only recently, after centuries of hesitancy. But in the Protestant and Jewish spheres the father continues to dominate as much as ever'. *Memories, Dreams, Reflections*, trans. R. and C. Winston (1963), ch. VII.

[2] Compare the chapter on the Androgyne in Suzanne Lilar's brilliant book, *Aspects of Love* (1965).

victory over the Soviet armies. Himself an exile after the Revolution, Merezhkovsky saw the Marshal, who was then head of state as well as commander-in-chief, engaged in a battle against the Antichrist. '*Le dernier combat avec lui serait livré ici.*' This is an apocalyptic kind of statement, but no less significant are the three Messianic prophets Merezhkovsky mentions in his pamphlet: August Cieszkowski, Andrew Towianski, and the poet Adam Mickiewicz. Three they are, of course, in keeping with the Third phase of mankind. But Merezhkovsky would not accept the Messianic claim that Poland was the Christ among the nations: '*Le Christ est dans la Pologne, mais la Pologne n'est pas le Christ.*' The way of the cross does not end here on earth, either for men or for nations.

The three names, however, seem to suggest that Merezhkovsky, a voracious reader, must at one time have been interested in the works of the Polish Messianists. This interest, too, is a link with Archbishop Kowalski who found Mariavite ideas in the same three writers. With the increasing awareness that he was destined to formulate the Mariavite creed and put it on record, he diligently assembled theological and literary materials which supported his claims, and what was not available in Polish he translated himself.

Both Towianski and Mickiewicz were God-sent prophets to him, and in Mickiewicz's case he was lucky: he could use the correspondence (newly edited 1933–6) which sheds much light on Towianski's circle. The Archbishop had among his books the three-volume Turin edition (1882) of Towianski's works.[1] Andrew Towianski (1799–1878), a Lithuanian Pole, is still regarded as a religious maniac who threw Mickiewicz into conflict with Rome and caused much dissent among the frustrated *émigrés* in Paris. There were also hints at his collaboration with Tsarist police. Why did the involvement of this crank with a great poet mean so much to Kowalski in Plock ninety years after the event?

A lawyer by profession, Towianski saw himself as a man of God sent to fulfil a mission. At the age of twenty-nine he experienced an 'illumination',[2] and in 1840 arrived in Paris during the reburial of Napoleon at the Invalides. He met Mickiewicz while the poet was in a deep depression, cured his insane wife, and won his confidence. It is difficult to imagine why this stocky, bald-headed man, with narrow tight lips and wearing blue glasses, should have fascinated women as much as he did. He had some hypnotic

---

[1] The critic T. Boy Żeleński, who visited Kowalski in Felicjanów, reported (in *Brązownicy* (Warsaw, 1930)) seeing this edition by his bedside. 'Towianski's Work of Mercy began a new era for mankind in 1840,' wrote Kowalski in *The Kingdom of God on Earth* in 1937.

[2] The teaching of the French Illuminist Saint-Martin (1743–1803) spread to eastern Europe through the Masonic lodges, and exercised a strong influence on both Towianski and Mickiewicz.

powers and a charismatic touch. During an intimate face-to-face meeting he would bring a person to a cathartic crisis, as one brings water to the boil, and then take full possession of his or her soul. For Towianski's mission was to 'govern souls', and Mickiewicz laid his soul at the Master's feet. Thy will be done.

With the poet's help Towianski announced his mission (*Sprawa Boża*) to a gathering of Polish exiles in Notre Dame, on 27 September 1841. Towianski's spiritual technique resembled modern group therapy. He had about fifty followers in the Circle (*Koło*) who called themselves Brothers and Sisters, and were organized in groups of seven. Each group had a leader, and within their own circle they prayed, confessed their sins to one another, and often wept. Purification was achieved through a series of crises. The leaders sent spiritual reports to the Master, Towianski. Among Mickiewicz's letters we find such reports dating from 1842, after Towianski was expelled from France. He settled first in Belgium and then in Zurich, where he lived, surrounded by women, until the ripe age of eighty.

Like Rozanov, Towianski died reconciled with the Church, but a small group of his followers remained faithful to the Master's teaching and collected his works. Alas, the writing is turgid, verbose, and singularly devoid of inspiration. By comparison Kowalski at his worst seems to have a bullying sort of style.

The Master's system is a Swedenborgian concoction with Saint-Martin and the cabbala thrown in; the belief in the evolution of spirits through metempsychosis forms a movable centre. Man lives in the dark, but the 'columns of light' are about him, planted in the earth which is 'the factory of spirits' and also the theatre of expiation (his two memorable phrases). We see only a variety of forms through which the spirits pass invisible to us. Each of the seven epochs revealed in the Apocalypse has its own servant of God who brings us nearer to the Kingdom of God. The progress of the spirit through time is manifested in great men, hence the cult of Napoleon who was 'a miracle in history'. Mickiewicz preached the Napoleonic gospel of Towianski in his lectures at the Collège de France, and on occasions the female members of the Circle staged hysterical scenes, throwing themselves at the feet of the bard.[1]

There are several points of resemblance between Towianski's sect and the Mariavites. Both practised devotion to the Virgin Mary: Towianski and his followers prayed before the image of the holy patroness of Vilna at the

[1] See a perceptive study by S. Pigoń in his *Z epoki Mickiewicza* (1922), the biography by T. Canonico (Turin, 1897), and K. Kantak's *Mickiewicz i Towiańskiego Sprawa Boża* (London, 1957).

church of St. Severin.[1] Both movements believed that the official Church was dead in spirit and both were duly condemned by the Pope (Towianski by Gregory XVI in November 1843).

The Mariavite therapeutic system of self-accusation corresponds to the open confessions within Towianski's groups of seven. Both sects upheld the function of a spiritual crisis, and showed an aptitude for frequent tears. 'Souls' were laid at Towianski's feet in much the same way as they were entrusted to the Little Mother. The belief in the migration of souls (metempsychosis) was accepted by both Towianski and Kowalski: a great soul is an instrument of the Will of God, fully attuned to His design.

Women were liberated in both movements, though on a much larger scale, as we shall see, in the Mariavite church. 'Souls have no sex distinction,' said Mickiewicz. Towianski's magnetic power over women resembles Kowalski's. He, too, bestowed kisses of initiation on them and absolved married women from fidelity to their husbands. (He even said *Absolvo te*, as one of them reported.)

Inevitably, all religious cells divide sooner or later. A split occurred in Towianski's Circle, as it did later in the Mariavite church.

The most important parallel, however, concerns the Eucharist. Mickiewicz said that all sinful priests were murdering Christ each time they celebrated Mass. In her Revelation Maria Frances Kozlowska received an angry message about the immoral priests who abused the sacrament. Their sacrifice could not be acceptable to God. For similar reasons, the miracle of La Salette (1846) upset many devout church-goers at the time because the Virgin spoke to the peasant children about the sins of priests whose sacrilegious hands held the body of Christ. Her words were harsh: '*À célébrer les saints mystères par l'amour de l'argent, l'amour de l'honneur et des plaisirs les prêtres sont devenus des cloaques d'impureté. Oui, les prêtres demandent vengeance.*'

Archbishop Kowalski quoted these words in his *Work of Great Mercy* and later.[2] To him they were a confirmation that the warning received by the Little Mother had to be taken seriously. In 1906 the Mariavite priests had argued that they took Christ with them when they left the Roman churches after the papal anathema. In 1918, with tears in her eyes, Kozlowska informed her priests that she had an 'understanding' about the end of the sacramental presence in all Roman Catholic churches. Christ was gone for ever from their golden monstrances. Mickiewicz seems to have made a

---

1 Where there is still a copy of the Virgin of Vilna, which Towianski brought to Paris (now in the main nave on the left).
2 He mentions in 1937 *Le secret de la Salette* disseminated by Leo XIII in millions of copies.

prophetic remark when he wrote to Towianski (15 March 1844): 'The sacrifice of priests has to end, and it will take a different form.'[1] Kowalski's cry: Christ is no longer in your churches! annoyed the Catholics and embarrassed the Mariavites' allies in the Utrecht Union.[2]

Many attempts have been made to cleanse the poet's reputation of the tarnish of a sectarian influence over a period of five years (Mickiewicz broke with the Master in 1846). The name of the poet's mistress, Xavera Deybel, a prominent member of the Circle, was expunged from his correspondence, and patriotic apologists did their best to preserve the bardic façade. But one could with some perverse satisfaction build up a case for Mickiewicz being the first nameless Mariavite.

As for Andrew Towianski, he was reaching out towards our age with his parapsychic tentacles. Clumsily perhaps and with little charm, he sent his greetings to the future astronauts and to travellers in the outer space of thought like Teilhard de Chardin. There are indeed traces of precognition in Towianski which remind one of Teilhard when, for instance, he speaks of matter, all matter, as part of God's body.[3] Teilhard de Chardin was silenced by his Jesuit superiors, Towianski clashed with the papal authority and was condemned. Would he be condemned today?

The idea of universal brotherhood envisaged by Woodrow Wilson in the League of Nations, for a time revived interest in the nineteenth-century philosopher, August Cieszkowski (1814–94), who wrote in Polish, German, and French. Cieszkowski begins his monumental though unfinished work on the Lord's Prayer, *Our Father* (*Ojcze Nasz*),[4] by showing the work of Providence in history, which leads man epoch by epoch to the Kingdom of God on earth since the heavens 'are the whole universe in which our earth is a single particle'. Man should realize that 'the very fact of his living means that he is already in eternity'. Cieszkowski accepts the necessity of metempsychosis to allow for the progress of the soul. Merezhkovsky must have found much in the Polish philosopher that appealed to his own mystical

---

[1] His inspiration told him that the Master should give them 'communion in the spirit', but the Master replied that he was against such innovations.

[2] This, incidentally, was one of the reasons why in 1924 the Old Catholics were to sever relations with the Mariavites.

[3] Also his belief in the cosmic evolution, in which our soul-bodies participate, is virtually the same argument as that of Teilhard. Towianski's 'cosmic Christ', however, differs from Teilhard's in one respect: he is the Christ of the Arians at the pinnacle of the creation; his 'column of light' pierces the darkness of the world.

[4] Cieszkowski published the first volume of *Ojcze Nasz* in 1848, then re-planned the whole project as a work in nine volumes. Four of them appeared posthumously, but many chapters remained in manuscript, unfinished. Excerpts from the work were translated into English by W. J. Rose, a Canadian, who published them under the topical title, *The Desire of All Nations* (1919). My quotations are from his translation.

curiosity. Both wanted to unravel the progressive revelation of the persons of the Holy Trinity. What kind of God had man so far experienced? Or rather, what state of God?

'As long as God manifested Himself in the first state, He was to us a cold and terrible God as if of ice.' And Christ melted all this. The self-manifestation of the Third Person is the Trinity realized in a mystery so great that 'all myth, all rites, all prophecies, all errors and heresies have pointed to it'. This, incidentally, is quite close to Léon Bloy's conviction that everything in the creation must be part of the Trinity. So even 'errors and heresies' have been inspired by the Holy Ghost. In other words, the so-called errors are part of the divine context. What Cieszkowski says is intelligent in its non-sectarian acceptance of all religious phenomena. You cannot condemn a man for his mystical state of mind. Telepathically speaking, Cieszkowski sends off his *absolvo te* to the man who will admire him in the next century, the Archbishop of the Mariavites.[1] Both want to see the phrase 'Thy Kingdom come' realized down on earth.

Irony seems to persecute visionaries. Cieszkowski could not finish his ambitious commentary on the Lord's Prayer. It took him a sizeable volume to ponder on the meaning of 'Our' only. He got stuck, significantly enough, on 'Thy Kingdom come'. Christ who first addressed the prayer to his Father did not speak volumes. He was brief.

3

In his letter-report of 25 November 1842 Mickiewicz informs the Master from Paris that the Circle is in touch with a religious group of Frenchmen calling themselves L'Œuvre de la Miséricorde. Mickiewicz describes the visit of a priest representing the group, Charvaz, a humble man; he also mentions a few women followers who struck him as genuinely pious and devoted to their cause. The whole letter, is in fact, about L'Œuvre de la Miséricorde and its prophet Pierre-Michel whose real name was Vintras.

'In the revelations of Pierre-Michel there are things which agree with those we have received from you', Mickiewicz reports to the Master. 'Even their cross is white, without the figure of the suffering Lord, the same one you displayed at your place and whose meaning you explained to us. They also believe in the destiny of Israel, and their relations with the clergy

---

1 Kowalski acknowledged his debt to Cieszkowski in his pastoral letters and major works, e.g. his commentary on the Apocalypse, as he had acknowledged Towianski whom he defended against his denigrators, notably in a series of articles, 'The Sons of the Kingdom', printed in *The Kingdom of God on Earth* in 1929.

are the same as ours: they are rejected and persecuted by the Church authorities.'

Then Mickiewicz mentions the miracles and signs attributed to Pierre-Michel and tells of the group's desire to join the Circle provided there is no objection from their prophet. They in turn have asked the Poles to consult their Père Andrew (i.e. Towianski) about this proposal. Mickiewicz accepts Pierre-Michel's reputation as a miracle worker and a mystic ('he speaks and writes in moments of ecstasy'), but the poet doesn't think much of his written works.

Now the case of Eugène Vintras (1807–75), known as 'the prophet of Tilly', is not only analogous to the story of Towianski (their teachings were condemned by the same Pope and in the same year, 1843), it also reveals a curious link with the Mariavites. The names of their respective missions which were to prepare the world for the coming of the Holy Ghost are almost identical. In 1893 Maria Frances Kozlowska was called by God to do 'the Work of Great Mercy' which echoes Vintras' L'Œuvre de la Miséricorde. He received his mission in 1839 from Archangel Michael who appeared to him in Tilly-sur-Seulles, a village near Caen.[1]

Vintras was told that his new names were Pierre and Michel. By some mystical coincidence Kowalski chose Michael for his Mariavite name, was compared to the Archangel by the Little Mother when they met on St. Michael's day, and later himself propagated the symbolism of the name. Vintras initiated redemptive rites and, like the Mariavites at the outset, attracted a large number of followers to the cult of the Eucharist. Except that in his church the sacrificial meaning of the host was visible: the hosts bled or, as it was said, sweated blood, or strange signs would appear on them. The prophet himself at the beginning of his mission saw the host being transformed before his very eyes. In *Le Livre d'Or*, the book which recorded Pierre-Michel's visions,[2] we find this entry for 28 October 1839:

> Au moment où le prêtre se prosterne pour adorer la sainte hostie, j'ai vu cette hostie s'entourer de lumière; puis elle s'est trouvée changée en une couleur de la vie. De ce cœur sortaient des rayons lumineux qui allaient se

---

[1] '. . . ce Vintras, cet enfant naturel, élevé par charité à l'hôpital de Bayeux, successivement commis libraire à Paris, ouvrier tailleur à Gif et à Chevreuse, marchand forain, domestique des Anglais à Lion-sur-Mer, commis chez un marchand de vins à Bayeux, puis en dernier lieu associé à la direction d'une petite fabrique de carton à Tilly-sur-Seulles et qui reçoit un beau jour la visite de l'archange saint Michel !' This is how Maurice Barrès introduces the prophet of Tilly in his novel *La colline inspirée* (1912), ch. IV.

[2] *Le Livre d'Or, Révélations de l'archange Saint Michel* (du 6 août 1839 au 10 juin 1840), publié par M. Alexandre Ch. l'un des nombreux témoins (Paris, 1849). 'Ch.' stands for Charvaz, the parish priest of Montlouis near Tours, the chief proselytizer for Vintras, who visited Mickiewicz in November 1842. He is mentioned in *La colline inspirée*.

fixer sur le front de chaque personne qui était dans la chapelle, excepté sur une. . . . Je m'approchais de la sainte table pour la communion, je me trouvais avoir le bout de la nappe. . . .

Une couleur de la vie vividly describes the blood colour of a living heart. Vintras was a simple man, of peasant stock; he must have seen animal hearts in the raw. Unlike Maria Frances, the Little Mother, he needed miracles to prove that the Lord was on his side and nothing, of course, looked more convincing than the blood on a raised wafer. Mickiewicz believed in the miracle and said so. Others were only too eager to accept such a dramatic manifestation of Christ's presence. But the frequency with which the bleeding hosts appeared (they were even handed out by the prophet of Tilly), threw suspicion on the phenomenon itself. The Bishop of Bayeux managed to uncover the fraud, Vintras was tried and sent to prison for five years.[1] Afterwards he travelled to England and finally re-emerged in Lyon where in his old age he met his spiritual successor in the priest Boullan.

Thanks to the liaison work of Father Charvaz, who approached the Towianski Circle shortly before the arrest of Pierre-Michel, the co-operation between the two Paracletean movements was established, the French prophet apparently willing to concede spiritual supremacy to Père Andrew. A certain Théodore Fouqueré acted on his behalf at the end of 1842 and the next year, in July 1843, a trusted friend of Mickiewicz travelled to Tilly. Later when Pierre-Michel was in jail, Fouqueré and other members of the sect declared their allegiance to Towianski and formed a separate French Circle. Women again played a prominent role in this mystical alliance, one of them, Alix Mollard, becoming a most ardent follower of the Master.

Since the Mariavites consciously adopted Towianski as one of their predecessors, with Mickiewicz heading the Romantic bards, they are in some ways mystical blood cousins of Pierre-Michel alias Vintras. The bleeding host apart, Pierre-Michel placed the Virgin Mary (the Mother-Spirit of the Gnostics) in the centre of his redemptive altar. A prayer after a night vision at Tilly (30/31 August 1839) ends with a significant invocation: '*Épouse du Saint-Esprit, priez votre divin époux.*' That's how Archbishop Kowalski addressed the Little Mother in the Eucharist. In the Work of Mercy, L'Œuvre de la Miséricorde, there is, to use the words of Father Charvaz, '*la promesse de l'épuration de la terre et de la renovation du Corps de l'Église, car elle n'a rien à changer dans son esprit.*' Maria Frances Kozlowska, who knew French, would have added nothing to this promise.

Assuming, however, that each ecstatic formulation has to be re-experi-

---

[1] Political motives contributed to his conviction. Vintras lent his prophetic support to Naundorff, the pretender who claimed to be the real Louis XVII.

enced, if a sect (or movement) is to survive the first 'revelatory' phase, one has to look for analogies in those who take over the heritage. Kowalski succeeded Maria Frances and assumed the title of Archbishop; Abbé Josèph-Antoine Boullan (1824–93),[1] by then unfrocked, proclaimed himself successor to Pierre-Michel in 1876, a few months after the latter's death (they had met only twice). He adopted the names of Jean-Baptiste, the one who will usher in the Third epoch, the realm of the Spirit.

What Boullan did to the Vintrasian church in Lyon is as controversial and soiled with scandal as Kowalski's reforms within the Temple of Mercy and Love at Plock. Both were ordained priests—in contrast to Towianski or Vintras, Boullan more thoroughly educated than Kowalski. Strong-willed and idiosyncratic, they both clashed with the Church authorities; Kowalski established his independence earlier and never recanted as Boullan did at his own request before the Holy Office. Physiologically, too, the resemblance between the two men is striking. Both were highly sexed and found spiritual demands constantly at variance with the passions of their bodies. Yet they wanted a *nihil obstat* for their actions from a supernatural source, an *absolvo te* for the rest of their sojourn on earth.

The sexual rites introduced by Boullan were in their secret content reserved for the elect only, as was the case with polygamy and the erotic ritual kept by Kowalski between the lines of his own Song of Songs. What they actually practised within their respective rituals is much easier to establish for Boullan, since he recorded all his 'crimes' in a written self-accusation.[2] Kowalski readily accused himself before the elect in the privacy of the cloister, but he spilled no beans, however spillable they were, at his trial in 1928.

Kowalski established the mystical marriages. Boullan practised his doctrine of *unions de vie* with the elect of his circle, breaking the limits of the erotic in order to ascend the ladder of perfection in an act of collective redemption. By means of a *union de vie* those who were on lower rungs were lifted up by the elect who had reached a higher point. A sexual lever in operation. Vintras abused the host, and there is always a lingering suspicion about the rites which are supposed to purify the flesh. In his healing experiments, for instance, Boullan used consecrated host mixed with urine and defecated matter, and he tried other obscene concoctions.[3] As for his

---

[1] See the chapter on the Abbé Boullan in Richard Griffiths's well-researched study, *The Reactionary Revolution* (1966), on which I base some of what follows.

[2] He did, in fact, commit a serious civil crime. In December 1860, while celebrating Mass, he murdered a child which Adèle, co-foundress of his religious community, had borne him.

[3] Apparently he devised special postures for his nuns, should they have intercourse with any of the saints or with the Lord himself.

sexual fantasies, he had the *unions de vie* in which to act out the sublime and the sordid. At Kowalski's trial similar suspicions were raised concerning the abuse of the Eucharist, but nothing could be proved.

It is a pity that Vintras did not meet Towianski, who may have pinched some of his ideas. Boullan died the year Mariavitism was born, 1893. But did the Archbishop know of the man who most resembled him in the previous century? There is a possibility that during his discussions with the Old Catholics he heard of the followers of Boullan who were still active in Lyon.[1] Did he try to establish contact with them? He was curious enough to do that, but I was unable to find any proof of it. When I asked Kowalski's successor about the Abbé Boullan, he said he had never heard the name.

Compared, Kowalski and Boullan reveal the same paradox of a mystical succession which is continuity in contrariness. As a result the founder is posthumously confounded in an anti-cult. This happened to Saint-Simonism when Enfantin took it over. Merezhkovsky was right, after all: the Son must stand up to the Father (or Mother as in Kowalski's case). Otherwise the secret of the Three might cease to be a secret.

4

The message of La Salette was apocalyptic: it threatened man with destruction. Both the Abbé Boullan and Kowalski understood the miracle as applicable to their missions of mercy. Boullan's deepest thoughts, however, were diverted to the acceptance of suffering on behalf of others. Which means carrying someone else's cross. For the Pole the miracle of La Salette presaged the Revelations of the Little Mother, in which the same warning was repeated.

One of the Mariavite ideas which originated from this apocalyptic fear was the Book of Life, a beautifully bound volume in which thousands of names were entered. Whosoever has his name inscribed in this book will be saved on the Day of Wrath. The condition demanded of the person was that he should honour and venerate the Eucharist. During their travels abroad the Mariavite leaders collected names for the Book of Life. Christians of all denominations responded, even Jews.[2] After all, it was like an insurance policy and the premium cost nothing.

Kowalski caused a scare among the peasants when he made his own apocalyptic prediction: the day of reckoning was due in 1924. 'The whole

---

[1] According to Richard Griffiths, the sect continued its practices in secret until the Second World War, and may still exist.

[2] Philip Feldman in his memoir describes how names were collected on a visit to the United States (1930).

earth will be consumed by fire', he announced on 31 July. The day arrived and destiny had to be postponed. But the Book of Life was filled to capacity: an additional volume has since been added and nobody knows how many thousands of names are entered in both.[1] I heard the figure of 60,000; someone else said, No, it must be twice as many. I tried to count the names on one page, but soon I confused the lines.

What is the moral of this register? True, it seems to be a valuable document. But it does emphasize, for me at least, the bookishness inherent in the apocalyptic tradition. St. John, whichever John it was, wrote a book about a sealed book. A concept within a concept, guarded by seven seals. The seals are broken, but the text remains turned inward on itself. The image of the scroll describes the reader's experience: it is an enfolding experience, you are drawn into the dark centre. In this lies the fascination of the Apocalypse. Seer after seer stares into it, each mind reflecting something strange at the bottom, but in the end it is only the reflection of the eyes.

Archbishop Kowalski fell victim to this fascination. Once he started seeing the Johannine church of Love round the corner of every other prophecy, he speeded up its arrival, and instituted the communion of love within the Temple. This is the inevitable result of peeping over God's shoulder into the unfolded scroll of His plans for man. You think the end of an age is imminent, the Third and the last is coming—the Spirit will free you from anguish. All apocalyptic seers do that, from the Gnostics to the followers of Joachim of Fiore and the Taborites, from Saint-Simon, Vintras, and Cieszkowski to Merezhkovsky and the Mariavites. Catastrophes are plentiful in each century: prophets of gloom can pick and choose.

Kowalski saw in the Bolshevik revolution a threat and a warning. In one of his comments on the Book of Isaiah he dispatched a prediction into the future: they will invade us again, just wait and see (this was written after the peace treaty between the Soviet Union and Poland in 1923), and his prophecy did hit the black spot in the future. But he missed many others, both black and bright. Such is the compulsive risk of compulsive insinuators. Provided you get one future event right, the rest will be put aside for further reference. You merely shift the foreseeable until it becomes unseen. The Calabrian abbot Joachim of Fiore fixed the year for the coming of the Holy Spirit: the Third Reign was to begin in 1260. Then he shifted the date, but Providence refused to co-operate.

After the miracle of La Salette Léon Bloy kept making appointments with

---

[1] The Book of Life is now on the altar at Felicjanów, under the monstrance, and I was allowed to photograph it for the record. The names are neatly entered in handwriting and every newborn Mariavite is registered there.

the Holy Spirit. Come Paraclete—come on 19 March 1880, on 28 March, 18 April, 19 September! The year 1880 was gone. End of expectation. But the bookishness remained. Another diviner would try to attach a date to a line of prophetic text, unaware that the two were equally elusive.

Cieszkowski took up the chiliastic scheme of Joachim of Fiore by airing the Lord's Prayer very slowly in big volumes; he strengthened his verbiage with the Hegelian spine of thesis-antithesis-synthesis. The result was a hopeful belief in a universal welfare state (work will be pleasure for all)[1] and a leap of fantasy into 'the communion of the worlds', which landed him among the spotters of flying saucers in our century. There will be no place for diverse religions in the Paracletean Era, he said; no need of a separate caste of priests, whether Christian, Buddhist, or Jewish. Artists, scientists, and social workers will be our priests.

Kowalski announcing the Kingdom of God on earth took some of his ideas from Cieszkowski. If God is to rule us directly, the clergy must disappear. In 1930 he acted on this assumption and established 'universal priesthood'. We are all priests in the Kingdom, but like those insecure rulers who keep a foreign bank account, he retained his title of Archbishop. Nevertheless, the apocalyptic fire burnt in his passionate heart, no matter what blissful changes were in store for his faithful flock. The mystical marriages were meant to be enjoyed in the Kingdom which had come earlier owing to the intercession of the Little Mother. But those who opposed the marriages were to be cast out from the Kingdom straight into the pit where there is gnashing of teeth.

On 21 April 1927 Kowalski published a pastoral letter 'On the Kingdom of God on earth'. It consists of 38 pages and is incorporated in the second edition of the New Testament in his translation.[2] There he cheerfully repeats that all those whose names are not recorded in the Book of Life (including you and me) 'will be cast out from the midst of the just and thrown into the fiery furnace, that is into the world which like Sodom and Gomorrah will be burnt and cleansed by fire'. He echoes the prophecies of doom from the apocryphal Book of Esdras: 'Fierce flames are being kindled to burn you' (2.16). However, there will be no end of the globe according to him, but an end of sinners. After such a cleansing holocaust Christ the King will establish His rule.

This is a repeated pattern in apocalyptic thinking. Merezhkovsky

[1] See Andrzej Walicki, *Filozofia a mesjanizm* (Warsaw, 1970) (in reference to Polish Romanticism).
[2] The pastoral letter comes after p. 1002, and its pages are numbered 1 to 38. Kowalski was fond of adding such pieces to new editions, which increases the difficulty of finding them.

interprets the apocryphal Book of Enoch as the record of the first cleansing by water. The Flood destroyed mankind polluted by the Sons of God, the fallen angels, who had come down and possessed the fair daughters of men. The world was demonized through unnatural unions and particles of the original contamination are still in our bodies. Merezhkovsky quotes Lermontov's poem 'The Demon' to show the redemptive power of love and the spiritual loneliness of the dark angel. The demon wants to be at peace with Heaven, to love and to pray; he 'the free son of Ether' has already renounced all thoughts of revenge. Needless to say, Kowalski pounced on the same example, translated it, and printed it in his periodical *The Kingdom of God on Earth*.[1]

After the first apocalypse (the Flood) in which Atlantis was destroyed, Merezhkovsky predicts the apocalypse of the fire before the Mother-Spirit reconciles the opposites within the Trinity. Everything will be permissible in the Kingdom, writes Kowalski in his pastoral letter of 1927, our freedom will be like the freedom of God. Three persons will be chosen by Christ from the elect to govern the Kingdom in the light of His Will. Guided by his inspiration they will be equal to one another, 'perfect in their Trinity.'[2]

D. H. Lawrence was dying, like Rozanov, when he wrote his Apocalypse. He could not give it his final revision. It is therefore an uneven book. Yet Lawrence is convincing in his criticism of the apocalyptic fury of destruction. 'How the Apocalyptists *envy* Babylon her splendours, envy, envy.' He sees, however, throughout the first part of the Apocalypse flashes of true cosmic worship. But the concept of the book is detestable to him; it is 'the work of a second-rate mind', and 'it appeals intensely to second-rate minds in every country in every century'.[3] Perhaps too dismissive, but worth remembering.

One has in the end some sympathy for the seers. Throughout the ages they looked at the catastrophic calendar and shifted dates according to their miscalculations. They had to tackle over and over again 'this business of postponed destiny'.

[1] In the last number, 1 September 1939—another symbolic coincidence.
[2] The present council of the Kowalski group consists of three people: two women bishops and one Archbishop. Theirs is a figure of the Trinity.
[3] *Apocalypse* (1932), ch. III. The germinal influence of Lawrence can be detected in Austin Farrer's analysis of the Apocalypse, *A Rebirth of Images* (1949).

5

The Mystical Marriages

EACH nun is a bride of Christ, wears a wedding ring, and waits for death to be united with her beloved. She gives her dowry to the convent, remains chaste and, as long as she stays on this impure earth, prepares herself for the nuptials in heaven. All this is so well known that even the caustic comments of anticlericals no longer have power to damage such symbols. Yet there is a subtle secret door to this symbolism of marriage; the nun frequently takes the sacrament in which, according to the Catholic belief, her bridegroom is present. He welcomes her with his body and blood.

If logic can be imposed on mysticism, one has to conclude from this that the nun is consummating (the word is apt) her marriage each time she receives communion. More obviously so, it would seem, than any lay woman, however pious. For the nun chose and is chosen; she is one of the elect. But why should there be so many brides and so many wedding rings between the visible and the hidden, for Christ is hidden in the Eucharist, as the phrase describes it.

Now all this may sound like casuistry in the worst manner of the lesser Fathers of the Church. But I want to quibble because Kowalski stumbled on such casuistic questions while he was exploring Mariavite mysticism after the Little Mother's departure to the Third Heaven, her heaven. Down on earth, in September 1921, he found himself surrounded by women who hung on his lips for spiritual advice. The new Mother Superior could not be elected for a year. And he was already producing interpretations concerning the Eucharist which would have been called dogmas, had he been Pope. His manic search for parallels increased as he plunged into the translation of the Old Testament, a work he had begun during Kozlowska's lifetime and which was to take him ten years altogether.[1]

Rendering the cryptic message of the prophets coincided with the writing of his own Mariavite scripture, *The Work of Great Mercy*, in which he was building another temple, this time in honour of the dead foundress. The

---

[1] His translation of the New Testament was finished in 1921. The Old Testament version of 1925 is more important for Mariavite ideas, as it contains a daring commentary.

Title-page of *The Work of Great Mercy* (1922; printed 1924)

nuptial language of adoration permeates this guilt-ridden, often irritating, but very human book. Kowalski was the four evangelists in one (this merely spurred his ambition) and the John of a new Apocalypse as well, brandishing Michael's sword along with his ferocious pen. Below the angelic orders he most willingly identified himself with King Solomon who erected the temple and wrote the Song of Songs, a fitting text for any temple of Mercy and Love.

> Let him kiss me with the kisses of his mouth: for thy love is better than wine. Because of the savour of thy good ointments thy name is as ointment poured forth, therefore do the virgins love thee.

And in chapter 6 of the Song there is a passage which begs for a reflection on Solomon's royal virility:

> There are three score queens, and four score concubines,[1] and virgins without number. My dove, my undefiled is but one. . . . Who is she that looketh forth as the morning, fair as the moon, clear as the sun, and terrible as an army with banners?

[1] In his version Kowalski translates concubines as *miłośnice*, i.e. loving women.

If this song is sacred because it is part of the Bible, then the King's many women deserve closer attention. Kowalski knew, of course, the Shulamite's prophetic identity: she was none other than the Little Mother, and when he came to provide his commentary on the Song, he wrote a hymn of praise to her, all in footnotes and the footnotes occupying on the average three-quarters of each page. The text is literally a pretext. Dark and comely, the bride of the Song of Songs is the chosen one above the other wives and concubines. The King raised her as high as himself.

In another gloss which directly concerns the mystical marriages, Kowalski explains that the Kingdom of God is being realized after the Little Mother's death, because she opened what was closed until now. A secret door to the indescribable: 'what the human eye hasn't yet seen nor the ear heard, and what hasn't yet entered the human heart'.[1] So it is his sacred duty to be a chronicler of this Kingdom (Queendom) and he proposes to describe 'the wedlock that took place between the Mariavite Priests and the Mariavite Sisters because through these unions a new and renewed human race [*rodzaj ludzki*] began on this earth, cleansed of every blemish of sin and renewed in body and soul so that it could become the tool of the Power of the Holy Spirit on earth'.

He does repeat himself as people often do when they are pressed for a clear yes-or-no answer. Whenever he doesn't want to be explicit he hides somewhere between the parallels and he is clever at doing this: 'And what is conceived and born according to the Will reflects in itself the likeness to the Most Holy Trinity, which was lost in Adam. Therefore it is pure, sacred, and immaculate . . .'

Sure enough, the Virgin Mary closes the parallel. The likeness to the Trinity is of particular importance, equally so the mention of Adam. Kowalski promised to get rid of original sin into which the first Adam dragged us all. But the promise holds for the elect only. 'From this wedlock there will arise a new human kind born without original sin.'

Babies were already crying in the cots at the cloister when this pronounce-ment reached the Mariavites. It comes from an introduction to a set of thirty-two Testimonies (*Świadectwa*), short and long, which together form a sequence of 426 pages, a book in themselves, in the second edition of *The Work of Great Mercy*. These were all written at Kowalski's order, by priests and nuns whom he had joined in mystical matrimony. Published in 1929, these fascinating documents have one weakness in common: they defend a

---

[1] In the Second Epistle to the Corinthians St. Paul describes how he 'was caught up into para-dise, and heard unspeakable words, which it is not lawful for a man to utter'. Kowalski never tired of alluding to this passage, especially when his reforms were under attack.

controversial issue after the event, when some of the polemical dust has already settled on the grey habits. They are, of course, for and not against Archbishop Kowalski (the title he assumed after the Little Mother's death, to show his supreme authority to the city of Plock and the world). He wouldn't have published them otherwise.[1] Yet their value lies in authenticity at least attempted here for the greater glory of truth; some secrets are veiled (as was to be expected), but this only adds flavour to the writing.

The first two mystical marriages were solemnized in secret on 3 October 1922, the night before the anniversary of St. Francis's death. The Franciscan tradition was observed even in this extraordinary departure from the Rule. Circumstances forced Kowalski against his will, but presumably with the Will of the Lord, to announce the existence of the marriages in a pastoral letter dated 18 April 1924. The persons concerned wrote their pieces a few years later, and although excerpts were read from the pulpit in Mariavite churches, neither then nor later were they meant to be read by outsiders.

No Mariavite documents are easy to obtain, but the Testimonies about the mystical unions seem to be the hardest of all to get hold of. Many copies have been wilfully destroyed. (This is also true of Kowalski's other publications.) When I learnt of the Testimonies half-way through my research, I knew I couldn't possibly discuss the Mariavite marriages without reading them. The people whom I asked to provide me with a copy usually made some vague perhaps-one-day promise, others flatly denied that such documents were ever printed.

One expects to find a touch of persecution mania in most Mariavites—understandable in their case—but hammering my enquiries month after month I began to feel like one of their persecutors. Frustrated in my efforts I thought that, short of becoming a Mariavite myself, I would never see the elusive evidence. But my luck changed, and then I smiled, for I had, in fact, guessed right. At the end of the Archbishop's introduction from which I have quoted, there is this advice: 'We print them [i.e. the Testimonies] only for the Mariavite Brothers and Sisters, with the request that you should not give them to non-Mariavites to read.' For religious adults only.

Above 'The Testimony of Father Archbishop Michael' there is the heading, *On the divine origin of the conventual marriages.* The whole evidence is to prove that the Archbishop's 'understanding' came from the Almighty, the usual procedure with dogmas. But the intention to keep the understanding secret from the majority of the Mariavites was there, clearly stated: 'At the beginning Father Archbishop thought [Kowalski writes his own testimony

[1] The cloister had its own press, from which, after 1922, Kowalski published much. See p. 153.

in the third person] that the marriage unions were meant for the four Fathers [i.e. himself, Jacob, Philip, and Bartholomew] whom the Little Mother called pillars and that they would be kept secret from the world.'

Soon, however, he received a divine intimation that the twelve foundations on which the New Jerusalem is built in the Apocalypse (ch. 21) are the twelve Fathers who will hold special offices in the Kingdom. The twelve pearls signifying the gates to this Kingdom were 'the God-minded', the Sisters chosen for this office by the Little Mother herself.[1]

So the number was increased to twelve marriages, all from the top conventual drawer. Here perhaps lay Kowalski's boldness. He involved in his scheme the nuns spiritually most advanced, the contemplative. It's not surprising that some of them were struck dumb at first. There, the Archbishop thought, the series would end. But another 'understanding' hit him from above. If twelve, why not all the priests? So he proposed three series of twelve priests. This seemed unfair to the dead Fathers who had missed the new bliss but, combining ingenuity with justice, the Archbishop included them in the enlarged set and found live wives for them. Thus the first Mariavite apostle, Father John, was now wedded beyond the grave.

What was originally meant to be exclusive became a proper marriage colony, and the Archbishop took all the credit for dispensing the marital blessing. A cynic, however, would observe that once the rumours spread and priests in the provinces began to be scandalized, Kowalski had no choice but to rope in as many of them as possible. The vow of obedience kept the timid in check. The strong-willed questioned the Will of God as administered by Kowalski. To see how the problem developed one has to go back to the Testimonies.

2

There is a joke about a nun being kissed in the street unawares. What was that? what was that? she asks her wimple. The Will of God, answers the wimple. Say one *Ave Maria* and three 'Thank you, Lord's, and be quick about it.

At the Mariavite Temple of Love it started with a kiss, too, then kisses multiplied, but no nun had any doubt where they came from. The Most Reverend Father, as they called Kowalski, kissed them in turn. The Most Reverend Father could have explained—he was eloquent in explanations—that it was the first verse of the Song of Songs he was re-enacting. 'Let him kiss me with the kisses of his mouth.' Or, at least, trying it out on those Sisters whom he had to meet often in the course of his duties.

---

[1] Their number was the apostolic twelve. Kowalski had a cabbalistic interest in numbers, but not in the zodiac, as far as I could ascertain.

Sister Honorata, the *vicaria* general of the convent, was in charge of the nuns after the Little Mother's death, and Isabel, a cultured young sister, was to become Mother Superior, though she had no inkling of it yet. Kowalski saw them both, Isabel twice a week, for such was his command (he wished to prepare her spiritually for the high office). He worked now in the Little Mother's room, slept on her sofa, used her prayer books and received callers in her antechamber. The best substitute for living in her womb.

When the Most Reverend Father kissed Isabel's temple and her eye for the first time, he asked whether she was scandalized. No, she said. Her reactions seemed to be slow, she got frightened later. Sister Honorata, on the other hand, was positively enchanted. She had worshipped him from the time when they were all with Kozlowska in Rome, in 1903. After the election of the new Pope she naïvely remarked: 'Why didn't the cardinals elect our Most Reverend Father Michael? With the Little Mother at his side he would reform the whole church and the clergy.' A kiss from such a man was grace straight from heaven. But she had to curb her jealousy. Isabel made her feel inferior: she was beautiful, well-mannered, and she helped the Archbishop with proofs and copied his manuscripts. Moreover, she would soon be above all the nuns. Honorata knew that from Kowalski, who could be blunt when revealing secrets, so she suffered much.

As for Isabel, her timidity and languor made her even more desirable. Being a perfectionist of a coy sort, she worried about her inadequacy and this tired her out. A lethargic stupor set in. The double kiss shook her out of it, then she started worrying again—could she be the source of his temptation?—but the woman was already awake in her. Kowalski knew how to confound her uncertainties. To begin with, he explained the mystery of the 'pure unions' between the Little Mother and the four. 'I didn't at first understand the need for such unions,' writes Isabel. Slow again. Then he did what he had done in the presence of the Little Mother: he confessed to Isabel his sins against chastity during his whole life, and asked her to confess hers. This was the sure way of bringing the intimacy to a quick spiritual boil. It worked for a time. But the scruples of a perfectionist are, like humility, endless.

Now Bishop Jacob heard most confessions at the convent. The Little Mother always advised the nuns to go to him. They had to confess once a week. Jacob knew his theology (like Kowalski, he had studied at the Catholic Academy in St. Petersburg), and he was a strict observer of the Rule. A man of routine, set in his ways, as he described himself in his Testimony, he gradually learnt from the nuns in his confessional that something odd was going on between them and the Archbishop. Kisses, kisses—on the mouth, on the eye, on the temple—even the elderly Sister Alexandra got one; they were all in rapture and remorse over them.

Honorata later admitted that she had used Bishop Jacob to vent her jealousy. The scrupulous Isabel simply worried him stiff with her worries: she was good at that as other nuns were to realize once they began their spiritual sessions with her.[1] Jacob collected the whispered bits and pieces and didn't like at all the emotional confusion in the cloister. It was his duty to probe further with questions, and what he heard upset his theological thinking. Could these credulous creatures have misunderstood the Archbishop's words?

When did it all start? Only two months or so after the Little Mother's death: Father Bartholomew mentions November 1921 in his Testimony. Jacob the confessor ordered Isabel to be firm and resist.[2] Castigated, she almost relished the proof of her worthlessness. She cried much. Jacob wanted to stop the rot and directed letters *ex officio* to his superior. But the spiritual son was going through a new rebirth; he readily confessed his guilt only to repeat the Solomon experiment at the next opportunity. He, too, cried and the nuns noticed it. He often attended the night Adoration of the Eucharist. While he celebrated Mass tears would stream down his face. Obviously, Kowalski had had one of his crises brought on by the death of the woman he truly worshipped, and now he saw her in the Eucharist. How could he possibly detach her from any act of adoration? It was like imposing one cult on another: the Christian St. John's eve, for instance, merged with the pagan festival at the solstice. The pattern already existed for him to emulate.

Despite his power as Archbishop, Kowalski felt at a loss and desperately needed approval. The possessiveness turned the other way round: he wanted to see his own identity confirmed in the possessive love of those who identified with him. For they, too, felt at a loss, just as he did—from the 'God-minded', who prayed and adored, to the 'doers', the nuns who performed menial tasks, cleaning, cooking, sewing, making shoes. Even during the Little Mother's illness the decisions made in the cloister had ultimately been hers. 'In all things he [Kowalski speaks of himself] depended on her.' They all trotted up to her cell like children, the elderly and the young: tell us what to do, and she told them, her cancerous belly swelling ominously.

There is a touching scene in Isabel's Testimony, which shows up the

---

[1] I have this confirmed by a number of older nuns who loved and admired their new Mother Superior. 'You brought your worries to her,' one of them told me, 'she fretted over them with you, and so you left her more worried than before.'

[2] A well-informed Mariavite nun told me that in her opinion Bishop Jacob's panicky reaction indicated that Kowalski had already gone beyond the kisses. Otherwise the urbane Jacob would not have been so shocked. I am inclined to agree with her.

priest's loneliness. Seeing her at work on his manuscript in the Little Mother's room, Kowalski said: 'I used to spend days and days alone, translating the Scriptures, and I had such a desire in my soul to have a companion in my work. Well, now the Lord has given me this comfort.'

But, above all, he needed signs, whether they came as dreams, parallels, or coincidences in dates. He lapped them up, ready for more. One obstacle was temporarily removed: from May to October 1922 Bishop Jacob was on a tour of parishes, conducting retreats (*rekolekcje*). In July Father Philip fell seriously ill with pneumonia and death hovered over the Temple once again. A month later the Archbishop got what he wanted: a sign through Philip.

It happened on the anniversary of the Little Mother's death, almost to the hour. Kowalski entered the room, fearing the worst, and at four in the morning he and the Sister tending the sick man felt Kozlowska's presence. They knelt. They thought she had come to take Philip away. Suddenly, Philip clasped Kowalski's hand and in silence repeated the four Mariavite vows. According to his Testimony, the Little Mother wanted him to add something else, so he waited and then repeated after her (in his mind) the following phrase: 'This is my marriage bond with you for ever.' The words seemed to puzzle him.[1]

Then Kowalski rose and asked:

'The Little Mother was here, wasn't she?'

'Yes,' answered Philip, but in his semi-conscious state he couldn't say more.

A few days later Kowalski told Philip that he could now inform him of his and the nuns' suffering and of Jacob's conflicts of conscience during those ten months since he had received an 'understanding' about the marriages in the convent. Philip knew nothing about them. And prompted by yet another understanding Kowalski passed the mystical buck to the sick man. 'Whatever Philip says, I will abide by it.'

A confession was at once repaid with a confession: Philip described in detail what had happened the other night and told him of his strange marriage vow. Yes, it all came from the Little Mother. Kowalski is guided by the Holy Spirit.[2] With tears in his eyes, the Father Superior of the Mariavites kissed Philip and announced that his new name would be Jonathan. At last Kowalski had an ally through whom divine approval was

---

[1] They are identical with the words which Christ apparently addressed to the Little Mother: *Ten jest węzeł mój małżeński z Tobą na wieki.*

[2] The curious thing about this 'happening' is that it was so readily accepted, almost as a miracle. But a man subjected to high temperature could have imagined anything. One is asked to take Philip's account too much on trust. Sister Raphaela, under whose care he was, describes how his fever made him jump up in his bed, wanting to run away. Apparently in his old age Philip himself confirmed that his 'vision' was the result of his high temperature.

voiced. He could go ahead at full speed, bestow kisses and soften up the indecisive Isabel.

On the day of her election to the office of Mother Superior (8 September 1922)[1] he produced a different oath from the approved one, demanding from her absolute obedience, love, and faith in everything that he would give them to believe in accordance with the Will of God. Hesitant and doubtful, as was her habit in the early days, she said No, and the Archbishop asked her to tear up the new formula. That was that. After the election he delivered one of his memorable speeches to the assembled Sisters, ceding to Isabel all spiritual guidance over them. In a sombre voice he apologized for the offences he had caused them (he meant the 'kisses'). The Sisters wept and, as he was leaving, some threw themselves to the ground, kissing his hands and feet, so afraid they were that they might lose their Little Father as well.

Kowalski won the battle of the tears. He knew the women were on his side. Poor Isabel after reaching her moment of glory tumbled into despair and felt abandoned, like the others. So she rushed to the Archbishop's room, fell at his feet and sobbed, begging his forgiveness. How could she, so weak and inexperienced, live without his guidance? And 'thus the Lord forced me to carry out His dispensation', and she quotes the Book of Genesis (ch. 2) in her account: 'It is not good that the man should be alone; I will make him a help-meet for him.'

Yes, now she wanted to take the oath she had rejected. Ah, said Kowalski, I don't remember what it was, you tore it up in small pieces, my child. Isabel wasn't slow this time, she reconstructed the formula and swore on it, promising him love and unconditional faith in all his inspired 'understandings'.

The act was not quite perfect, writes Kowalski, because it was done out of anxiety for herself. But he nowhere says that his formula resembled the dogma of papal infallibility in matters of faith, the very thing the Mariavites attacked. Feigning great sadness, he nevertheless bestowed a kiss on his betrothed.[2] He had earlier asked Isabel to occupy a room adjoining the Little Mother's cell, then she had moved out to give no further cause for gossip in the cloister; now she could officially be installed in the room next to him.

But her doubts still remained, 'and she was only as a sister to him, not as a spouse', writes Kowalski in the tone of his Biblical translations. 'About the incident over the writing of the new oath formula, however, Father Arch-

---

[1] In her Testimony Isabel confuses the chronology of events. She places the crisis in Philip's illness, 23 August, after her election. There are quite a few such discrepancies in other accounts.
[2] The betrothal had happened months earlier. While she was kneeling by the sofa, Kowalski kissed her and said in a matter-of-fact voice: 'This is betrothal.' Brief and simple.

bishop spoke to nobody.' Another secret. It is surprising how often Kowalski put a confidential seal of silence on his theological work in progress. One suspects secrecy in other undertakings which he didn't bother to record.

After gaining divine approval through Philip, Kowalski felt confident enough to tackle the upright pillar of the Temple, Jacob the confessor. He did it in the usual way. 'Self-accusations', repeated vows, confessions going back over a whole life were the Mariavite kind of therapy. Hear my sins, I will hear yours. Nothing could work better for the stubborn Jacob. Confessor, confess yourself.

When the busy man returned from his tour of the parishes, Kowalski gave him an order: Go to Philip and open your soul to him, accuse yourself. Which meant: Let him interfere with your convictions. And Philip did it, skilfully. Had Jacob not obeyed, Kowalski would have thrown him out.

Jacob had so far been consistent in his defence of the Franciscan Rule. Marriage, however purified, was incompatible with the vow of chastity. Knowing that Isabel was to become Mother Superior he had, quite logically, made a frontal attack on her, and had also learnt much from her rival, Sister Honorata. Here, incidentally, one must observe that the frequency of confession within a community as enclosed as a convent can lead to the unconscious abuse of information, especially if the priest regards himself as a moral supervisor of the whole group. Among the Mariavite top priests the knowledge of one another's secrets was tinged with pathological interest. They began practising soul nudism at a time when 'soul' was a favourite word in literature and art.[1]

Events accelerated. After much prayer and many neurotic hangovers Kowalski passed the whole issue to Philip who was convalescing and had no duties at the cloister. And Philip pronounced for the marriages. Like Honorata, he had unconsciously desired them. His decision came on 26 September. On 3 October 1922 (the day on which the first marriages were effected), Bishop Jacob denuded himself before Father Philip (a much younger man), and was told of the 'happening' and its consequences, but this apparently did not convince him fully. Still, he swallowed his pride, went back to Kowalski, asked his pardon and made the same vow as Philip. Did he say 'my marriage bond with you'?—I wonder.

Once again he went away, still perturbed. Now it was for the all-forgiving Father, the Archbishop, to choose a suitable wife for him. Kowalski not only invented the mystical marriages, he was also a heaven-

---

[1] The leader of the Modernist group in Polish literature, Stanislaw Przybyszewski, never grew tired of showing his 'naked soul'. His manifesto of 1898 appealed to the anti-bourgeois bohemians.

Sister Love

Sister Celestina

The third Adam dividing an apple with Isabel, left, and Cherubina.

(*Left*) Isabel among the lilies; (*above*) Clemensa in the robes of a Mariavite priestess (worn also by Gertrude, below).

Honorata

Gertrude

inspired marriage broker. When Jacob returned to the Temple at the end of October, Kowalski asked him: 'How do you feel, Father?' To which he replied: 'I am still suffering.'

The following Sunday he was summoned to Philip's room in the evening.

'How do you feel, Father?' Kowalski repeated.

'I suffer much,' he said, and added to his own surprise: 'But I am ready to do your Will.'

Kowalski told someone to fetch Sister Honorata. This was the wife chosen for Bishop Jacob.

It is fascinating to read Bishop Jacob's Testimony, a document which traces the progress of a confirmed bachelor to marriage and finally to polygamy. Jacob's account reminds one, somewhat uncomfortably, of the abject confessions at the Soviet trials. How the poor man praises the inventor of the mystical marriages, how grateful he is for being allowed to come round to the Will of God. Praised be the Lord and the Most Reverend Father!

To justify his enforced conversion Jacob the solemn quotes examples from the Bible, resorts to theological subtleties, and is visibly at pains to convince other doubters of his sincerity. The Archbishop knew that Jacob's opinion would carry much weight with them. Jacob goes on for a page about the kisses in the cloister, which had caused him so much distress. Now the Song of Songs and the epistles of the apostles came to his rescue. Didn't St. Paul say, 'Greet one another with a holy kiss'? And didn't St. Peter say the same in his first epistle? Nothing convinces better than being convinced oneself, and Jacob tries hard to appear that he is.[1]

But the real worry at the back of his mind was the possible downfall of Mariavitism through Kowalski's action. 'I sacrificed my family, career in the Church, and comfortable living for our cause.' He throws in this bitter sentence, and a whiff of melancholy lingers between the lines. At one point he recalls the Little Mother's appraisal of Kowalski in 1903, then quickly castigates himself for being hurt by it at the time. He had thought he was her 'first-born', and she said of Kowalski: 'I sensed a new Adam in Michael.' And now this Adam was sowing the seeds of a new Genesis.

It is Jacob who in his Testimony mentions the first children born in the Temple of Love. At least he doesn't try to hide behind the myth of virginity.

3

And the good Archbishop was pairing them off in the likeness of the upper Paradise. The Little Mother apparently had a vision of it in December

---

[1] His piece, no. 5 in the series, is entitled, 'Bishop Jacob's Testimony to the Divine Will'.

1902; the heavens opened, and what did she see? Just pairs—pairs—pairs. St. Paul must have seen the same when he was whisked into the Third Heaven. He knew that he couldn't reveal what he had seen, writes Isabel; people were not pure enough to accept the secrets with dignity and 'would have used them to satisfy their sinful wishes [*zachcianki*]'. How considerate of St. Paul (Isabel came from a good family and observed the proprieties).

Now the Mariavites were ready to do all the unspeakable things which Christ had concealed in parables and St. Paul kept to himself. And the Archbishop was giving new names to those about to enter the Philadelphic Church of Love, the church of St. John.[1] A new name indicates a rebirth: this way Kowalski could adjust parallels. Isabel he called Abishag, the one who warmed old King David because he 'gat no heat'. The Archbishop wasn't that old, just over fifty, but Isabel had once rubbed his cold hands, a sign of warmer things to come. Philip became Jonathan, a God-sent gift to Kowalski–David; Sister Honorata became Mary the sister of Moses (because she sensed the marriages in prophetic dreams); Sister Raphaela was given the name of Michaela because she came to be united with Archbishop Michael; and so on.

Like Adam in his Paradise, Kowalski loved inventing names.[2] To the reader of Mariavite documents this can be a headache until he sorts out who is who in Kowalski's Kingdom. And there are dreams to sort out as well. One could compile a catalogue of them, for Kowalski recorded his and asked others to remember theirs. During the crisis over the marriages dreams hatched in the worried minds of the nuns, prompted by the kisses and confessions, and it is easy today to see their significance. Whenever the Little Mother appeared in them, the dreamers took their meaning literally.

Sister Honorata saw the Little Mother's tomb open and heard her words, 'I am buried here with the martyr of love' (meaning Kowalski). In her second dream she did even better: the Little Mother rose from the dead and in the illuminated Temple led Isabel, wearing a bridal crown, to the great altar. Kowalski was in pontifical robes. In Bartholomew's dream the Little Mother said: 'I am so sorry for you' (his mystical wife did not want him), and after that things improved. Some dreams expressed what the nuns really wanted once the kissing touched on their suppressed desires. One felt a baby

---

[1] The Philadelphic Church is one of the seven churches of Asia Minor, mentioned in St. John's Revelation (ch. 3) and exempted from reprimand. Cf. the significant phrase: 'he that hath the key of David, he that openeth, and no man shutteth.'

[2] The Little Mother imitated St. Clare in this respect, so we find among her Sisters names like Illuminata, Hortulana, Felicita. Kowalski showed a preference for Old Testament names, like Ruth, but he also produced some rare ones: Esperata, Humiliana, Redempta. The new Adam named about 300 nuns.

sitting on her chest, and her bliss was immense. Another saw her future husband walking towards her naked, and then realized in her dream that she, too, was naked. A plain directive, straight from Adam and Eve.

In a way Kowalski's dream messages indicated the same source of disturbance. He wanted confirmation: Yes, you are right, you are pure. On his wedding night he saw the Little Mother lying on her sofa, and there was intense light which startled him.[1] 'Who is it? What is it?' he shouted and woke up his wife 'whom he did not touch until then' (the phrase is significant). This was the sign for Go ahead: she is your rightful wife.

But did she or did he, for that matter, lose virginity that night? A silly question in view of what later came out at the trial. Despite all the self-accusations in which he counted his sins against chastity, Kowalski claimed to have miraculously preserved his virginity. A remarkable achievement for a full-blooded man exposed to the hot breath of the Demon of Noon. There is a curious coyness in his printed comments on sex, even in his autobiographical novel, *My Ideal*. He couldn't help it; he was born into an age of prudery.

The word 'virginity', however, seems to have a double connotation in Kowalski's mystical vocabulary. In his pastoral letter on the marriages, of April 1924, he described them as unions 'without the loss of virginity'. The letter was published eighteen months after his own wedding night. What did he want to convey to the credulous? That no copulation took place? or that the elect entered another body like ghosts passing through walls?

The more plausible explanation is to be found in Sister Honorata's Testimony where she extols her hero through quotations from the Psalms and from Apocryphal writings. In the so-called Book of Zacharias (ch. 3) Jesus is wearing soiled (*plugawe*) clothes which are removed at the command of an angel. A footnote, presumably added by Kowalski, explains that 'the soiled clothes signify the impurity of the body which was taken away from him'. This is a Gnostic comment all right. It is through Our Most Reverend Father, writes Honorata, that we will be liberated from the shackles of the body. His sacrifice is offered for the lowest sins—sensuality and impurity. And here she quotes the cryptic saying of the Lord to Kozlowska: 'Give your soul to me, and your body to Michael.' Did the Little Mother then liberate him from the stains of sensuality and thus make his physical acts pure—in reply, as it were, to St. Paul's dictum that 'unto the pure all things are pure' (Epistle to Titus, ch. 1)? In a letter to a nun Kozlowska wrote: 'All things that God creates are pure; only the evil will of man made them un-

---

[1] Again the evidence is one-sided. Isabel did not see the Little Mother ('because I was turned the other way'), but she woke up thinking it was already daylight.

clean through sin. . . . A little child walks naked in front of everybody and is not ashamed.'[1]

A sanctified body too, like that of a child, is outside shame. St. Francis threw off his clothes and stood naked before the people to show he was reborn. No pious prudery here. But examples like these depend on the state of faith. Sin well, said Luther, but keep your faith. 'The soul of sweet delight can never be defil'd', wrote Blake. Moreover 'the lust of the goat is the bounty of God'. We are on the ancient track of Gnostic and Manichaean paradoxes.

> The Lord Jesus united me with the Most Reverend Father. . . . I kissed him with such faith, love, and reverence as one kisses the holy Martyrs of God. The reverence I felt for the Most Reverend Father, for his pure and mortified body . . . part of this reverence poured as it were onto Father Czeslaw; he was becoming less loathsome to me.

This is Sister Boguslawa in raptures over the Archbishop who coupled her with a priest she couldn't stand. To her copulation with Kowalski was sinless. Give your body to Michael and he will cleanse you. Back she goes to her mystical husband, reborn. Virginity is not a physical *status quo*—it is spiritual rebirth. Very likely, Kowalski believed that in his church of Love constant rebirth would rule out ordinary conception. The body-spirit would be preserved intact.

He became angry with one Sister who couldn't grasp the supernatural law of the Kingdom, insisting that children were bound to come, sooner or later. What's the point of these marriages if there won't be any children? Pray, said Kowalski, the Holy Spirit will enlighten you. But he couldn't tell whom she would get for a husband. 'I want nobody but you,' she felt sanctified in his presence. 'Not only my soul but also my body and even my habit was dearer to me because he touched it.' When Kowalski told her to see Father Philip to be further instructed, she burst out: 'I don't want Father Philip. I give myself to you alone', and she clasped Kowalski's neck.

The whole Testimony of this passionate nun (her name is Melania) has a sinister end. The Archbishop in one of his inscrutable 'understandings' found an answer: he married her off to the ghost of Father John (the first propagator of Mariavitism), and the obedient ghost turned up to claim his marital rights. Melania's testimony, one of the longest in the book (16 pages), is splendid stuff, with echoes of Bürger's *Lenore* and other macabre ballads. The nun's hysterical style goes well with the subject.

---

[1] The letter was written in 1918 to Sister Gertrude and quoted by her in her Testimony (see p. 95). Afraid that it might cause offence, the Little Mother asked her to destroy the original, but Sister Gertrude translated the contents into French.

First, there has to be an apparition in a dream. The dead Father John bends over her bed and, kissing her, whispers: 'We must be wedded.' Sometime later Melania moves to the parish where the dead priest used to live and she stays in his room. 'It was on 13 December,' she writes,

> at nine in the evening. As soon as I went to bed I heard a rustle of wind. Fear seized me, I trembled and my heart beat like a hammer; I thought I was about to die. Suddenly, as if someone had told me it was Father John, I felt he was coming nearer. I moved close to the wall, wanted to shout, but at this moment Father John embraced my neck and began to kiss me with great love. Fear left me and I was so filled with joy that I cried out: 'Oh, my beloved Father!' Said Father John: 'Quieter, quieter.' I stopped talking and felt shy. When I felt that love joined us into one being [i.e. Melania probably experienced orgasm], Father John said, 'I am united with the Little Mother.' I understood it was through me. I wanted to ask him something but he interrupted me and went on with his kissing.

Melania receives a new name from him and on his departure notices the colour of his eyes. They are blue.

'Overflowing with happiness, I was so weakened that I could not raise myself. Then I looked at my watch. It was twenty minutes past nine.'

The love affair from beyond the grave had lasted twenty minutes. Melania described it all in a letter to Kowalski who was pleased and pronounced the happening to be true (he recognized the symptom of awe before the visitation). When the love-sick ghost turned up again (twice), the wedded nun couldn't control the fear preceding his visit and jumped out of bed.[1] But the happier memory remained with her and sometimes she longed for his ardent embraces.

The Mariavite ballad of Sister Melania and Father John stands apart from the rest of the accounts. There were other arbitrary choices which Kowalski imposed on reluctant couples. He would join an elderly nun with a young priest, or vice versa; sometimes he seemed to be testing the limits of human incompatibility, as with Boguslawa and Father Czeslaw, or Sister Cherubina and Bartholomew, whose testimonies describe the physical repulsion they had to endure.

For her prophetic backing and unconditional co-operation Sister Honorata deserved at least a choice that would have appealed to her sentiments. The Archbishop knew she desired him exclusively. However, he wanted someone loyal who would keep an eye on Bishop Jacob, so he paired them off. Thy Will be done, in heaven and in hell. For Sister Honorata suffered mental tortures 'and like a condemned soul ran about the cloister garden'.

---

[1] Whereupon Melania received a further proof to convince those who didn't believe her: rejected by Melania, Father John consoled himself by calling on a priest he had known.

I understood, she writes, what it is to be denied the presence of God for ever.

The Archbishop was for her a sacred being: she felt his presence in David's Psalms and in Messianic writing; it is in her Testimony that a footnote appears connecting Kowalski's date of birth with that of the Nativity.[1] And now his Will pushed her into the arms of the man who had opposed that Will and was loathsome to her physically. Honorata entered her hell for the sake of Kowalski's Kingdom, but when the split in the sect occurred in 1935, she left Bishop Jacob and followed the Archbishop, faithful to a bitter end.

Her contorted evidence, like that of Sister Boguslawa and Bishop Andrew (who was given a nun with a hump), throw a grotesque light on Kowalski's decisions. Now and again he produced what I would describe as a mystical joke, double-edged and in its intention not unlike the Sufi way of upsetting our moral security. 'If you don't know where you are going, any road will take you there.'

During the crisis of 1921 Archbishop Kowalski discovered that he possessed a transmittable power, similar to the *baraka* of the Sufi visionaries, which he had to give away with his whole body-spirit. After the mediatrix he the mediator.

One can detect a pattern in the preparation of the elect for the 'nuptials of the Lamb', his favourite phrase for the marriages. It must have been evolved in consultation with Father Philip who was the chief celebrant of this Philadelphic Church of Love within the Temple. The Testimony of Sister Celestina maps out her own progress. It is, I think, the least confused account of what happened to a nun once she was chosen for the inner circle.

Three years after taking her religious vows Sister Celestina became a sacristan and began to notice that something mysterious was going on between several of the priests and Sisters. The Sisters, in particular, talked to one another with great affection. She was an outsider and felt anxious, then heard rumours about 'pairs', and the wall of secrecy depressed her. One day an inner voice consoled her at prayer: 'Nothing can be evil in a place where the Holy Sacrament is venerated.' A strange longing possessed her. She cried.

In March 1923 Sister Honorata told her to go to Kowalski. The Archbishop kissed her and asked, did it upset her? No, it gave her strength. Good, said he, accuse yourself now of all your sins against chastity. She did and was kissed again. Much grace was to come to her. Would she like to offer a triple vow to him: of love, fidelity, and faith in all that the Holy Spirit

---

[1] As early as 1907, Honorata had stumbled on Slowacki's poem about the Slavonic Pope, which was later recited at Mariavite entertainments. (See p. 102.)

would inspire in him? Gladly she agreed, and he in turn vowed her eternal love and care. Sister Celestina received a new name, that of Beniamina ('It means a double gift,' said the Archbishop). There and then he told her she now belonged to the choir of the 'God-minded'. They went together to Mother Superior Isabel, who kissed her with great love. Celestina couldn't believe all those graces were hers. Almost too much joy for one day.

The procedure is psychologically interesting. By means of the 'self-accusation' Kowalski finds out what sexual fantasies disturb the woman he has just kissed. The triple vow commits her to any future inspiration (or fantasy) he may wish to act out. He also has her discretion. No wonder that Isabel, on whom the special vow was first tried, had qualms about its possible consequences. Now she acts as Kowalski's partner; she welcomes the new insider and will appease her, should there be guilty second thoughts.[1] The elect is immediately upgraded, joins the choir of adoration which gives her certain privileges. In the church of Love the Lord rewards his favourites.

For further inside information the elect were sent to Father Philip. Without his assistance and that of Isabel and Honorata, Kowalski might never have succeeded in putting his audacious scheme into practice.

As for Sister Celestina she had to pass through an ordeal but not a prolonged one. Her husband was to be Father Policarp, whom she didn't fancy much, but she prayed hard to have only Christ and the love of the Archbishop. Unlike Sister Honorata she got her pious wish. 'On the 22/23 of October 1923 [she means the night, of course] the Lord Jesus bestowed a high grace upon me by uniting me in a still greater love with the Most Reverend Father.' The 'still greater' must refer to the fact that she became one of Kowalski's wives. This time he changed his 'understanding' for better and not for worse.[2] Sister Celestina was twenty-four, he nearly fifty-two.

As for the ceremony of marriage, it was apparently simple. The couple came to Father Philip's room. The Archbishop read appropriate passages from the Bible and the couple repeated marriage vows, swearing to do the Will of God. There was no binding of hands with a stole, no kneeling. The couple kissed each other and were kissed by those present. Twelve persons (the Archbishop's apostolic twelve) attended a meal after the ceremony, and

---

[1] As there were indeed in a number of cases. Some nuns felt that they had broken their first vows, some eventually left the cloister. Others weren't in the know, and Kowalski tried his best to observe some secrecy. A nun who worked in the press, in the basement of the cloister, remembers how his favourites would sneak by on tiptoe and climb up the stairs to his office which was immediately above the compositors' room. Nobody else saw them.

[2] From the beginning he kept changing his mind about who should be coupled with whom. He would switch husbands at the last moment.

the couple spent their wedding night in a room near the great altar. They lived in their separate cells afterwards.[1]

Sister Gertrude describes the evening of her betrothal. Pears and apples were handed round. 'We shared them as the fruit of Paradise.' Alas, her wedlock brought her much unhappiness.

In the original Paradise, Adam had no marriage ceremony to perform. There was only room for one couple, and they didn't do well.

4

Luis de León, poet and monk, got into serious trouble with the Spanish Inquisition over his interpretation of the Song of Songs. Archbishop Kowalski, three hundred and fifty years later, had his translation confiscated for being both blasphemous and obscene.[2] In fact, the source of his offence was in his commentary, not in the text. The whole interpretation glorifies the mystical marriages and the Little Mother.

Kowalski did more to the poem than any of its numerous translators and interpreters in the past. He *lived* it with a group of people, line by line. This was, one could say, a continuous translation in flesh and blood. On the printed page, however, he is relentless in fixing his parallels once and for all. The Song of Songs is the prophetic matrix for the mystical marriages, except that now they have at last become a reality. It is the Little Mother who asks for Christ's kisses—'Let him kiss me with the kisses of his mouth' —and it is only through her that the mystical marriage with Christ is achieved.

> She alone has the power to admit to her Husband's marriage bed those of her Virgins and Daughters whom she likes well and whom she wishes to usher to the nuptials of the Lamb.

This is the Church of the Elect (*Kościół wybranych*), and Kowalski is the mediator whom the Lord Jesus and the Little Mother have made their passive instrument (*martwe narzędzie*). Thus 'the Little Mother continues to unite body-souls with the Divine Spouse, for she herself is not jealous'. The last observation could well have been inserted to temper the jealousies, big and petty, among his own wives and the other nuns who feared competition from the beautiful newcomers. We must remember this is the year 1925, and he had had a few emotional troubles already.

---

[1] None of the printed Testimonies describes the marriage ceremony in any detail. I have had to rely on conversations with the nuns who were themselves married. They prefer to remain anonymous.

[2] This explains why his translation of the Old Testament is not to be found in any library.

In the beginning was the Kiss ('whosoever once tasted this kiss will not forget it and crave for it always') but to receive it one must possess absolute purity and virginity ('unless it be miraculously restored by God as was done to Mary Magdalene').[1] The miraculous restoration is a characteristic aside. Kowalski's own virginity, as he repeatedly asserts, was 'miraculously preserved'. Perhaps with the help of the Little Mother he became a male Mary Magdalene, one more name to his collection.

A comment on the phrase 'I am black but comely' (Song of Songs, ch. 1) explains that the Little Mother was all through her life blackened by the Roman clergy who were supposedly defending the Virgin Mary. A nice touch this, since the famous shrine in Poland is that of the black Virgin.

'Behold his bed, which is Solomon's; threescore valiant men are about it' (ch. 3). This, says Kowalski, corresponds to the thirty pairs of the mystically married and he lists them all for the record, name by name, in order of initiation (the four 'pillars' with their first wives at the head). He also alludes to the number of years Christ lived on earth. Strangely enough, when all the couples renewed their marriage vows on 19 April 1925, standing in a row before the main altar, their number was precisely thirty-three.[2]

'Still, this is not the end. As Solomon had only one Queen and wife, but a thousand concubines, so the Lord Jesus, having only the Little Mother for his wife. . . allows to this marriage union many others, chosen by Himself' (with Kowalski mediating as his 'passive instrument'). He therefore mentions six Sisters who were 'in a special way' joined through him with the Heavenly Couple.[3] This is a veiled admission that Solomon's example has been followed to the letter. At the height of the cloister's expansion there were about two hundred nuns at Plock. The Archbishop would, no doubt, have preferred the figure to be closer to that of Solomon's concubines, but he couldn't grumble; he had plenty to choose from.

What mattered to Archbishop Kowalski, however, was an allegorical matrix. He has a lot of fun with the animals, the parts of the human body, and the objects mentioned in the Song of Songs. He can even afford to turn the nickname 'goat-bleaters', frequently flung at the Mariavites, into a word of praise. For in their pastoral Kingdom they are indeed a herd of goats,

[1] The son of one of the bishops told me how furious his father was on hearing that he, the son, was no longer a virgin. He should have waited to lose his virginity with one of the elect in the Temple of Love. This would have been proper. And there is a mystical wife who believes to this day that her hymen remained unbroken until she gave birth to her first child.

[2] No 'secondary' wives were present, however. Philip Feldman mentions the ceremony in his unpublished memoir, but he breathes no word about polygamy. He suppressed the most interesting event in his personal life. Why write memoirs then?

[3] They are Sister Love, a newcomer who is given second place after Isabel, then Clementina, Dilecta, Celestina, Michaela, and Alina. (The last died before the publication of his translation.)

tended by the Goat-lady (Kozlowska's name being derived from 'goat'). The whole catalogue reads like a religious incantation, which it is meant to be.[1]

Kowalski lets his imagination fly into the absurd nooks of hagiology. Here is his list of correspondences:

For the *scarlet lips* of the Beloved read 'the blood and bile with which they were covered' in the Little Mother's agony.

The *two breasts* are 'her two spiritual sons, Fathers Michael and Jacob' (this probably quenched Bishop Jacob's ambition).

For *thou hast ravished my heart with one of thine eyes* read 'the blinded right eye of the Little Mother'.

The *north wind* will blow in the next war 'which will destroy sinners'. This is the seer's ancestral voice prophesying war. And the war came. And it destroyed him as well.

The Beloved's *hair* signifies all the conventual Sisters of the Little Mother; her *teeth*, the Mariavite Fathers; her rounded *hips* are the four choirs at the convent; her *navel*, likened to a *goblet*, is the cup with the Saviour's blood.

The *mandrake*, a plant believed to be a cure for sterility, indicates the Little Mother's grace which made the Virgins of the Plock Temple conceive and bear 'children without original sin'.

And so on and on, with cross-references and nodding asides. One can just imagine the learned professors of Catholic theology throwing up their arms in horror, and hissing: Anathema! anathema!

Parallelism offers one obvious advantage to its maker: he can glide in and out of it at a whim's notice. But somehow Kowalski felt obliged in his gloss on the wise King Solomon's vocabulary to define the difference between the mystical and the ordinary marriage. The reader holds his breath. Well, he merely repeats what he has said often enough about the perfect love of the Heavenly Husband united now with his Bride, but he expresses little hope for the ordinary marriage which is doomed from the start by the inherited sin of Adam. Self-love, pride, anger, and greed weaken it all the time, while adultery breaks it asunder. Broken or weak, such wedlock must end with death. Only the mystical marriage is for ever.

This was precisely what got Sister Honorata, Sister Gertrude, Sister Boguslawa, and other nuns so hysterical. They wouldn't mind being with the Archbishop for ever—he was already a top husband in heaven—but why

---

[1] The Book of Kings (ch. 11) blames Solomon's wives who 'turned away his heart' so that he worshipped, among others, Astarte of the pagan Sidonians. Could perhaps the Song of Songs be a tribute to that ancient goddess of love? There is, after all, a Sumerian love poem which offers a very striking parallel.

with pedantic Bishop Jacob? or timid Father Czeslaw? or some priest from the provinces?

Bishop Andrew was astonished at the choice of a hunch-backed nun ('But she is so deformed!').[1] During the wedding night he did his duty, but 'felt a loathing for Sister Gertrude'. She returned to her cell at four o'clock in the morning as upset as he was. She admits in her Testimony that at the age of forty-seven she knew nothing of the physical nature of marriage. Their characters clashed: she was quick-tempered, he was slow, but one day in December something happened to the poor mystical husband. 'In these marriages the Holy Spirit itself awakens the erotic urge.' Just as the Most Reverend Father said.

Then Andrew makes an intelligent observation: 'Even in a religious order a man feathers a comfortable nest for himself, in which his nature with all its faults can rest undisturbed. . . . Only the intimate relationship of marriage will bring to light the most deeply hidden faults of a person, and also test his virtues.' This echoes a moving confession of his oversensitive wife: 'This union lifted me out of my abnormal state, bordering on maniacal oddity, into which I was driven by my confessors who magnified every scruple I had.'

A young nun like Dilecta expresses a different mood when she tries to describe her trust in Kowalski: 'With a child's simplicity I embraced him as if he were my own father, because I felt like a child in the presence of the Most Reverend Father.' She was only sixteen when she entered the cloister (1923). She became one of Kowalski's wives and the mother of his only child. In her Testimony, however, she describes herself as a spiritual wife, 'one of the many'. The language is for the elect. They knew the nuances. And she was a *dilecta*.

Kowalski's success with the nuns at Plock is not sufficiently understood either by his followers or enemies. What happened in 1921 after Kozlowska's death was a shift of archetypal images, instinctively felt by all—from the Great Mother to the Great Father. Hence the crisis suffered by the progenitor himself, John Maria Michael, because he feared the force of conflicting emotions which her death and his assumed 'parenthood' unleashed simultaneously. As the father figure loomed bigger within the cloister walls, the sexual urge gradually came to the surface. He had a choice, of course: he could either suppress the urge brutally by ascetic means or let its voice be heard within his 'understandings'. He knew what was at stake, but

---

[1] Andrew, Bishop of Lodz, was very popular with the people and much respected, even by non-Mariavites. Sister Gertrude knew a number of languages, was in charge of foreign correspondence, and helped the Archbishop with his publications.

could not stop the overpowering desire of the split body-soul to be reunited.

The men he led into this risky experiment, including himself, were at a critical age, sexually. At the time of the first four marriages, he was fifty, Bishop Jacob nearly the same age, Father Philip thirty-seven, and Father Bartholomew forty-four. Mother Isabel was thirty-one at the time of her marriage, Sister Honorata forty-four. I think that in the circumstances, with the hysterical passions around him and most of them aroused by his kisses plus, Kowalski had to opt for a more complex pattern, and willy-nilly fell into the trap of polygamy which in the end destroyed his organiza-tion.[1] Still uncertain of the ways in which his Will operated, he strengthened his conviction by convincing others. And he had one considerable ad-vantage: he knew his Old Testament well, he was translating it. Finally, he could impose a special vow on the elect. They were answerable to him only. His word was law, each of his inspirations a dogma.

As for Kowalski's treatment of his love-bound women, he summoned them at his convenience, and none of them ever dared to say no. A witty nun told me: 'He behaved like a Victorian husband. Either I have a wife, or I haven't, he would say, meaning the one he desired that day. Fetch her at once.' And the Sister on duty, or his ever-patient Spouse Number One, would rush to deliver his marital ration of purified flesh.

But how could he cope with all those women whose energy, too, was released and indirectly threatened the father image in him? A charming Sister told me with a twinkle in her eye: 'For the older ones a kiss on the forehead, a pat on the cheek, or a flicker of a smile was enough. What they really wanted was to be assured now and again that the Most Reverend Father loved them. One physical act meant so much to them that they could live on it emotionally for months.'

The Archbishop then could spare his energies—and they were consider-able—for the younger nuns, especially when his own appetites grew. I imagine that James Boswell, as curious and indefatigable as Kowalski, would have loved a long discussion with the Archbishop on the 'plurality' of the female species and the ways of reconciling man's lust with his religious aspirations.[2] Did the Divine Authority approve of Solomon's concubines,

---

[1] Because of the marriages he lost some of the most active priests in the parishes, who later testified against him at the trial. And the experiment resulted in a rift with the Old Catholics of the Utrecht Union, who showed bias against women. When Kowalski turned up with his senior nuns at a conference of Old Catholics in Bern the women were not admitted, and the decision was taken to expel the Mariavites from the Union (15 September 1924). Apart from the mystical marriages, the Old Catholics objected to the Little Mother's Revelations, especi-ally the one concerning the invalidity of Roman Catholic Masses.

[2] See Boswell's diaries from the years 1776–8, *Boswell in Extremes*, ed. C. McWeiss and F. A. Pottle (1973).

or did the King find himself in the Book of Books by some providential oversight?

Polygamy is difficult socially and may prove tiresome emotionally. As the Archbishop soon found out. All the nuns he introduced to the mystical nuptials held him in great esteem and affection.[1] The combination of lover and father seemed ideally suited to a religious community as earnest as the Mariavites were. All the nuns loved Kowalski except Sister Love (*Miłość*) who was the youngest and to him the most beautiful of his wives. Isabel suffered much over Kowalski's obsession with Sister Love. Her name was supposed to protect the love of nuns for their Mother Superior. What a curious way of appeasing rivalry. There were also Sisters Faith and Hope to complement the symbolism. He did single her out, though she was too young and inexperienced, and then she ran away, which only increased his passion for her. On her return he made the other nuns kiss her feet in homage (good for obedience, this). At a banquet with dancing organized to celebrate the occasion, the Archbishop paraded with his Sister Love, thrusting her hand out to be kissed. The poor woman could not take that amount of public attention, and Kowalski could not accept the possibility of her leaving the convent for good.[2]

Sister Celestina describes a scene when she called on Kowalski (3 May 1928) and found him ill in bed, in a morose mood, talking of his love for Love in the presence of the self-effacing Isabel. He exchanged rings with Celestina (she was already his wife). Hers was the ring of love and his, which she took, was the ring of mercy. 'Remember,' he said, 'should Love return to us, have mercy ready for her.' This is not the Solomon of the Song of Songs, but a lover rejected by his image of the goddess of love.

He was, after a fashion, loyal to his Queen Abishag, Isabel the beautiful martyr. He would tell a nun: 'Go now to the Mother Superior and ask her permission to be kissed by me.' Isabel would receive such petitioners with motherly tenderness and kiss them too. The protocol had been observed. But as a nun cherishing Isabel's memory remarked to me: 'Kowalski made a real person out of her. Before she was flabby and frightened of her own shadow.'

As for the priests who lived at the cloister but were outside the inner group of four, they could hardly risk voicing a protest. Some convinced themselves so much that they actually enjoyed having intercourse with their wives soon after Kowalski had entered them as Father Mediator. The husbands felt in closer touch with the bliss of the Third Heaven.

1 This I have heard repeated by every Mariavite nun I talked to.
2 She stayed until she was thirty, when she left Kowalski's paradise and married. (See p. 230.)

A visitor from England who saw the Mariavite bishops and their wives a few weeks before Kowalski's jubilee in 1934, made this comment to me:

'They all looked so incredibly young. Philip Feldman must have been nearly fifty at that time, and he looked no more than thirty. Bishop Jacob, too, didn't appear old. As for the women, they looked youthfully happy, every one of them.'

'Even Sister Gertrude,' I asked, 'the one with a deformed spine?'

'Yes, Mother Gertrude, too. My companion was positively infatuated with her. They all radiated something, well—from inside.'

'And the Archbishop?'

'I noticed his eyes, yes, his glaring blue eyes. They had a peculiar expression. I saw a pair of eyes like that recently, in a young boy. He became mad.'

I didn't ask the obvious question until my interlocutor, musing for a while, interrupted the silence and said in a quiet voice:

'Archbishop Kowalski' (he pronounced the name Ko-o-lski) '—that look of his. I believe he was mad. Don't you think he was mad?'

I made no comment, merely jotted down what he said. And it occurred to me on my way back from our interview that Kowalski, whether sane or insane, had broken one of the powerful taboos connected with convent life. People feel sentimental at the sight of a nun. The purveyors of pornography use the nun's habit as one of their kinky outfits. The dirtiest way of defiling a woman's image is through her virginity, of which the nun is a symbol.

Now Kowalski upset all these traditional associations. He replaced pornography with sexual health, and sentimental fantasy with the reality of highly efficient Mariavite Sisters. He saved himself, if not the women in his power, from the mean violence of suppressed passions which would have turned their piety into a mockery of love. Archbishop Kowalski never forgot that Mercy is the twin sister of Love.

He took risks and allowed hysteria, including his own, to release its latent energy so that the identity of the person could be fully visible. Exasperating, domineering and often silly in his arrogance, he nevertheless carried out a major sexual revolution in the name of God, whatever he and we mean by it; and he achieved this over fifty years ago in a sanctimonious provincial town on the outskirts of Europe.

6

Erotic Ritual on Trial

I

I HAVE yet to meet a Mariavite, young or old, who when faced with a direct question about the trial of 1928 does not behave as if he were still standing in the dock. He usually has a pat reply: The trial was rigged. And a few names of villainous riggers are mentioned. Unfortunately, this is how the majority of lost cases are defended by the losers, whereas in terms of law only new evidence leading to a retrial can alter the verdict. There was no retrial of Archbishop Kowalski. He had threatened many journals with libel suits, but the threats were soon abandoned. Apart from a few vague repudiations that appeared in his own periodicals after the verdict no substantial body of material presenting the Mariavite side in the trial was ever collected and published. A curtain of indignant silence dropped, and it is difficult to imagine that any of Kowalski's followers would wish to raise it now, thirty-three years after his death.

The evidence, then, is mainly hostile, both on the trial itself and on the events leading up to it. Important among the latter was the publication in 1926 of those 'disclosures' (*wynurzenia*) of Mrs. Tołpyhowa which had made my aunt Casimira's face purple with disgust. The lady who decided to tell all in the pages of a Plock periodical was not a nun, Mariavite or otherwise. Under the title, 'A Year's Stay at the Mariavite Convent', she addressed her public as Mrs. Janina Zygmuntowa Tołpyhowa, using her husband's Christian name as well as his surname, which emphasized her status as a respectable married woman whose report could be trusted. She had no grudge against the Mariavites to begin with. After her husband had lost his job, they generously invited her to come with her sick son to their centre at Plock. During her work at the convent she met not only Archbishop Kowalski, Mother Superior Isabel, his wife, and Sister Love, his love, but also many other members of the community, including the very young girls who later gave evidence against Kowalski at his trial.

Tołpyhowa was admitted as a potential convert and within a short time won the confidence of other women in the cloister. They didn't regard her as an outsider, though later she proved to be just that. By disclosing the inner secrets which were apparently confided to her, Tołpyhowa did in a sense break the code of friendship. She broke it again two years later when she appeared in court as a witness against Kowalski. In the eyes of the Mariavites this was betrayal, and it mattered little whether she reported their secrets accurately or not. To some people a traitor is also a capable liar.

Tołpyhowa shows herself in her story under a halo of saintly indignation. She encourages the mystical wives to tell their bedroom tales, becomes obsessive about the different kisses administered by Kowalski to his chosen ones, receives a few fatherly smacks herself, and finally when the generous Archbishop lures her to a kissing session by the sacred sofa, she runs away in panic and writes an indignant letter to him resigning from her job in the cloister. She then summons her lawful husband who arrives and is apparently intercepted by Kowalski. Virtue triumphs in the end. The husband is not taken in by Kowalski's version of the story, stands firmly by his spouse, and the family trio escapes from the clutches of the villains. A sort of moral happy ending.

The narrative of these stormy events exudes a musty provincial odour, reminiscent no doubt of Tołpyhowa's own upbringing. When, for instance, she describes Kowalski's advances to the pretty mandolinists in his convent orchestra, she reprimands him for tempting the girls with home-made wine, cakes, and sweets. The convent parties, and there were many of them, must have suited the genteel tastes of the participants.

Tołpyhowa's account contained nevertheless three important disclosures which were exploited by the press before and after the trial. The first concerned the nature of the mystical marriages. They were all interlocked with one another through Kowalski, Tołpyhowa reported, and he himself had not one wife but six.

The second concerned Kowalski's role as mediator, the only one who could unite his mystically bound lovers with Christ and the Little Mother, now joined in their eternal nuptials. It was the Little Mother who, complying with God's ordinance, 'organized and is now continually creating her new church, the church of Love. . . , in which the souls and bodies of the elect are united in no other way but through her spiritual son and spouse' (i.e. Kowalski).[1]

The third assertion concerned the sexual offences against several girls who were under age. Some of them had already left the Mariavite cloister.

[1] Tołpyhowa is quoting from Kowalski's commentary on the Song of Songs.

It was Osinowa, mother of one of these girls, who in the same year, 1926, formally asked the public prosecutor in Plock to bring charges against Kowalski for depraving her daughter Mary. Her appeal set the wheels of the law in motion and the process of investigation began.

In 1927, Dr. M. Skrudlik published the first part of a book with the defamatory title, *The Crimes of the Mariavites in the Light of Documents*, in which Tołpyhowa's disclosures were quoted. And all through that year attacks on Kowalski in the press were intensified, with the object of forcing the public prosecutor to act. In particular, articles appeared that summer in the *Warsaw Morning Gazette*, a daily reflecting the views of the leading Opposition party, the National Democrats, hinting at the government's reluctance to put Kowalski on trial because of his prompt support for the *coup* which had brought Marshal Pilsudski to power in 1926.

These allegations created such a stir that the Mariavite bishops felt impelled to answer them, in an 'open letter' published in August in the free-thinking periodical *Epoka*.[1] The bishops, defending their leader, claimed that the well-planned and well-financed campaign of the National Democrats was in fact a joint action with the Catholic clergy. Protesting that the Mariavites had been libelled, the bishops made various claims (in themselves libellous) against individuals who had left the cloister and were now giving evidence against the Archbishop; they appealed to the Minister of Justice to appoint an impartial commission which would look into the true state of affairs in the cloister. The last sentence mentions sixty libel writs which the Mariavite hierarchy had initiated to ward off further attacks in the press.

The sixty lawsuits were never heard in court. They were quietly withdrawn. Instead, the public prosecutor opened a case against Archbishop Kowalski on 28 September 1928.

2

Outside the newly decorated hall of the County Court at Plock, on the day the trial began, crowds had been gathering since early morning, but nobody was allowed in without a ticket of admission. The public which packed the court consisted mainly of women and the Mariavite priests. When Archbishop Kowalski arrived at nine o'clock, driven by his chauffeur, some of his female followers knelt in the street. To them he was their Slavonic

---

[1] Five Mariavite bishops signed the open letter: Jacob (Próchniewski), Andrew (Gołębiowski), Francis (Rostworowski), Philip (Feldman), and Bartholomew (Przysiecki). The Archbishop of course did not sign, though touches of his impassioned style are detectable in it, or so it seems to me.

Pope, as he had been called in print by one of his bishops;[1] to the curious and, no doubt, sexually excited onlookers he was the Jan Kowalski, a most uncommon bearer of the most common name.[2]

At the time of his trial the Archbishop was nearly fifty-seven. Of peasant stock, well-built, with a confident face and a powerful neck, he looked tough even in distress. The admiring eyes of his co-religionists, fixed on him in the courtroom, must have alleviated his feelings of betrayal when he looked at the witnesses who had once been his priests and nuns. The ex-Mariavites were now sworn in as Catholics, and this further emphasized the religious division among the witnesses. Only the Mariavites offered to testify for the defence, no Catholic was to appear on Kowalski's behalf. For this reason alone the trial could not alter or mitigate the passionate involvement on both sides, which remained the same from the beginning to the end. To observe impartiality the judges had to forget about religion and stick to the criminal offences with which the Archbishop was charged.

The material assembled by the prosecution over more than two years had been reduced to 23 typed pages which were read out in court that day, together with the formal charges against Archbishop Kowalski. At first the prosecutor had asked for the whole trial to be held *in camera*, and the defence had gone even further, demanding that the full text of the charges should also be read out behind closed doors. The court decided on a compromise: only parts of the proceedings were to be conducted *in camera*. The public therefore heard every page of the long document and was—as the press reported the next day—duly scandalized.[3]

According to the law of the land Kowalski was charged under articles 513, 514, and 515 of the penal code, all of which referred to sexual acts (*czyny lubieżne*), whether with children under fourteen or between fourteen and sixteen, or with persons over sixteen, if they were raped or forced in

[1] The so-called *Mysterium*, compiled by Bishop Philip (and later published), consisted of extracts from the works of the Polish Messianists, which were acted by the children of the convent school. The culminating point invariably came in Slowacki's poem mentioning the Slavonic Pope: the girl reciting it would point to Archbishop Kowalski whenever he was present in the audience. In 1924 a Mariavite periodical announced 'the transfer of the apostolic capital from Rome to Plock'.

[2] Kowalski is the equivalent in Polish of Smith, Schmidt, or Kuznetsov (*Kowal* means smith), and Jan (John) is as popular a Christian name in Poland as anywhere else. By an odd coincidence, on the very same day another Jan Kowalski appeared in the court reports of the *Warsaw Courier*. He was a spy, and the Court of Appeal sentenced him to four years' imprisonment.

[3] The court archives at Plock were destroyed during the German occupation, and the only surviving member of the court which tried Kowalski is, as far as I know, the then recording clerk, Z. Deczyński. I have had, therefore, to depend on reports of the trial in the daily press. Those printed in the *Warsaw Courier*, a moderately conservative daily founded in 1820, while far from impartial at least tried to sound aloof; those in the *Plock Daily*, as the provincial newspaper of the town where the Mariavites had their centre and where the trial was being held, were no more impartial but much more informative.

any other way to have intercourse with the accused. There were some legal subtleties within these articles as to the manner, for instance, in which defloration could take place with or without direct copulation. Penalty for each offence varied from one to eight years' imprisonment. The most serious offence, of course, concerned the depraving of children, in this case girls from the convent school.[1]

At the beginning of the trial, the hearing of witnesses was expected to take a fortnight. In fact, the trial lasted nineteen days,[2] until 12 October. One has to exclude from the reported testimony a number of irrelevant matters or mere red herrings which cropped up, as they always do in prolonged cases. They were brought in for the purpose of discrediting the sect as a whole. Did the Mariavites or did they not welcome the enemy in the Russo-Polish war of 1920 when the Red troops occupied part of Plock during the decisive battle of Warsaw? In the tenth year of Poland's independence it was still a touchy subject, but what did it contribute to the examination of the Archbishop's sexual habits?

In the tense and often hysterical atmosphere of the courtroom, the women witnesses, in particular, tended to give poor evidence, they sounded repetitive and confused. One of them during a hearing *in camera* was so carried away by her intimate confessions that people in the corridor outside could catch what she was saying at the top of her voice. Such occurrences fed the imaginations of rumour-mongers. Naturally enough, some statements which must have repeated word for word the evidence already written down, do not seem all that convincing today; others read like smuttily coy vignettes in a pornographic fantasy.

From bits and pieces of this evidence the prosecution at the trial put together a representation of the Mariavite beliefs as applied by Archbishop Kowalski to his own actions which the civil law considered criminal under three articles of its penal code. This distinction between beliefs and civil law is vital. The mystical wives of the Mariavite priests were, for example, all chosen by the Archbishop and they had first to pass through his mediatory bed. How was the law to judge such a mystical *jus primae noctis* in a feudal paradise?

A system of this kind could not have been evolved without secrecy, ritual, and initiation. In order to protect the ritual, degrees of initiation were established. There were apparently three. During the first initiation Kowalski joined the elect with Christ through a deep kiss. He simply put his

---

[1] Five of these girls are mentioned by name in the court report and in the verdict. According to one of the witnesses, some of the depraved girls were only seven years old.
[2] i.e. days of the actual proceedings, excluding three Sundays.

tongue into the mouth of the initiated. One of the girls complained that the Archbishop's first-degree kissing bruised her lips and made them swell up.[1] During the second initiation the elect had her left breast uncovered and touched by the mediator's hand. The third degree of initiation meant a full sexual union in a kneeling position. By passing through these stages of initiation the elect would finally join the secret church within the official organization, the inner circle of kinships which Kowalski called the Philadelphic Church of Love. There the arch-mediator presided over the mysteries with his appointed wives. As to their number, opinions varied. Some witnesses said there were six,[2] some seven, and some said twelve. The last number would presumably correspond to the signs of the zodiac which played an important part in the symbolism of the Apocalypse.[3]

In crude terms then, Kowalski's system gave him every right to enjoy his women. But there were jealousies among them; some of the elect felt more elect than others, and fear of the pretty newcomers increased passions. This psychological factor was not sufficiently recognized by the prosecution in evaluating the statements submitted by women who had left the Mariavite convent for one reason or another. The jealous undertone was heard clearly in a number of testimonies at the trial.

Former Sister Baptista,[4] for instance, explaining to the court how the kinship with Christ was achieved in practice, quoted her own question put to the Mother Superior: why was it that only pretty nuns were chosen to receive the grace of kinship? To which she apparently got an evasive answer. The same Sister Baptista described how the other nuns who did not enjoy the Archbishop's favours had to labour like slaves in the convent and in the workshops which were known outside for their efficiency.

Former Sister Teodota, one of the chief witnesses, who recanted after the trial, also spoke of favouritism. She had come to the convent via Kowalski's confessional, he had taken her to his room, 'kissed her violently' after her confession, and then had arranged for her to be brought to Plock from a provincial place.[5] She was accused of stealing linen and stockings while at work in the convent, was threatened with dismissal by the Mother Superior

---

[1] 'The kiss had a purifying meaning,' reported the *Plock Daily* (22 September), 'for it was Christ himself who through Kowalski's mouth was kissing his new beloved.'

[2] Six was the figure given by the witness Paluchówna and by Tołpyhowa.

[3] Cf. Austin Farrer's structural analysis of St. John's Revelation, *A Rebirth of Images*.

[4] Out of discretion, whenever possible I use the witnesses' religious names rather than their full surnames which appear in the trial reports.

[5] A similar episode occurred, it was said, during the Archbishop's visit to another provincial centre. The Archbishop told a young nun to see him after confession. She came to the dining room where he was alone, 'he seated her on his knees, opened her habit, and began to fondle her indecently.'

and went to Kowalski to plead her innocence. He began to caress her, and while doing so had a spiritual confirmation of her innocence. Then he told her 'he had the same feeling for her as for Sister Love and called her his little wife'. After supper the Archbishop summoned Teodota to his room. She had to wait while another sister (Clementina) was kept inside for an hour. Sister Clementina left the room 'very red in the face and excited'. Then Teodota went in and found Kowalski in his bed. In her testimony she speaks of the orgiastic excesses which followed.

'One was horrified,' writes a reporter,

> to listen to the details during the reading of the charges, in which the witness described various foul acts which Kowalski had ordered her to perform. It is not certain whether she repeated the same evidence last Saturday at the proceedings *in camera*. However, from some snatches of conversation between the people who were present at that hearing, one can conclude that the testimony of the witness under oath was far more incriminating than that given during the investigation.

This quotation, from the *Plock Daily* of 24 September, is typical of the way in which the trial was reported in the press, guesswork and innuendoes being offered by journalists in lieu of confirmed facts. As it happens, it was Sister Teodota who later wanted to withdraw her damaging evidence, and is still of the same opinion today.[1]

Among the stage properties of the sexual fantasies which were attributed to Kowalski there was also a musical instrument: the mandolin. Kowalski must have loved its tremulous sound for he had a cloister orchestra wholly composed of pretty mandolinists. A photograph reproduced in the press showed five young girls dressed up in a curious folk costume with a head-dress resembling a crown. But why was this particular instrument chosen? A former mandolinist explained to me that it was thought easy to handle and therefore suitable for young players. They were taught to play classical pieces, and had an excellent tutor in Sister Salomea. The number of girls in the orchestra was always twelve.

One after another the hostile witnesses described how the Archbishop made the girls sit on his knees, how he fondled them and administered his deep kiss of initiation. Whenever the mandolinists were summoned to his

1 A few months after the trial Teodota met the Archbishop by chance at a Mariavite church in Warsaw. She burst into tears, was forgiven at once, and then agreed to sign a statement. Kowalski could have taken her to court on the charge of perjury, but (according to Teodota) he didn't want to harm her. I found her explanations not wholly convincing when I talked to her in September 1971. What seemed obvious to me was the Svengali-like power of Kowalski, which she couldn't resist.

small room,[1] they found him lying in bed, usually with his wife Isabel or with some other unveiled beauty. The girls had to entertain him and his bed companions with the songs he liked.

One of the mandolinists gave this account:

> Each of us went up to Kowalski and greeted him by kissing his hand. He told us to sit on the floor by the sofa. We strummed and sang folk-songs and the 'nuptial hymns' from the Song of Songs as, for instance, 'Come, my beloved'. After playing a few pieces we stood in a row to say good-night to Kowalski. When my turn came, he began to kiss and cuddle me, whispering: 'My wee little spouse, may the Lord Jesus bless you.' Kissing me he put his tongue into my mouth and sucked my lips so much that they still ached the next day. . . .
>
> Once when the curtain was down, Kowalski chased me all over the stage, then he caught me and began to kiss me by putting, as usual, his tongue into my mouth, which the convent brothers saw, and Kowalski wasn't in the least embarrassed. . . .
>
> After the concert Kowalski asked [Bishop] Feldman whether he kissed any of us and he said no, so Kowalski ordered Feldman to kiss us well after God's fashion, which he did. And [Bishop] Próchniewski also kissed us. One Sunday we went to dance in the refectory and during intervals sat at Kowalski's feet, and he said that all twelve of us would get wedding rings as the Lamb's brides [oblubienice Barankowe]. That Sunday the dancing ended at half past ten. Saying good-night, Kowalski went up to me, gave me a kiss and asked in a whisper whether I would like to come to him straightaway. A shiver ran all over my body, but I managed to excuse myself in a small voice: no, I wouldn't. Kowalski pushed me aside and walked out. Kasia Z. confided to me that she went to Kowalski for the whole night and was also Feldman's wife.[2]

A hostile witness, the former Mariavite priest, Banasiak, whose own morals were much questioned and his evidence later challenged by the

---

[1] According to a number of witnesses, it was Raphaela (Bishop Philip's first wife) who often conducted the young girls up to the Archbishop's room. She discharged her night duties with diligence.

[2] Even four years after the trial Kowalski couldn't conceal his interest in small girls. His autobiographical novel *My Ideal* (serialized in 1932) describes erotic temptations besetting a young seminarist. His friends have a pretty eight-year-old daughter, Zosia, and he plays with her, kissing her often and being kissed by her in return. Zosia's mother thinks it all innocent until she realizes how serious the attachment has become, and begs the seminarist to stop caressing the girl. 'Why? She's only a child and can think no evil.' To which the mother replies: 'It may seem so to you, Father, but she is in love with you. She can neither eat nor sleep, and wants only to be with you. . . . A child has the same heart as a grown-up.'

So the seminarist stops fondling the little Zosia, but before long he is tempted again, this time as an ordained priest. Whenever he gives communion to very young and beautiful women, he wants to touch their lips or teeth with the very fingers which are holding the host. And he desires to kiss them, although he is shocked that even in such sacred moments 'he cannot control his sensuality'.

Naïvely written and didactic at the end, the novel is a revealing document of the Archbishop's obsession with virgins, kissing, and subliminal sex in ritual. So is his unpublished memoir.

defence, claimed to have been present at yet another wedding of Kowalski, this time with Sister Salesia. At that ceremony, too, the mandolinists were singing love songs, seated as usual at Kowalski's feet, while he 'kept calling them his royal daughters'. Again and again, the evidence described his uninhibited advances to the mandolin girls, and as the hearings went on, the instrument itself became an erotic object whose very shape was suggestively feminine, and tellers of dirty jokes now had an ideal prop for countless anecdotes. Even today I find it impossible to think of the mandolin—strings, plectrum, and all—away from the absurd connotations it acquired at the Plock trial. Kowalski, it seems, raised this poor cousin of the lute to sublime kinship with the ridiculous.

And there was still more to be deduced from this fetishistic transformation. The public whose curiosity was being titillated did want to be shocked, but it could not go on being shocked with the same intensity. It found comic relief in objects like the mandolin and in unexpected happenings, whether inside the courtroom or outside. On the third day of the proceedings, for instance, a Mariavite chauffeur who had brought some priests to the court building attacked one of the onlookers with an iron bar, and when the police intervened, he hit a policeman as well, but only with his fist. When he was being taken away, the crowd wanted to lynch him. Reporting this incident, the *Warsaw Courier* lost its temper and rebuked the Mariavites for their crooked ethics. It did not, however, point out the crooked desires of the crowd.

Every night the monstrance at the top of the Temple was brightly illuminated and this annoyed the inhabitants of the town. One evening the lights failed, but a few young Mariavites climbed on to the cupola and mended them, while the mob in the street below kept roaring with fury.

On the ninth day of the trial, newsreel cameramen from Warsaw turned up in Plock. Soon after came taxis which brought a group of foreign journalists: German, Russian, and American.[1] They were allowed to attend a session behind closed doors, then visited the Mariavite estate at Felicjanów, where they stayed for lunch. 'After that, convinced they already had enough information, they all left for Warsaw.'

Each day, inside the courtroom, the eager public watched out for sudden traps in the legal procedure, especially when witnesses for the defence were confronted with those whom they had previously accused of lying. Mariavite nuns and priests facing ex-Mariavite nuns and priests were bound to get worked up and increase the dramatic tension.

[1] Both *Izvestiya* and the *Chicago Tribune* sent representatives. There was nobody from the English press.

On the fifth day of the trial the prosecution called as a witness one Pągowski, who still wanted to be regarded as a Mariavite priest, though he and his parishioners had kept their allegiance to the Old Catholic Church after 1924 and did not acknowledge Kowalski's supremacy.[1] He was sworn in as a Mariavite despite strong objections from the defence, but his testimony proved disappointing. He had heard this and that from other priests: about the Archbishop, for instance, lecturing them on anti-pregnancy measures;[2] or about the way in which a married priest could be united with God only through his wife after she had visited Kowalski's mediatory bed. Finally, Pągowski accused the Archbishop of calling himself the son of God. This was blasphemy, he said, particularly foul in view of the obscenities already described.

But on the twelfth day of the trial the tables were turned when a Mariavite nun accused her own sister who, according to her, had been expelled from the convent for 'unruly behaviour and debauchery with [the priest] Pągowski'. And another nun told the court she had seen the ex-nun W—— 'enter the dormitory in her *négligé* and jump into the beds of other nuns'.[3]

Odd items of inside information surfaced, especially during the cross-examinations of finicky witnesses. Much was said and even more implied about the Archbishop's bathing habits, and the pond with the shower adjoining on the Mariavite country estate became, like the mandolin, charged with erotic significance beyond its ablutionary capacity. Apparently, Kowalski liked to bathe together with his nuns, he was seen taking there Isabel, Sister Love, and the very young Sister Regina, every one of them naked; some other witnesses spoke of orgies in the water. Pond and shower apart, there were splashing frolics in the nude elsewhere, in rivers and in the Baltic Sea. Photographs were shown in court of one such scene at the seaside. Cross-examined, Bishop Philip denied any impropriety, and instead began to argue about the colour of the nuns' bathing costumes. They were

[1] On the day Pągowski gave his evidence (24 September), the *Plock Daily* reported a rumour that some Mariavite bishops were preparing themselves for a possible verdict against their leader. In such an event Bishop-elect Philip (Feldman) was to take over.

[2] Had the pill been invented earlier Kowalski's mystical experiment would not have landed him in court.

[3] Such sparks of unintentional humour occurred from time to time, as on 29 September, when Kowalski's prophecy about the end of the world came into the testimony. The Mariavite cloister had bought a vast quantity of goods in preparation for this calamity and ran into heavy debts. Goods had to be returned to the merchants. On the witness stand the priest Nowakowski explains that the Archbishop prophesied not only the destruction of the Polish capital (a prophecy tragically 'fulfilled' in 1944) but of the whole globe.

The presiding judge: 'Why did you then make all those purchases?' The witness: 'Everything is in the hands of God.' An outburst of laughter in court. Quickly the defence comes to his rescue and the witness rewords his statement. No, he meant the end of the world for sinners, they would be wiped out, so the cloister bought whatever it needed, that's all.

designed by the Mother Superior herself, their colour was blue, and 'here they look white'. Which, in view of the black-and-white reproduction, sounded odd.

If the Archbishop sinned by preferring the natural state of the human body, he certainly had Adam and Eve on his side, and he said so on those occasions when some of his companions were reluctant to strip. Kowalski would then make his round of embraces to dispel shyness.[1] After all, was he not supposed to bring up a new generation born without original sin, therefore free of shame?

He also took personal interest in the design of nuns' underwear. A looser cut for their old-fashioned drawers. No buttoned-up flap at the back. Nuns' shifts were until then in one piece and had to be put on over the head. Kowalski decided that they should open in front at the waist. A former vestiarian testified that before each visit to Kowalski the nuns had to change their underwear. On some days, she said, three or four nuns would come to her storeroom.

Insecurity at home, financial hardship, or plain poverty drove many women to seek protection and love at the Mariavite cloister. This they were given, and much more. The social background of the Kowalski affair was not as shabby as the press tried to make out. Two aristocratic names glittered on a long list of witnesses, one of them belonging to a cousin of Prince Radziwill. These well-born gentlemen were Mariavites and both praised their Archbishop heaven-high.

The oddest religious name mentioned during the proceedings was the Holy Ghost Junior.

3

The trial was drawing to its close. Archbishop Kowalski had so far spoken very little, and only when asked by the court; otherwise he observed *belle indifférence*. His answers, according to the *Warsaw Courier*, were dull and did not suggest the agility of mind which was attributed to him. When he arrived to hear the speech of the public prosecutor, his strong face was showing tiredness. Exposed to ridicule day after day, the proud man must have suffered greatly.

The presiding judge, Momentowicz,[2] who was known for his severity,

---

1 The prosecution alleged that girls from the convent school were also present at these nude sessions. The Felicjanów park provided seclusion: it had a clearing which was called the 'frying-pan' (*patelnia*) by those who sunbathed there naked.

2 For the record, the chief personages at the trial were: judges, B. Momentowicz (presiding), W. Szczepiński, J. Sołomerecki; prosecutor, S. Rogowski; recording clerk, Z. Deczyński; advocates for the defence, Śmiarowski, Kobyliński, Główczewski, and a Mariavite priest, Tułaba. The chief judge of the Court of Appeal in Warsaw was also present.

had ordered that all previous tickets of admission should be cancelled. On Monday 8 October the public besieged the court to get new tickets. On Tuesday, at 11.20 a.m., the public prosecutor, S. Rogowski, began to address the court. His speech lasted two hours and fifteen minutes.

'First of all I must emphasize the specific nature of this trial,' began Rogowski. 'Lustful, immoral acts are attributed to a person standing at the head of an association (*zrzeszenie*)[1] which in its insignia carries the words: morality and poverty. At the time of its beginnings the association professed in particular the vows of chastity. There is a discrepancy then between the official position of the accused and the charges brought against him.'

And so on. The prosecutor denied the existence of a Catholic-inspired conspiracy whose aim was to destroy Mariavitism.[2] He also rejected the charge of collusion between the witnesses for the prosecution, e.g. between the women Tołpyhowa (the lady of the disclosures) and Osinowa and the Catholic priest Krygier.[3] Osinowa was outraged by what she heard from her daughter and acted spontaneously. At that time she could not have envisaged that a trial would finally take place. 'The horrific orgies described by Badowska[4] seem almost improbable, and yet, remember, she had been in the convent since the age of seven, and they did not teach her about orgies. If she described them with such realism, it is because she was their victim. She told us exactly what the accused had done to her. Therefore one has to accept her testimony as true.'

Here the prosecutor began to interpret Kowalski's commentary on the Song of Songs, quoting examples from it to establish links between his teaching and the erotic practices he initiated. To discredit the Archbishop's character on the basis of his early inclinations, Rogowski repeated the words of a witness, alleging that Kowalski as a schoolboy visited prostitutes. After surveying the whole career of the accused from this erotic angle, the prosecutor tried to demolish the veracity of the testimonies given by those Mariavites who were under Kowalski's jurisdiction. Finally, he mourned the deterioration of morals in the country, as all prosecutors do; said that Kowalski had known what he was doing and grossly abused his authority;

---

[1] The term chosen by the prosecutor is intended to be subtly a-religious. Throughout his speech he never refers to the Mariavites as a church. Rogowski had a reputation as a religious fanatic, I was told by a number of lawyers who remembered him.

[2] The counter-charge made in the Mariavite bishops' open letter of August 1927. See p. 101.

[3] A member of the Warsaw Council, said to have bribed the Mariavite renegades with the promise of jobs.

[4] Janina Badowska, chief witness for the prosecution. Brought up in the convent, she had a mind of her own and, being the oldest in the school, dared to challenge Kowalski's authority. 'He can do what he likes,' she said to a friend, 'why shouldn't I?' She fell in love with a young priest and left the convent.

then, turning towards him, exclaimed: 'The very lack of contrition [*skrucha*] on his part is an incriminating circumstance.' At this point the Archbishop laughed, the best comment he could make in the hostile atmosphere. 'His guilt has been proved', the prosecutor announced to the judges and sat down.

The first advocate for the defence, Główczewski, appealed to the exemplary record of religious tolerance in the Polish tradition, which was historically true, but almost in the same breath accused the Catholic clergy of fanaticism and criticized the behaviour of the press, for which he got a bad press the following day. Then he spoke for two hours behind closed doors.

On Wednesday, 10 October, Śmiarowski, the second advocate, delivered his well-argued peroration. He accused the Catholic clergy of trying to destroy the Mariavite movement through an individual, i.e. Kowalski. He mentioned a libel case brought by the Little Mother in 1907, when she was accused of equally absurd crimes.[1] He dismissed a number of irrelevancies, mainly of political character, which were brought in to blacken the reputation of the Mariavites.

Then Śmiarowski produced his precise counter-charges in Kowalski's defence: (1) It was not true that he had six wives, otherwise he would have been tried as a bigamist. (2) It was not true that the women who were presented as Kowalski's victims had ever had intercourse with him. They had been examined by a doctor and their virginity was confirmed.[2] The fact that they agreed to be examined was sufficiently telling. (3) The room in which the orgies were supposed to take place was too small to contain the number of people whom the witnesses mentioned. (4) The witnesses for the prosecution were motivated by revenge, grudging regret, and desire for material gain. They were all subject to mass hysteria.

This last point the advocate elaborated at some length, giving examples from the past.[3] He also tried to prove that Tołpyhowa and Zarębski, the two accusers of Kowalski, were not trustworthy characters.[4] Finally, Śmiarowski reminded the court of the admirable social work done by the Mariavites at their centre.

[1] Kozlowska sued for libel the editor of the Warsaw weekly *Niedziela* and lost the case. The court was prejudiced and she was subjected to abuse.
[2] He mentions both Żytkówna and Sister Love, who were witnesses for Kowalski, and Badowska who was one of his most violent accusers. The medical opinion, however, was contested at the trial.
[3] Those who are now familiar with the gruesome story of the Loudun possessions would certainly agree with Śmiarowski's line of defence.
[4] Zarębski, a Warsaw businessman who had had financial dealings with the order, was at first much involved in Mariavite affairs and even agreed to have his son educated in the cloister. He admitted at the trial that, though he was a Catholic, he took Mariavite communion.

The third advocate, Kobyliński, spoke in the evening of the same day but, as far as one can judge from the press reports, he concentrated mainly on the history and ideology of Mariavitism; his refutation of the specific charges as, for instance, the one dealing with the financial transactions during the end-of-the-world scare, proved less effective than the counter-arguments used by his predecessor. Nevertheless, he impressed the public with his legal skill.

One of the obvious points he made concerned the mystical marriages. It does not matter what you call them, they are real marriages, and marriage precludes debauchery. As for some sporadic excesses among the boarders at the convent school, they happen, he said, in all boarding schools in all countries.

After the three big speeches, the Mariavite priest, Father Tułaba, who was a member of the counsel for defence, made a very brief plea: 'I ask for complete discharge of Archbishop Kowalski. That is all.'

It was now the prosecutor's turn to reply to the defence. He reiterated his arguments. If there was a conspiracy among the witnesses for the prosecution, as the defence claimed, what proof was there that a similar action had not been organized within the walls of the cloister?[1] He dismissed the view that a cultured woman from a good home (i.e. Isabel, Kowalski's wife) could not because of her background take part in Kowalski's orgies. Highborn Russian ladies gave themselves wholly to Rasputin. This is your proof, said the prosecutor, you cannot rely on the psychology of women—it is a riddle (*zagadka*). The future of the Mariavites and their cloister had nothing to do with the case. Kowalski must be punished by law for his own crimes.

The last word was to come from the accused himself. Archbishop Kowalski rose and faced the judges, his silver-grey habit sending out rays from the Mariavite monstrance embroidered in gold on his massive chest. His voice was hesitant at first, but as he spoke on, he regained confidence. His defence was that of a religious martyr. All reformers, he said, had to suffer persecution. 'There is no saint who did not have calumnies thrown at him, though later they canonized him. I am surprised neither by the parties in this lawsuit nor by Providence. The Little Mother prophesied that Mariavitism would have to pass through the trial of the holy Church, that is through the trial by Christians. This trial is now taking place. Every injustice must pass through Trial in order to elucidate Truth. I am therefore not surprised and have no regret in my soul, for there is nothing to regret.

[1] In fact, the Mariavite oath was often under attack at the trial. Their witnesses could not tell the truth, it was alleged, because Kowalski had ordered them to disregard the authority of any civil court.

I am innocent, I have done no evil to anyone. Through the examination of the witnesses you have learnt, gentlemen, who is guilty and who is not, therefore I believe that the verdict will be not guilty.'

Then the Archbishop proceeded to apologize for his omissions, whether in the articles about the case published before the trial by his press, or in the polemics with the Catholic Church. Again he quoted the Little Mother who, like Christ, had commanded them to love their enemies. He appealed to the judges to let him go free and 'allow the Mariavites to exist'. His last sentence was moving because it had the unmistakable tone of humility:

'In the name of the love of God, in the name of the love of our country, in the name of mercy, I ask you for forgiveness in this case.'

The court ended its proceedings at twenty minutes past four, in the afternoon of 11 October, and the judges retired to consider the verdict. Half an hour before midnight they returned to ask ten questions concerning the guilt of the accused, adding the eleventh question put by the defence. Then the court retired again.

At two o'clock in the morning of Friday 12 October 1928, the Plock County Court, presided over by Judge Momentowicz, pronounced sentence on John Maria Michael Kowalski. He was found guilty of sexual offences against girls under age (*nieletnie*) and other women at the Mariavite cloister.[1] He was sentenced to four years' imprisonment, but as amnesty was applied, the sentence was reduced to two years and eight months. The court allowed Kowalski to remain free on bail which was a thousand zloty.

4

The immediate reaction to the sentence was a high-minded condemnation of Mariavitism in the press. The leader writer of the *Warsaw Courier* called the trial one of the most gloomy spectacles ever conducted in a Polish court of law. He pontificated on the weakness of a civilization which permits scoundrels and swindlers to exploit the credulity and superstition of the masses. 'Kowalski is certainly not an ordinary criminal. . . . A mystic? What a mystic indeed, this man endowed with an exceptionally robust health and plunged in despicable filth, showing off his physical lust'—and so on. The article ends with loud breast-beating. *Mea culpa*. We have all sinned because we let our religious ties weaken, while the insane anti-clerical propaganda pushes 'the village Mariannes, Catherines, Johns, and Matthews straight into the arms of the Kowalskis'.

[1] The minors named were Osinówna, Tomasikówna, Żytkówna, Fijałkowska, and Badowska (the first three played in the mandolin orchestra); the other women were Prochówna, Niewiadomska, and Bittnerówna.

The high costs of the trial were discussed by journalists interested in professional fees. The *Plock Daily* reported that the advocate Śmiarowski was paid 1200 zloty per day. In 1928 this sum represented the average yearly income of an office clerk. For the nineteen days of the trial, then, the chief advocate alone was to receive from Kowalski 22,800 zloty, a minor fortune in the decade of a general economic crisis.

Forty-five years after the trial, however, the question is: Did the Archbishop get a fair trial? A lawyer practising in Plock, who was a young man in 1928, wrote this in answer to my query:

> The trial was not free from the tendency to compromise Mariavitism publicly. But one must rule out a supposition that the whole trial was rigged. . . . This or that piece of evidence may have been at variance with the truth, but Archbishop Kowalski undoubtedly had a number of wives and introduced the priesthood of women whom he 'sanctified'. He had enormous authority, and the girls were afraid to resist him. . . . All this does not alter the fact that the trial was conducted in a special atmosphere, and the reports of it were artificially blown up in the press.

In my view the defence is much to blame for the impression it left with the public. It tried to demolish the evidence against Kowalski by accusing the witnesses of immoral conduct, and since practically all of them were ex-Mariavites, a reverse effect was often produced. There must have been strange goings-on inside the cloister, if most counter-charges brought up by the defence were concerned with sexual licence.[1]

A Mariavite nun, for example, told the court how one of the priests who was later expelled by Kowalski had tried to pull off her dress but gave up when she was about to faint. A scene of confrontation followed. The ex-priest, Dziewulski, was called in and he, in turn, told the court how the same nun who was accusing him now had nearly seduced him while he was ill. She came in, shut the door, sat on his bed and began a conversation. After a while she took off her veil, then she took off more. . . . At this point of dramatic suspense Dziewulski exclaimed: 'How can a nun still wearing a habit tell such lies!' To which, according to the *Plock Daily*, the confronted nun replied with scarlet blushes.

In its attempts to discredit the testimonies of the former Mariavites, the defence was capable of stooping to petty accusations. Another ex-priest was described as untrustworthy because he had a dog with a bell on its tail and they had tinkling walks together. 'He loved this dog more than his mystical wife,' said the witness.

---

[1] The 1927 open letter of the Mariavite bishops speaks of the 'apostates who were expelled from our Church for immoral acts, in most cases erotic in character'.

Badowska was accused of scandalizing other children at the convent; Tołpyhowa was accused of lies. Such counter-charges, and they were many during the second half of the trial, only too often sounded like squabbling among children in a very big family, all of them eager to tell tales against one another, and shouting when caught out: You did it, yes, you did it!

In his winding-up speech the prosecutor made a sarcastic comment on this aspect of the trial: 'The witnesses for the prosecution have been slandered, and various details from their past life described. . . . But where did they live, these immoral people? At the Mariavites!'

Who was lying, then? Or rather, who was lying more: those who accused Kowalski or those who defended him? Secrecy wears a mask, but betrayal shows an ugly face to the world. Somewhere between the two perhaps breathes the truth overshadowed by fear and guilt, the inevitable partners in any human conflict.

The Court of Appeal, which on 3 December 1929 upheld the original verdict on the Archbishop, made a point of saying that Kowalski 'raised sexual intercourse to a religious cult'. He let erotic energy into spiritual passion. Kowalski was not the first blender of such divergent energies. From the early days of Christianity some believers found the claims of the soul over the flesh too demanding. To castigate evil usually meant to castigate the flesh, evil being a greedy flesh-eater. The Manichaean conflict could not have penetrated so deep into theological thinking, had it not been for its acceptance of evil as a necessary counter-force.

Two trials, relatively recent, resemble Kowalski's. The first was that of Enfantin, the extreme disciple of Saint-Simon, who after the split in the movement (1832) established a commune on his property and as self-styled priest practised polygamy, searching for a female Messiah. When arrested he demanded that two women at least should defend him at his trial. This was refused.

The American founder of another religious commune, Benjamin Purnell of the House of David, was also accused of immoral relations with his female disciples and was brought to court after successfully evading trial for several years. When he died in 1927, he left behind him 22 charges of immoral conduct on the files of the court, every one of them pending.[1]

Supposing Archbishop Kowalski did practise sexual rites for a religious

---

1 When I wrote to the House of David asking for some more information about Purnell's trial, I received a courteous reply which consisted of references to passages in the Bible. 'I am firmly convinced', the letter said, 'that the trial was necessary to fulfil the scriptures (II Tim. 3:12; II Thes. 1:4; II Cor. 12:10; I Cor. 4:12; Luke 17:25; I Peter 2:8 & 1:20 & 4:12 & 4:17; Rom. 8:18; Luke 24:26; John 15:20; Matt. 5:11; II Thes. 2:11, 12)'. Archbishop Kowalski would have loved decoding this numerical answer.

purpose: how should we look at them? The prosecution before and during his trial probed into the evidence and was both astounded and horrified. But what was it precisely that made the facts appear so horrific? Since many of them were investigated behind closed doors, the press could not describe the nature of the alleged practices in any detail. Guesswork and the sniggering knowingness of jokes had to provide pseudo-information. Much of it is still used by people who have no access even to secondary sources. For there is a type of historical hearsay which can fill up the darkest gaps in the past. Nevertheless, hostile historians do perform some service for the truth.

Dr. Skrudlik based his *Crimes of the Mariavites* on the evidence assembled for the trial at which he himself was a witness. He appears to know something about the facts which were examined *in camera*. On page 43 of his book he used large bold letters to draw his readers' attention to the unmentionable character of Kowalski's ritual.

> We have to omit the most hideous moments described by the witness when she speaks about the 'black' liturgy of the sect, about Kowalski and his companions fusing together the foulest debauchery with divine worship; about the signs and phrases taken from the liturgy of the Church and used by them in their ritual which was rigorously observed as a necessary completion to the acts of licentiousness.[1]

The witness in question, Badowska,[2] was, according to her own statement, admitted to the highest rank of 'understanding' within the secret inner circle. If we believe her, the erotic liturgy was celebrated by the elect of the highest rank, while ordinary sexual acts were prescribed for lower degrees of initiation. The same witness told the court how Kowalski's wife had encouraged her, when she was still very young, to submit to his wishes. All three would drive out in a carriage, the girl sitting on Kowalski's knees and his wife next to him. During mutual caresses the Mother Superior would kiss her too, telling the girl how fortunate she was to be receiving so much grace from Christ. One begins to grasp why the little mandolinists were so early admitted to this system of kinship. They were in a mystical family, they had to grow up in love.

Liturgy provided the elect with a clear framework as well as with ecstatic stimuli. The sequence of such a ritual would follow that of the Mass, culminating in consecration and communion. The sofa on which the Little Mother died would serve as a kind of bed-altar. The sexual organs would

---

[1] 'Nothing of the kind happened, nothing', a witness for the defence (Sister Love) protested to me of her own accord. 'How could he speak of orgies behind the altar! I prayed there and I wept.'

[2] Identified by Skrudlik as 'J.B.'

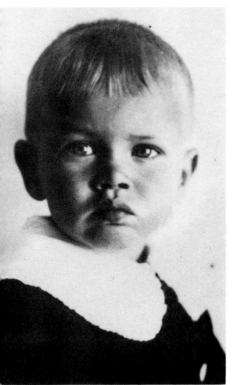

Some of the children of the mystical marriages; Kowalski's son Michael
at left above.

The Archbishop's trial, 1928: Kowalski standing in the centre (marked with an X).

Mariavites on a holiday excursion, 1931, travelling in secular dress;
front row, from left: Jacob, Celestina, Isabel, Kowalski, Philip.

act as the instruments of dual energy, charging the flesh with the manifestation of the spirit. The priest's phallus would have a consecrating power and
the female organ, like the chalice, would receive it during communion.
These two suggestions horrified all practising Catholics, and an obvious
analogy with the Black Mass intensified the shock. And yet, if we accept
that this could be a ritual of divine love celebrated in the flesh, neither wilful
mockery nor the blasphemous reversal of the Mass would apply to this type
of sexual adoration. The participants were probably very serious about their
gestures and acts, especially if they venerated Kowalski's presence in the
sacrament as was alleged by some witnesses.

Obscenity in religion results from a sudden super-imposition of a moral
code on to erotic worship. It happens especially when two very different
cultures meet as they did in India during the reign of Queen Victoria.[1] The
obscene is indeed in the shocked mind of the beholder. Sanctify the shame,
as Kowalski would argue, and you will return to primeval innocence. The
naked Adam did not notice his nudity until he was told to feel ashamed.

But whatever Kowalski tried to prove through his ritual, he was incon-
sistent at his trial. He could have challenged his accusers by turning their
charges into the glorification of love in all its possible forms. He could have
answered them like a king with his own Song of Songs. Was he afraid that
such a confession might ruin him and his church? Was he, like the first
Adam, too startled by the divine intervention to reject the wages of guilt?
As for the judges, they sentenced him according to the accepted code of
morals, and, no doubt, felt fully justified. But the deep secret remained with
the convicted man. Perhaps that is the ultimate responsibility which erotic
ritual imposes on those who worship with their bodies.

If Kowalski had been tried in the court of Love with Anteros prosecuting
and Eros conducting his defence, he would still have lost, for society, no
matter how promiscuous, does in the end listen to the voice of Anteros.
Kowalski had no chance to win either way.

The trial of 1928 humiliated him, but did not make a martyr out of him.
The Archbishop was left with his angry visions and his women, and when
the subsequent appeals failed and he finally served his reduced sentence in
1936 in the jail at Rawicz, he meditated on the presence of the Little Mother
and was granted an 'understanding'. In the margin of his own copy of *The
Work of Great Mercy*, he wrote:

The Little Mother said to me that she was present at the creation of the

[1] See Wendy O'Flaherty, 'Obscenity in Religion', *Times Literary Supplement*, 28 January
1972.

world and arranged the world. She told me that the words in Holy Scripture 'God possessed me at the beginning of his ways' . . . referred to her. These things I would not publish at once, because I did not then understand them well. The Lord Jesus said also this of me: 'He will overturn the tables of the merchants in my Temple.'

7
Subterranean Channels

R ELIGIOUS institutions are in a crisis. But there always has been an institutional crisis as long as religions have existed. The frame presses on the content which has a tendency to expand while the frame remains the same. All this is happening on the surface—institutions occupy the flat areas of life—whereas below the social consciousness there is a constant flow of streams, sources, and channels which feed the human psyche. Religion has been described as a trusting acceptance of the unknown; it is also a profound experience of the continuity of life, in which our individual existence is only a minute sequence.

Mariavitism, as I understand it, developed horizontally and vertically. Its horizontal growth on the surface was a social phenomenon, in many ways typical of the times: the Mariavites offered their services to the community, they were self-sufficient and egalitarian, they also cared for hygiene. Their modern outlook manifested itself in welfare organizations, workshops, and schools, they attracted to their ranks peasants and factory workers. It is symptomatic that the Mariavites had strong centres in the industrial district of Lodz and in Silesia. Their social success owed much to the idealism of the foundress.

As for the vertical growth of the Mariavite church, it was a slower process and, in my opinion, it wouldn't have reached the subterranean channels without Kowalski. It was his obsessive groping in the dark after the secrets of the Holy Spirit that made him descend the ladder of 'understandings' into the Gnostic abyss. Once he and Bishop Philip established the secret church of the elect (1922), the real tapping of the subterranean resources began. And at this point the Mariavite beliefs merge with the old heresies of Christianity. Some of Kowalski's utterances are incomprehensible unless we place them in their comparative context. The need for such a treatment revealed itself during the lengthy trial of the Archbishop. He was, of course, secret-bound while those who sat in judgement over him did not really know how to unlock the mysteries of the Philadelphic Church. The Catholic theologians could have helped but they were too prejudiced to start with, and their learning usually got stuck in some blind alley of dogma

The question of whether Archbishop Kowalski was a sectarian magpie pinching ideas wherever he found them, or a very intuitive pattern-maker, cannot be answered without selecting a number of parallel examples from the history of Christianity and Judaism (the Messiahs). What one must watch out for is the way in which 'heretics' and reformers would take one aspect of Christianity or Judaism, enlarge on it, and build a pattern around it to hold the whole thing together. These, for instance, are the six determinants applicable to Kowalski's innovations: (1) Christ imparts special knowledge (gnosis) to the chosen few. (2) The cult of the Eucharist evolves a secret ritual, in which the host is used (in the Eastern rite together with consecrated wine). (3) The pure in spirit perform strange acts which contradict the accepted code of morals. (4) Reincarnation is attained in the process of redemption (great souls pass through a succession of bodies). (5) The sexual act is seen as a means of reaching God. (6) Polygamy prefigures the heavenly marriage (Christ the bridegroom of many).

One can dip into the dark Gnostic stream at any point in the Christian tradition—dip but not too deep—for the spiritual science it conveys flows elusively from age to age. Gnosticism is, of course, older than Christianity, but the new religion did not succeed in suppressing it. There are two phases in the Gnostic revival: that of St. Paul (his mysterious asides in the epistles are meant for the elect), and that of Mani whose clear-cut duality poisoned the optimistic messages of theology.

To the elect Christ was the cosmic teacher who first imparted his gnosis to the apostles, but only gradually and not to all of them. What happened on Mount Tabor during the Transfiguration profoundly altered the relationship between the cosmic Teacher and his disciples. They saw him as he really was, their eyes were initiated into the perception of the divine. Without Christ's self-revelation on Tabor the disciples would not have been ready to accept the Eucharistic mystery of the Last Supper. For this reason John the Evangelist dwells so much on Christ's final message, the sacramental gospel of love.[1] The cult of the Eucharist had a significance projected on to the event on Mount Tabor. In other words, the presence of the Master in the sacrament must be understood in Gnostic terms, for he himself continues to impart spiritual knowledge to those who receive his body.

Reading St. John's gospel and the Acts of the apostles one is aware that some passages could invite Gnostic speculations. During his agony in the garden of Gethsemane Christ was accompanied by three of his disciples,

---

[1] In a long sequence of five chapters there is, however, no mention of the breaking of bread. Was it too obvious for the elect?

Peter, James, and John (the elect?), but they kept falling asleep. Whose eyes then and whose ears witnessed the whole agony? Was the witness a recording angel or a human being? If it was a man and not a higher spirit, his experience in the garden could be described as gnosis. He was given a knowledge beyond the human range of perception.

The word 'simonism' goes back to a scene in the Acts (ch. 8). But the question is: why should the laying on of hands have impressed Simon, the converted sorcerer, so much that he wanted to buy that power with money? Unless, of course, Peter appeared to him as a new kind of magician, that is a possessor of Christ's secrets. However you cannot purchase gnosis, for it is God's unsolicited gift. You have to be initiated, tested, and perfected through suffering. This happened to St. Francis on La Verna (again a mountain of transformation) when he received the stigmata.[1] Many speculations and legends have grown out of this extraordinary event. If Christ did administer communion to the saint, he fed him with his own body-spirit for a purpose. The final act of initiation. Then he is supposed to have revealed to the saint some of heaven's secrets. Were they the secrets of the Third Heaven seen by St. Paul in a vision and surmised by the Little Mother before Kowalski's experience in 1922?

The Archbishop knew that the mysteries of La Verna belonged to the other tradition of Christianity, the hidden one. He also grasped the significance of the form in which Christ appeared to St. Francis. The form was that of a seraph, six-winged and aflame with love, as Lorenzetti depicted the scene in his fresco. This would suggest that the saint reached a spiritual level at which he could face Christ the angel, for it is impossible for man to see God. The later facts support this view. After his initiation into the angelic sphere St. Francis withdrew from the affairs of the order he had established; he was, one might say, no longer of men.

The seraphic apparition raises other issues which perturbed the Gnostics in the early centuries of the Christian era. Was the son of God fully a man, in body and in spirit? To Apollinaris in the fourth century he was not: Christ could not have a human soul. Nor was his body made up of ordinary flesh and blood. There were, in fact, two tendencies among the diviners of the nature of Christ: one inevitably led to the denial of his humanity, the other to the denial of his divinity. And, as always with opposites, a compromise solution emerges, a hopeful alternative, in this case reincarnation. Great spirits not only take on the flesh, they put it on again and again. The progress of the soul is therefore a progress through many bodies.

[1] The sacred mounts are associated with a number of cults: La Verna in Italy, Monserrat in Catalonia, Jasna Góra (the Bright Mountain) in Poland.

To the Cathars, who were obsessed with the impurity of the creation, the origin of life was a divine compromise with the dark side of the spirit world. God let some souls be enslaved by the flesh. To procreate was to allow the enslavement to go on. Only the higher spirits could carry out a rescue operation by wilfully entering the lower forms.

Since Christ existed in the Three from the beginning, they reasoned, he must have revealed himself inside the creation in different forms and ways. He was the Logos before his birth from the Virgin at the time of the Emperor Augustus. He was Archangel Michael too,[1] and other mighty spirits who activated the latent forces of the creation and tried to correct the spiritual errors of which our globe was a sad example. One could argue, somewhat perversely perhaps, that the cosmic Christ of Teilhard de Chardin is not only shaping the evolution but is also guiding the spirit through the diversity of forms. The metempsychosis of evolution is not such a heretical concept, after all. Nor are the Cathars wholly to be blamed for trying to account for the pull of contrary powers in the ever-changing universe.[2]

It is easy to ridicule Kowalski for his interpretations of the Little Mother. She was, said he, both the Bride of the Song of Songs and the angel comforting Christ in Gethsemane. According to the meta-logic of reincarnation the spirit is free to travel, it passes through the physical walls of existence with as much ease as the powerful cosmic rays travel through space.[3]

2

Let's think the Gnostic way and admit a few holy indiscretions to our cause-and-effect habits of reasoning. Supposing at some point in the creative evolution there was a 'wilful miscalculation' to test the contradictory wills within the universe. We don't know why such an out-of-order procedure was adopted and why the Creator stepped, as it were, aside to allow the unaccountable to account for itself.

In the ancient Book of Job, Satan is still on speaking terms with the Creator. He comes round to co-ordinate his disruptive activity with the

---

[1] The Jehovah's Witnesses, a relatively modern sect, believe in these manifestations of Christ.
[2] 'Il est facile de voir que le dualisme cosmique commence vraiment à la deuxième ère avec l'opposition de la lumière et des ténèbres. . . . La genèse du monde ne s'expliquerait pas sans la primauté de l'Esprit et de la vie par rapport à la substance.' Déodat Roche, *Catharisme et science spirituelle* (Arques, n.d.).
[3] 'Duchy ludzkie to duchy wcielone. . . . Mogą one nieraz wcielać się lub schodzić w przedmioty martwe, rośliny lub zwierzęta (Human spirits are spirits incarnate. . . . Again and again they take on flesh or descend into dead objects, plants or animals),' Kowalski wrote in *Nowy Hexahemeron*, a discourse on the six days of the Creation. Slowacki, a poet much admired by Kowalski, wrote a treatise on spiritual evolution in which Christ is considered as the Alpha and Omega of all creation: *The Genesis from the Spirit* (1844).

plans of the Almighty. Thy will be done even when it appears to be against Thy will. Job's comforters have been much maligned. In the distorted light of divine justice they argued in a crooked way—how else could they argue, with Satan pulling off a great confidence trick in the name of the Creator? All ends well for the good servant Job, his body bulbous with boils. A sinister happy ending if you take the Catharist view on procreation. For the worn-out old man is encouraged to leave behind a breed of children, boil-free for the duration of chance.

According to the apocryphal Book of Enoch something went demoniacally wrong with the genetics of Genesis, and even the animals had to perish in the Flood. If you pursue this line of thought one thing is certain: you cannot trust yours or anybody else's body. The Cathars in the West and the Bogomils in the East[1] took the Biblical hints in earnest and said: Let's leave the wretched body as quickly as we can. The Cathar and the Bogomil *perfecti* did not eat any flesh, that was logical; little food and fasting liberated the mind to cope with higher necessities such as getting out of the physical entrapment. Eat and multiply was a message for slaves and mercenaries; all that the elect wanted was to opt out.

It is not surprising that in Russia where religion is a matter of intensity rather than of morals, the sect of the Skoptsy should have arisen in the eighteenth century and taken the distrust of the body to its extreme. After an orgiastic farewell to the genitals the Skoptsy castrated themselves.[2] The bigger the penis the better the sacrifice. Nobody could accuse them of duplicity—they cut their passions at the root.

The followers of the Spanish bishop Priscillian (*c.* 340–386) were not expected to go that far, although like the Cathars later they abhorred the idea of marriage. No meat and no wine. Instead they let the devil-inspired passions go to the devil. Sexual release through excess, if necessary, seems to have been the spiritual prescription of the Bishop of Avila. And he had many female disciples who thought his solution more than satisfactory. They met at night in woods, and there conducted their rites. These, as their accusers suggested, ended in communal sex, after which, feeling less body-bound, the participants left for their homes.

Now the difficulty in discussing a clandestine movement of this type is the doubtful reliability of facts handed down in the documents obtained by the prosecution. The main source in Priscillian's case is the chronicle of Sulpicio Severo. What do we learn from it? That the movement operated

---

[1] For a work in English, see Dimitri Obolensky, *The Bogomils: a Study in Balkan Neo-Manichaeism* (Cambridge, 1948).
[2] The penis was completely severed, women had their breasts cut off.

through small groups of women, each centred on one man. Outwardly their purpose seemed to be wholly ascetic, but the Priscillian asceticism was in fact a Gnostic paradox, hence the query whether these communities practised polygamy or not. Since they participated in collective acts of *turpitudo*,[1] it is easy to deduce some communal system of relationships. What did the Bishop of Avila confess under duress at his trial? That he prayed naked with various women.[2] He admitted having studied the doctrines of magic, but denied that he put any of them into practice. The nocturnal character of his reunions, however, cast suspicion on the Bishop's spiritual allies. If he regarded the body as a cage forged by evil, did he perhaps try to render unto the demons what was theirs in the dual nature of man?

All this of course was taking place when Christian beliefs were still very close to the pagan world—Priscillian was himself a convert. The concept of offering virgins to God had a long history in pre-Christian Spain. Gnosticism was therefore rooted in the old as well as the new. This inevitably created a spiritual tension, often beneficial to an inquiring mind, as was the case with St. Augustine's Manichaean involvement. When the Church was seeking a means of co-existence with the secular powers, the prosecution of individuals like Priscillian had a political motivation as well. After all, he himself had once benefited from this state of affairs. The secular authorities ignored the charges of Manichaeism and re-instated him at Avila. Later, however, Bishop Priscillian was less lucky: he appealed to the usurper Maximus—mystics should never side with political losers—and his enemies pounced on him. This time he had no chance to refute the allegations of magic practices, whether they were fabricated or true (in the Gnostic sense of superior knowledge).

For the Priscillians were *electi deo*, they discarded their physical passions in order to communicate with God soul to soul. Though his Manichaeism was not proved, Priscillian had to suffer death. He was executed at Trier in 386 together with six of his disciples, half the apostolic number.

The political pressure exercised during the trials of 'heretics' is a concomitant factor in all successful prosecutions. The Mariavites should take some bitter comfort from this, since their Archbishop too, whether guilty or not, was crushed by the same combined power, the Church and the State. Among the condemned Bishop Priscillian stands out as a memorable figure, but he is one of many: Basil the head of the Bogomils in Constantinople was burnt at the stake with his twelve apostles. Tsar Boril of

[1] The word suggests sexual licence, an accusation made by a certain Itacio. See José M. Ramos y Loscertales, 'Prisciliano', in *Acta Salmaticensia*, tomo V, no. 5 (Salamanca, 1952).
[2] 'Una de las acusaciones formuladas contra Prisciliano en su proceso, y que el confeso ser cierta, la de haber orado desnudo con varias mujeres', writes Ramos.

Bulgaria destroyed his Bogomils in 1211. Pope Innocent III ordered a crusade against the Cathars which succeeded in wiping them out. After the capture of Montségur in 1244 their last leaders were put to death by fire. Philip the Fair of France subjected the Templars to a seven-year trial by the Inquisition and again the leaders were burnt at the stake (1314). A century later John Hus of Bohemia met with the same fate. His compatriot, Žižka, used military power to annihilate the Adamite group, once members of the Taborite commune, to which he himself belonged. Examples of cruel righteousness go parallel with authoritarian terror. Both demand victims for the greater glory of God.

Christ, the archetypal victim, prefigures them all: the cross, the stake, and the rack are his terrestial emblems. But Joan of Arc, more than any other martyr, symbolizes the helplessness of a visionary caught between the machinery of the state and the machinery of the ecclesiastical law.[1] From a Gnostic point of view she was one of the elect. She had ears to hear and they heard messages from above. Her knowledge came from the voices, and because she possessed gnosis, Joan of Arc, like the others before her, had to render her secret accounts on the altar of fire.

> Cuándo, mi Dios, del fuego
> de vuestro dulce amor seré encendido?
> Cuándo he de entrar en juego?
> Cuándo he de ser metido
> en el horno de amor, y consumido?
>
> *(Canción de la glosa soberana)*

Consumed by fire in the furnace of love. The conceit of St. John of the Cross is apt, but the memory of the righteous cruelty makes it sound like an epitaph for all the victims of religion.

Lux in tenebris lucet, we read in St. John's gospel which, understandably enough, is the text for the Christian Gnostics.[2] In it the darkness and the light are contrasted throughout: the demon of this world tempts the incarnated spirit from heaven; the people have eyes but are dark within, the blind have their eyes opened. Those who were initiated into the Eleusinian mysteries had to pass blindfolded through a subterranean passage, full of voices; they had to overcome fear through the senses of touch, smell, and

---

[1] Vintras, the prophet of Tilly, was lucky to live in the nineteenth century, otherwise he would have ended at the stake. Like the Bishop of Avila, he sided with a pretender and invited the wrath of both the civil and the ecclesiastical establishment. (See p. 69.)

[2] Far more than the Apocalypse. The fourth gospel records the mysteries of love in the words of the Master. It begins with the glorification of the Logos and ends with an oblique promise to the beloved disciple: 'If I will that he tarry till I come, what is that to thee?' The 'thee' is applicable to every one of us. The secret of the elect remains a secret.

hearing until they emerged into the light to be blinded again for a moment by the very experience of contrast.

Perhaps the Priscillians held their nocturnal rites for a similar purpose of illumination. *Lux in tenebris lucet* as the soul emerges from the prison dark of the body. A sexual act helps to loosen the shackles. Buñuel has captured the mood of Priscillian reunions in his film *La Voie lactée*.[1] There they are, the luminous figures of the *electi* among the shadows of the wood, praying in Latin, the breasts of the women uncovered for the ritual, the flesh glistening in the moonlight.

Each religious experience draws on the subterranean channels, none is heretical in relation to the unconscious forces in man. We are all heirs to the cosmic miscalculations which are imprinted on the dark matrix of our psyche. What is original sin if not a spiritual inheritance of some wilful error in creation? The Gnostic mind is not afraid to ask the sphinx at the entrance to Paradise or Hell: Tell me, what went wrong and why? The sphinx turns his questioning face on the Gnostic: You tell me first. And the Gnostic tries his best to tempt the tempter with a secret.

3

The eruption of the Free Spirit brotherhoods in the Middle Ages is a religious phenomenon of particular significance. The vagrant *vita apostolica*, the poverty and begging of these Beghards, as they were called, with the predominance of women[2] in the movement, bred much suspicion about their conduct, especially when nakedness was an outward sign of inner liberty. The Adamites of Bohemia seemed to practise what their name suggested. They tried to recapture the spirit of the first man as he was in Paradise: free from the fear of sin, therefore innocent. Before the Fall Adam's Paradise prefigured the Third Heaven.[3] The Bible had no practical use for the Adamites: it dealt with the events after the loss of primordial innocence. Marriage, too, served no purpose, so they had wives in common and dispensed with all personal attachments. So much so that intercourse could only take place by permission of the leader, Adam–Moses, as he was called in the commune.

---

[1] This is as far as I know the only attempt at discussing heresies in cinematic terms, probably Buñuel's most profound work. Two tramps are on the road to Compostela and enter the past at various points of their journey. Priscillian's identity escaped most audiences when the film was first shown.

[2] Commonly known as Beguines. For a discussion of the whole movement, see Robert E. Lerner, *The Heresy of the Free Spirit in the Later Middle Ages* (Berkeley, 1972); also Norman Cohn's pioneer work, *The Pursuit of the Millennium* (new ed. 1962).

[3] 'The Third Heaven, which was prefigured in Adam's Paradise, has been opened to us through the Little Mother's Sacrifice,' Kowalski writes in a footnote to Genesis, ch. 3. He says this about Adam and Eve: 'They recognized they were naked, that is denuded of God's grace.'

Did this mean that like the Adam of the Mariavites he had the right to sleep first with each woman of the commune? Among all those women one claimed to be the Virgin Mary. What seemed to shock the clergy most was the uninhibited display of their paradisiacal bodies. The Adamites went about naked, provided the climate wasn't too disagreeable. They also prayed in the nude and were supposed to take their sacraments in the nude.

The Adamite doctrine of retrievable innocence reached Bohemia early in the fifteenth century and became the cause of a struggle within the Taborite movement. The Taborites, who followed the teaching of John Hus (burnt as a heretic in 1415), were radicals who emerged as a group after Hus's death.[1] They took their name from the mountain of the Transfiguration and held their religious conclaves on mountain tops. They gave the name of Tabor to a Bohemian (Czech) town to which their first community moved. The town was later transformed into a military stronghold by Žižka, a soldier of genius, who like Cromwell managed to combine religious zest with tough practical measures. The Taborites had a special devotion to Christ in the Eucharist (the chalice with the host above it was the emblem on their banners),[2] they received communion in both kinds (*sub utraque specie*), accepted the Bible as the only source of faith, and used the vernacular in their services. Their priests married.

Superficially, the Mariavite church appears to be a very late offshoot of the Taborite movement. But which Mariavite church?—the outer (horizontal) or the inner (vertical)? The question is tricky. For sectarian patterns have a tendency to split in the early stages of their formation. This creates confusion in the doctrine itself and for a time the confusion serves as a protective screen. A sect, it would seem, has to mutate in order to survive. If it doesn't mutate quickly enough, it dies out or is swallowed up.

A new religious movement, especially a radical one, needs flexible minds to steer it away from self-destruction. St. Paul had such a mind, that's probably why he is so admired and so detested. The priest Martin Houska was endowed with great intelligence in political matters and in theology. It was he who planted the doctrine of the Free Spirit in Bohemian soil.[3] Houska

---

[1] Hus was venerated as a saint in the Mariavite church, his day in the Mariavite Calendar being 16 May.

[2] As shown in a Göttingen manuscript (sign. Theol. 1892); a relevant page is reproduced in *Výbor z české literatury husitské doby*, ed. Havránek and Hrabák (Prague, 1963). In the same illustration a priest carries a large monstrance at the head of the troops.

[3] The doctrine was probably brought from the west by a group of immigrants, the Picarts, or Picardi, an Adamite community expelled from Picardy. Whether Martin Houska had direct contact with them or not is still an open question. Lerner (op. cit.) is doubtful about the infiltration of the Beghards into Bohemia, but his argument is self-contradictory. The Free Spirit ideas travelled fast, from Picardy as far as Polish Silesia.

envisaged a millenarian society of the elect, pure in spirit, who would be nourished by a new 'angelic' food, the Eucharist of the Third Kingdom.[1] The Lord's Last Supper was the sacrament of love (the Real Presence in the Eucharist being ignored altogether, as in St. John's gospel). The Second Coming will be a wedding feast for the elect, the sacramental promise fulfilled. After his triumphant descent from Heaven Christ 'will prepare a great banquet and supper of the Lamb as a nuptial feast for his spouse, the Church, here on the physical mountains'.[2]

The vocabulary of this passage reminds one of Archbishop Kowalski's pronouncements at the time of the mystical marriages. Except for the mountains which he, the prophet of the plains, did not associate with the divine setting for the final revelation.

The Czech Adamites found themselves in conflict with the leaders of the Tabor commune and were expelled from the city. A chronicler reports their subsequent activities, but he is, of course, on the side of those who did the expelling. (As a rule it is a Bolshevik and not a Menshevik who writes the official history of a religious revolution.) He tells how the rejected brethren wandered through forests and over hills, and believing themselves to be in a state of innocence 'threw off their clothes' and went about naked. This was the Adamite gesture true to the Free Spirit that dwelt in their bodies.

'From the same madness', the chronicler writes, 'they supposed they were not sinning if one of the brethren had intercourse with one of the sisters; and if the woman conceived, she said she had conceived of the Holy Spirit.' This is exactly what a simple Mariavite nun was told by one of the elect. Without hesitation she replied that she too would like to have a baby from the Holy Spirit. Alas, the third Adam did not choose to mediate on her behalf.

Another close parallel between the Free Spirit brethren and the Mariavites under Kowalski is the belief in the sinless state of the children born of the mystical unions. The Czech chronicler writes: 'The children of holy parents [i.e. members of the Adamite sect] are conceived without original mortal sin.' But the holy parents and their offspring met with a gruesome fate at the hands of the Taborite brethren. Žižka hounded them relentlessly and

---

[1] The 'angelic food' is a recurring theme. St. Francis received it. The sinless children of the Kingdom of God, according to Archbishop Kowalski, would be sustained by it. Hence his order (see p. 157) to give communion to infants immediately after baptism, a practice also observed by the Taborites.

[2] A passage from the Hussite chronicle of Master Lawrence of Březová, the primary source of the Taborite history. This and the following quotations are given in Howard Kaminsky's translation, from his essay 'The Free Spirit in the Hussite Revolution', in *Millennial Dreams in Action*, ed. Sylvia L. Thrupp (The Hague, 1962).

finally, on 21 October 1421, the Adamites were annihilated. 'Thanks be to God,' said the chronicler of the massacre.

There is nothing equal in cruelty to a righteous sectarian butchering a brother dissenter. One Adamite was spared to give testimony of the Free Spirit doctrine. Render unto the truth what is supposed to be the truth, and magnanimously Žižka kept one solitary witness alive. As for his testimony, how objective could he afford to be after seeing such a thorough slaughter? Nevertheless, what we know of the Czech Adamites is based on that evidence. Historical documents, however, are full of data obtained by dubious means. Should one therefore take the story of sexual orgies among the Adamites as exaggerated, if not invented?

Half a millennium has passed since their time. Kowalski's trial happened less than fifty years ago, and it is already impossible to ascertain the truth of some of the facts. How far should we go in our scepticism? Some facts may be doubtful but the parallel patterns reveal the character of events despite inaccuracies and bias. Kowalski denied that he committed any of the sexual offences with which he was charged, and the press was blamed for distorting the evidence. Today there is no doubt in my mind that Kowalski protected the secrets of the elect. Erotic freedom reflected the sinless delights of the Third Heaven. In the fifteenth century Kowalski would have been expelled from Tabor just as he was to be expelled from the Plock Temple in 1935. The Taborites should have heeded Christ's warning, but they fought with the sword and perished by the sword.[1]

As Charles Péguy observed (*L'Energie spirituelle*, 1919), '*Tout commence en mystique et finit en politique.*' The realities of politics, whatever their ultimate aims, are always concerned with the imminent. The great fault of all millenarian thinking, from a mystical point of view, lay in the imminence of the Kingdom of God, which was preached with so much worldly passion. Prophets may and do bully their people, but bullying Providence on behalf of the elect can only achieve frustration. 'Surely the Second Coming is at hand', the poet's wishful cry in the wilderness. Like the luckless Adamites before him, Archbishop Kowalski at least tried to do something in the meantime. He paired off his elect and told them that the pleasures of the Third Heaven could be found in a cloister bed. Get some practice before that big wedding banquet of the Lamb. For the Lord is the bridegroom of many.

The Taborites and the Mariavites connected the search for the divinized (but deeply concealed) self with the angelic feast of the Eucharist. The divine

[1] After Žižka's death the rift between the two factions became more apparent, and the whole revolution ended with the battle of Lipany in 1434. Finally, the diet of Prague in 1444 condemned and banned the Taborite movement. The Free Spirit brethren were posthumously revenged.

in us is starved and it needs food. This notion can be traced via the subterranean channels to the Gnostic rituals in which the consecrated bread and wine were used for a dual purpose. Gnosticism distrusted the surface manifestations of religion: the deity on display, officially worshipped and within everybody's reach. There was a hidden God, the true one, who eluded the body-bound vulgar mob. Only through gnosis, that is through the secret and esoteric knowledge, a few human spirits could approach him. The gospels record Christ's sayings which point to this path. Many are called but few are chosen.

Which God then is hiding from man? Surely not the one who gives himself freely in the Eucharist? Perhaps the sacrament is meant to unlock an inner door, but only to those who are ready for the secrets of the concealed divinity.[1] Dark suspicions, however, hang over rituals in which the host was treated as an object of magic. The Phibionites, for instance, who were active in the third century, attributed a Eucharistic meaning to the sperm and the blood discharged at menstruation. Apparently, they swallowed both after uttering the liturgical words of consecration ('This is my body', etc.). They were also accused of consuming embryos of children born prematurely, and again this meal resembled communion.[2] Other practices which centred on the Gnostic Eucharist seemed to employ similar shock tactics, reversing, as it were, the concept of the sacred.[3] It is difficult to prove whether they continued in any clandestine form during the later centuries, when the 'horizontal' religion of the surface was firmly established.

Now and again, however, isolated outbursts of sacrilege seemed to suggest that the subterranean sources were still powerful. As the sacrilegious acts tended towards ritual rather than mere outrage, one may assume that they reflected something of the ancient matrix. In the seventeenth century, for example, strange things were reported from the convent of Louviers in Normandy. The nuns and their priest Pierre David prayed naked in the manner of the Priscillians, nuns came to communion with their breasts uncovered.[4] Consecrated hosts clotted with their menstrual blood were

[1] For Merezhkovsky and Kowalski the hidden God would be identifiable with the secret of the Three.

[2] The embryo was treated with honey, pepper, oil, and fragrant spices, torn to pieces and distributed among the participants.

[3] But was the concept sacramental? Hans Küng writes: 'It was only towards the end of the twelfth century and the beginning of the thirteenth that the *doctrine* of the sacramental character underwent methodical development.' *Why Priests?* (1972).

[4] See *Examen de la possession des religieuses de Louviers* (Paris, 1643). We have noted the allegation at Kowalski's trial, that in the second initiation to the Philadelphic Church the nun's breast was exposed. Another curious analogy is the confession of a nun at Louviers that she slept with the ghost of Pierre David. Compare this with Sister Melania who was married to the ghost of the first Mariavite priest.

apparently found buried in the cloister gardens. The last item, obviously Phibionite in origin, has a bearing on the continuity of the Gnostic rituals. If they were passed on by the Illuminati, how was the conveyance done? Obviously by word of mouth. The best way of preserving mystery is to lock it up tightly in a secret. A Gnostic would add: the hidden God is the secret of secrets.

In the nineteenth century Vintras won followers by showing the 'bleeding host'. In the ritual of his successor the Abbé Boullan, the consecrated wafers mixed with excreta and urine served a function similar to the Eucharistic meal of the Phibionites. If we detach our minds from the pathological aspect of this procedure[1] and treat it exclusively as a religious expression (however disgusting it may be to the majority of people), the question it poses concerns the sacramental transfiguration of the body. What happened on Mount Tabor constitutes a matrix. The Taborites knew its importance but failed to understand the transfigured Adam in the Adamites.

Christ's body performed the usual functions. It digested and excreted food, passed water and sweated. The early heretics who couldn't accept the physical nature of Christ, over-spiritualized him contrary to the evidence in the gospels. There Christ's daily life is lovingly described: he takes meals with friends, likes the company of women, eats meat and drinks wine, often journeys on foot, and rests when tired.[2] He knows thirst, hunger, and pain. Since all his acts are charged with meaning, one cannot help concluding that he wanted to emphasize his ordinary humanity. That's why the Transfiguration scene comes as such a contrast and fills the apostles with awe.

Now let's think the Gnostic way for the sake of an argument. At the Last Supper Christ said: 'This is my body.' He didn't say: This is my spirit. The spiritual illumination came later, at Pentecost, after the Resurrection. The physical is once again emphasized in the Eucharist, and it is emphasized by the son of man, as Christ insisted on calling himself. The thin white wafer given in communion spiritualizes the physical reality of the bread. Other symptoms of the same spiritualization have, in fact, weakened the living cells of the Christian matrix. Hence the sectarian temptation to go back to the beginning, either to the apostles or to Adam.

'This is my body' could be interpreted without any offence to the originator of the sacrament as his whole physical being, entrails and genitals included. Why this prudery then which makes us accept Christ emaciated

---

1 Otto Rank in *The Trauma of Birth* (1924; English trans., 1929) deals with a number of odd religious deviations. I want to avoid here a psychoanalytical interpretation.
2 The abstemious habits of the *perfecti* whether Bogomil, Cathar, or early Mariavite, deserve an ironic comment at this point. They are so unlike the natural behaviour of Christ. He used wine and not water for the mystery of his sacrament.

and clinically gutted? He died a horrible death. We owe his young body, while it was still alive, the fullest respect. But did the manic use of sexual excreta restore the full meaning to the sacramental body? It did not. Shame is a sneaking liar. Still, there was a perverse logic in the Gnostic argument. The extremists went all the way to the end of perversion, and, no doubt, felt liberated by doing so.

The four Mariavite bishops ('the four pillars of the Temple') believed they were the physical body of Christ. Kowalski, however, took care not to provoke the charges of Gnosticism. But the texts from which he often quoted were the ones favoured by the Illuminati: St. John's gospel, Revelation, St. Paul's epistles, the apocalyptic Book of Daniel and the apocryphal Book of Esdras. His own version of the Old Testament was banned as a blasphemous publication. They couldn't burn him at the stake. Against Kowalski's wishes, however, much too much leaked out at the trial. Did he or did he not perform secret rites in which the host was used? There are enough parallel examples in the past to suggest that he might have done. Those members of the inner church who consented to talk to me were either too shocked by my probing or feigned total ignorance. Two, however, supplied oblique comments which indicated that the vow of silence had been planted deep in their conscience.

The body of Christ was reincarnated in Kowalski and his bishops; the Little Mother opened the Third Heaven for the elect, the pure in spirit could not sin, and so on. A dark subterranean stream threw up these ideas and deposited them, wistfully it would seem, on the sandy banks of the Vistula, near the Temple.

4

Whoever claims to be a Messiah is by definition a free spirit. He sets his own rules of conduct. The rise and career of Shabbetai Zevi (1625–76), an oriental Jew from Ismir (Smyrna), was a display of the Messianic free spirit on a grand scale. His name is still a legend.

There are clearly marked phases in his life, which from a psychological point of view reveal the pull of opposites, each swaying his mind towards a claim of such a dazzling magnitude. In seventeenth-century terms he was a victim of the blackest melancholy which no amount of blood-letting, fasting, and meditation could cure. Today he is described by Gershom Scholem as 'an extreme case of manic-depressive psychosis'.[1] But the crises he underwent in search of the hidden God correspond to the violent disturbances

[1] See Scholem's essay in *Encyclopaedia Judaica*, vol. XIV (Jerusalem, 1971). His monograph, *Sabbatai Sevi* (Princeton, N.J., 1973), appeared in translation after this book was written.

which afflicted great mystics from St. Paul and St. Augustine to St. Francis, Suso, and St. John of the Cross. Why should we always assume that such upheavals within the psyche invalidate the experience which is reached at the end?

Shabbetai Zevi, like Kowalski, was a virile man who thought he could master his erotic obsessions. In his early twenties until 1648 he led a semi-secluded life. The news of the massacres of the Jews in the Ukraine during the Chmielnicki rebellion (1648–53) shocked the Sephardic communities in Turkey. The time was ripe for a spiritual event.[1] Shabbetai Zevi began to utter the unspeakable name of God in public; he broke the religious taboo, and the inner compulsion to assert himself drove him on. He spoke and behaved like one who had authority directly from Jehovah.

Undoubtedly, his learning in the cabbala helped him to impose a paradoxical meaning on his actions. He knew which hints to take from the Bible. The prophet Hosea provided one—he married a whore—so Shabbetai Zevi, too, chose for his wife a girl of ill repute.[2] He married Sarah in Cairo in 1664 and fourteen months later, encouraged by Nathan of Gaza, a learned visionary, he proclaimed himself the Messiah on 31 May 1665.

The rabbinical establishment in Jerusalem reacted strongly to the new claimant but a large number of Jews, the poor in particular, saw the signs of a divine hope in this handsome and imposing figure. Shabbetai Zevi was as keen on parallelism as Kowalski. He had his twelve apostles, each representing a tribe of Israel; he had his standard-bearer, the wise Nathan, who issued prophecies about his redemptive mission and about the age of trouble preceding it. And the Messiah of Ismir broke the rules: he ate the fats forbidden by the Mosaic law (*helev*), he called God by his sacred name, had concubines like Solomon, and, according to the evidence of his adversaries, celebrated a sexual ritual, during which again all taboos were wilfully broken.

Shabbetai Zevi was a poetic thinker—he preferred metaphors and allusions to a systematized discourse. In this he was not unlike the Gnostic and Sufi teachers. A metaphor doesn't argue, it demands an act of faith. Shabbetai Zevi dictated *The Mystery of the True Faith* and it later inspired a number of Shabbetaian hymns, but the real codifier of his theology was the indefatigable Nathan of Gaza (*The Book of Creation*).

---

[1] Apart from the impact of the massacre there were, in my opinion, other factors which caused the Messianic wave. In the seventeenth century all established churches suffered from inertia. Judaism, Christianity, and Islam needed revivalists. And they came. Germany had her *Pietismus* and mystics like Angelus Silesius. In the Turkish Empire Sufism flourished, and the Jews in the diaspora were shaken by the Messiah of Ismir and his successors in Europe.

[2] It is interesting that Kowalski also mentions Hosea's marriage to a whore as an example. To the pure in spirit everything is pure.

How original, Messianically speaking, is Shabbetai Zevi's cabbala? Its interpretation of the divine principle rests on a dual action which, in essence, resembles the Gnostic paradox of the hidden God. But, if anything, Shabbetai Zevi pushes the duality further.

According to him, both form and matter are in *En-Sof* (Godhead), while the whole process of creation works through the opposition of two lights: the 'thoughtful' and the 'thoughtless'. There is nothing evil in the opposition itself: the thoughtless light is there of necessity in order to annihilate the structures produced by the other light.[1] The Satanic force is simply 'the other side' (*sitra ahra*), the *En-Sof* in reverse. This, of course, makes the trials of Job sound even worse. The divine coin was tossed in Hellheaven and it fell on both sides at the same time. No point in asking which side wins. They both do.

In the beginning was Golem, the primordial matter, chaos and the absence of light. Yet why should the original illumination have turned against itself so radically that a redemptive intervention became necessary? The question changes into a silent sphinx. The Messiah prefigures all human sacrifice and suffering but to fulfil his mission he has to challenge the mystery of redemption and to break the tablets of the law. Enslaved in the lower part of primordial space, in the dominion of thoughtless light, his soul has tried since the beginning of the world to open up that lower part so that the thoughtful light could enter it. The demoniac domains are ultimately redeemable. The soul of the Messiah has to undergo indescribable sufferings to come closer to this act of cosmic liberation.

In the Christian religion the Messiah enters the Inferno after his death to redeem the souls of the just who are Lucifer's hostages. The Harrowing of Hell inspired medieval poets and painters, for it combines the myth of the underworld with the mystery of Christ the avenger.[2]

Is Kowalski a figure comparable with Shabbetai Zevi? The Archbishop was a fanatical Messianist on the way to becoming a Messiah. He saw his mission through the Romantic filter of the three bards who had predicted his new papacy.[3] Kowalski had no scruples in explaining the mystical marriages in terms of redemption. Though he found pleasure in discussing religion with a young rabbi in Plock, he knew little of the cabbala. What he did know of it came via the teaching of Towianski.

---

[1] I have relied here on Professor Scholem's *Encyclopaedia Judaica* essay (op. cit.), but the comments, for whatever they are worth, are mine.

[2] Both the Bogomils and the Cathars held that the devil was the son of God and the master of the world. In a Russian version of *The Legend of the Cross* we read that the tree of the cross was planted in Paradise by Satanael. (See D. Obolensky, op. cit.)

[3] See p. 102.

Myself I find the true affinity between Shabbetai Zevi and Kowalski in their spiritual *persona*, in the manner in which they projected themselves on to others. Both were iconoclasts, breaking the holy taboos, both put themselves above the moral law and, when deprived of the inner light, both would fall deep into a mood of uncertainty and dejection. But Kowalski was never made to face an alternative as dreadful as that presented to Shabbetai Zevi when he was brought to the Sultan's court and given a choice: conversion to the Mohammedan faith or death. And the Messiah of Ismir chose apostasy; he became a Moslem on 15 September 1666 and took the name of Aziz Mehmed Effendi.

This altered the whole nature of his Messianic claim. If he wanted to prove that he could do the unimaginable, this was the act. His wife and some of his disciples followed him into apostasy. Contrary to all expectations, the shock Shabbetai Zevi had inflicted on his believers did not ruin his mission. Most of them accepted him as a Messiah, and Nathan of Gaza soon had it all worked out: what Shabbetai Zevi had done was the darkest Messianic secret and the future would reveal its meaning. The faithful took it as a sign that the fulfilment of his mission would come through Islam. This didn't sound too remote. There were many Jews living within the Turkish Empire. The two lights seemed to be reflected in the paradox of an apostate Messiah.[1]

To justify this paradox Nathan searched the Bible, Talmud, and obscure cabbalistic texts. Appropriate quotations turned up as they usually do. A similar procedure was adopted by Archbishop Kowalski after the Little Mother's death. He crammed his pastoral letters with references to the sacred writings in the attempt to square the marriages in the convent with the vow of chastity. As he added more to the Mariavite system he found himself trapped by his own paradoxes. He was 'the passive instrument of the divine Will', it was therefore God who made him break the rules. The nuns with whom he had sexual relations talked to me of his martyred body, accepting and purifying the unclean desires of others. This is, indeed, an ancient juxtaposition greatly favoured by the *electi* from the days of the Eleusinian caves. The followers of Shabbetai Zevi explained his strange acts in much the same way. The Messiah had to absorb the destructive light emanating from those he came to redeem. Boullan's doctrine of vicarious suffering, which influenced Huysmans, belongs to this category of thinking.

If the Messiah allowed incest and other sexual transgressions, he did that

---

1 As Scholem observes (op. cit.) 'By placing the paradox of an apostate Messiah, a tragic but still legitimate redeemer, at the centre of the new, developing Shabbetean theology, Nathan laid the foundations for the ideology of the believers for the next 100 years.'

to free the demonized world from the fear of its unclean nature. Many things have been attributed to Zevi's erotic celebrations which seemed to flourish whenever he was in a state of elation, attuned to his own inscrutable law.[1] There are indications that the worshipped deity was a woman. If so, the incestuous forms of sex must have increased the pleasure through the violation of the Mother image. The Messiah had to break the taboo so that he could annihilate the frontiers between good and evil.

The incestuous cult of the Mother is probably the nearest parallel to Archbishop Kowalski's concept of the Third Heaven inhabited by the Little Mother.[2] In both cults the liberation of the spirit comes through the erotic force, breaking the barriers. The Archbishop placed the Little Mother in the Eucharist. Shabbetai Zevi (who died at the age of fifty) was also deified early in the eighteenth century by his clandestine followers in a sect led by Baruchiah Ruso (Osman Baba). Each of the thirty-six prohibitions of the Torah became a command. Thou shalt fornicate with thy mother and thy sister, with thy brother and thy daughter. The holy outrage abolishes transgression by transgressing it fearlessly.

Shabbeteanism had to go underground in order to survive.[3] It joined the dark route of Gnostic and cabbalistic secrets. Persecution achieved the opposite: it only helped to keep the interest in the sect alive, and scandals added flavour to it.

Finally, a new pattern, resembling Shabbetai Zevi's apostasy, emerged in Poland when Jacob Frank (1726–91), after spending some years in Turkey, returned home as a reincarnation of the Messiah of Ismir. The most striking thing about his cabbala, which draws on the ideas of Nathan and Baruchiah, is the concept of the Trinity that includes the feminine element. Frank saw himself, together with Shabbetai Zevi and Baruchiah, in the sequence of the messengers of the Big Brother (He-who-stands-before-God), for God himself is inaccessible and hidden. We are back with the secret of the Three, which is ultimately resolvable by the Eternal Feminine incarnated in the Virgin-Mother. Jacob Frank became a Catholic in 1759 and his apostasy,

---

[1] By contrast, his black depressions occurred when he felt at the level of the ordinary human condition.

[2] This brings us to the problem of redemption through the woman. Even in England. The prophetess from Devon, Joanna Southcott, imagined herself pregnant of the Messiah when she was over sixty. But the Messiah rushed back to heaven as soon as he was born, her followers explain. Joanna died in 1814, but she is still revered by the Panaceans, a small commune of the elect in Bedford. The Little Mother expected to give birth to the Antichrist. Both were believed to be the woman of Revelation. ch. 12.

[3] It surfaced now and again in Italy, Germany, and Poland. Towns like Leghorn, Modena, Frankfurt, Vilna, Żółkiew, and Kalisz had their Shabbeteans. The whole network of links came out in the open when the luggage of an emissary from Polish Podolia was searched in Frankfurt (1725).

like that of Shabbetai Zevi, caused dismay, but was accepted by his loyal disciples. This group of converted Jews became wholly assimilated; some of them were made nobles and played a considerable part in Polish life.

Jacob Frank's version of Shabbeteanism brings his highly imaginative theology close to Archbishop Kowalski's ideas concerning the Trinity, the female principle, and rebirth. Frank appointed twelve apostolic sisters who were his concubines; Kowalski, too, had twelve bishopesses annointed by him. The two Messianic traditions merge imperceptibly. Kowalski knew about the Frankists at least as much as any educated Pole. But it doesn't really matter how far his knowledge went. What matters is his discovery of a dark religious matrix. Those who are obsessed by parallels often make such discoveries. They hit an obstacle, and by tripping over it find a concealed underground passage at their feet.

Once Kowalski violated the Virgin in the sacred image of the Mother, his underground journey began.

8

The Priestesses

THERE was certainly something strange in the air during the last decade of the nineteenth century. Maria Frances Kozlowska received her Revelation in 1893 and thus became the chosen woman for the Mariavites. In 1896 the Virgin was seen by hundreds of people at Tilly-sur-Seulles and nearby villages in Normandy. This miraculous event occurred again and again throughout the year, confirming what the prophet of Tilly himself had predicted (Vintras died in 1875). In 1898 the Russian Vladimir Solovyov claimed to have seen St. Sophia the Incorporeal Mother in three successive visions.[1] 'The most significant thing that has so far occurred in my life.' He believed that the Eternal Feminine was to come down to earth and take on an imperishable body.

This was the return of the Maid of whom Virgil spoke in Eclogue IV, rolling the riant r's: *Iam rediit et Virgo, redeunt Saturnia regna.* But where was she returning from? In *Le Livre d'Or*, which records the visions of Pierre-Michel (Vintras), the entry under 5 September 1839 speaks of that place: '. . . *Marie fut dans le ciel jusqu'au jour de son immaculée conception, comme la Sagesse Fille du Père, et* Épouse du Saint-Esprit.'

She is the Wisdom wedded to the Holy Spirit. This comes close to the meaning of Solovyov's announcement in 1898 and to Archbishop Kowalski's 'understanding' of the eternal feminine, manifested in both the Virgin and the Little Mother. One day during his imprisonment in Rawicz in 1937 he saw 'an extraordinary light' in his cell and knew that the Virgin Mary was God. 'Tears of repentance' washed his face. It was then that he must have accepted divine bisexuality.[2]

---

[1] The first vision occurred in his childhood, the second in 1875 (in the Reading Room of the British Museum), the third a year later when, true to her promise, Sophia appeared to him in the desert near Cairo.

[2] As regards Christ's parenthood, Kowalski taught that 'the Heavenly Father became not only father but also the mother of his son'. This clearly corresponds to Merezhkovsky's concept of 'divine bisexuality' (see p. 62). In her Revelations, Dame Julian of Norwich too speaks of Motherhood in God. 'He willed that the Second Person should become our Mother.' About her own visions Dame Julian speaks, like Kowalski, of receiving them in her 'understanding'.

According to Pierre-Michel, 'la Fille du Père' before Her immaculate conception was a special act of creation which caused jealousy among the angels and led to the war in heaven. Since the Archangel Michael himself entrusted these holy secrets to the prophet of Tilly, how could he possibly doubt their veracity? The Archangel was there and moreover he did win the war. When you say *la divine mère de dieu*, he was told, 'your faith can be at peace'.

The striking feature of this recurrent wish for the Virgin's return is its connection with the idea of the Second Coming. Her appearances at La Salette, Lourdes, Tilly, and at Fatima in our century point to some irrevocable disaster in which the only hope is the mediatrix who could become a co-redeemer and save at least a small portion of mankind from annihilation. The recipients of her messages are usually girls before the age of puberty. Mature women, on the other hand, give birth to new religious movements, and in the last hundred years we have several examples to prove it: Mary Baker Eddy, for instance, of the Christian Science movement, Madame Blavatsky of the Theosophists, the Little Mother Kozlowska of the Mariavites,[1] Mrs. Ellen G. White of the Seventh-Day Adventists, and finally, Edna Ballard of the 'I Am' cult.

Salvation, it would seem, can only be achieved through the Woman who is clothed with the sun in the Apocalypse and hurls it towards the earth like a ball of fire in the frightening miracle of Fatima, twenty-eight years before the destruction of Hiroshima. Salvation will also be achieved *with* the help of women, whether as visionaries, religious reformers, or priestesses. The Second Coming no longer has an exclusively male connotation. But perhaps one could deviously argue, taking a feminine point of view, that the apocalyptic seers wishing a global disaster on us all were in the main frustrated males. Even the Lady of La Salette, angry as she is, wants to protect rather than to destroy. 'The world is going to destruction', writes Merezhkovsky in *The Secret of the Three*, 'because it has forgotten about the Mother. The male species is dominating the female.'[2]

It was the male prophet Benjamin Purnell, founder of the House of David, who at the time of the Little Mother's revelations, in 1895, proclaimed himself the last of the seven divine messengers. His task was to gather the 144,000 true Israelites, the apocalyptic number of the chosen. And he proceeded to look for them in Michigan, U.S.A.[3] The idea of the

---

[1] It is interesting that the English Catholic journal, *The Tablet*, described Kozlowska as 'the Polish Miss Eddy' (25 December 1909).
[2] As translated by Kowalski in *The Kingdom of God on Earth*.
[3] See p. 115.

elect or the chosen, wherever it happens to be realized, is bound to become a society for mutual protection. As early as 1906 the Mariavites started collecting signatures of those who accepted the sanctity of the Little Mother (45,000 signed willingly). The Mariavites have since protected their chosen in the Book of Life which they keep under the monstrance at the Felicjanów commune. But the 'Book of Survival' would be a more appropriate title in this age, so close to the apocalyptic holocaust. The aged King David of our civilization is in desperate need of Abishag's warm body. Queen of the elect, protect our bodies in the hour of survival.

Now Archbishop Kowalski (King David to the chosen among the chosen) already had his Abishag, the first of his mystical wives, who as Mother Superior helped him to establish the Kingdom of Love on the banks of the Vistula. A new Paracletean reign had begun: '*c'est ce Règne—*' in the words of the prophet of Tilly—'*où sera connu l'amour véritable.*' Vintras and the Abbé Boullan had priestesses who participated in the rites of the sect. Huysmans was so involved with Boullan that he kept a Vintrasian priestess in his house. This enabled him to observe the rituals performed by her in expectation of the Third Reign. Léon Bloy, as addicted to the mystical as Huysmans, did a similar thing when he took up with Anne-Marie, former prostitute turned prophetess, so that he could have direct access to a secret source in which the Holy Spirit bubbled up darkly.[1]

If we go further into the past, where the records are both fewer and less reliable, we still find sufficient evidence of the priesthood of women, not only in the quasi-pagan cults of the Christian era but also in most underground societies. Suspicion of witchcraft, however, hangs over such clandestine organizations. Hence the charges of Satanism flung at the Saint-Simonists, Vintras, Towianski, Boullan, Bloy, et al.[2] Hence also the wilful courting of Lucifer which is so noticeable in the *fin-de-siècle* writers, like Huysmans, Evers, and Przybyszewski. Every novel about Satanist rituals has a woman playing a prominent part in it. Kozlowska was suspected of a liaison with the devil, and the cartoonists often showed her in his company. She in turn suspected the devil of wanting a liaison, if not with her directly (she had been immunized against him during the purification process), then with some of her nuns and priests. The sinister Demon of Noon knew how to attract women to his angelic luminosity.

Archbishop Kowalski must have been fully aware of all those pitfalls

---

[1] When the power of the Spirit was withdrawn from her, she went mad. See Griffiths, op. cit., ch. VII.

[2] Rumour had it that on his estate in Lithuania Towianski had a chapel in which a woman celebrated Mass.

when he introduced the priesthood of women in the Mariavite church. True, he had an 'understanding' about it in 1929 and, as usual, rushed into action, but his decision was in the circumstances bold, not to say reckless. There he stood condemned by public opinion after his trial in 1928, ridiculed in the press and in cabarets all over the country, and still he felt compelled to test the courage of his convictions. To lie low for a year or two would have been the course of action any other compromised leader would have taken. But not John Maria Michael enthroned in the New Jerusalem at Plock, under the roof of the Temple of Love which he had built with the woman of the Apocalypse.

A cynic, of course, might observe that what the Archbishop carried out was a well-calculated counter-attack. Instead of trying to appease his enemies, including a number of his own priests, he provoked them. Instead of hiding behind a priestly mask, he showed again the defiant face of a reformer. Why should women be debarred from the altar if the Woman was to save the world? In 1929 one could not see the full implications of his act. Today when all Christian churches suffer from a shortage of those with a vocation, the admission of women to priesthood is not a subject for canonical debate but a necessity, if the church rituals are to be continued.

Kowalski did not enter into a debate; he ordained the elect among his nuns and once again acted in advance of his time.[1] No matter what one thinks of Kowalski's motives, a visionary light was present in his pastoral letter of 1929. It gave the Mariavite women the full sacramental rights of priesthood.

2

How did the ingenious Archbishop bring it all about? The mystical marriages had prepared the ground and, indirectly, weakened the main opposition among the conservative Mariavites. Those who had left the church had already testified against Kowalski at the trial. Nothing worse could happen, or so it seemed. As for the women, by being married they had more influence on the affairs of the cloister, especially those who, like Sister Honorata or Sister Raphaela, belonged to the inner group of four. Isabel grew in stature, encouraged and bullied in turn by her overbearing husband. She had taken the humiliations of the trial with great dignity, which the press and the clerks of the court duly noticed.[2] The testimonies of the married

[1] Forty-five years later, in January 1974, Pope Paul VI decided to allow the first woman acolyte to serve communion. I predict that by the end of this century the priesthood of women will be instituted in the Catholic Church.

[2] This was confirmed by the lawyer Z. Deczyński, who was present at Kowalski's trial.

nuns, too, indicate the change in their status. Marriage gave each of them
more confidence, even if they had to suffer from bad conscience at the
beginning.

Kowalski exercised his skill in combining surprise with showmanship.
On Maundy Thursday, 28 March 1929, he ordained twelve conventual
Sisters, including Mother Superior Isabel who, on the same day, was also
consecrated bishop together with Philip and Bartholomew, two of the 'four
pillars' of the Temple. The hierarchy of the inner circle was now obvious
to the outsiders.

The ceremony of ordination must have been a colourful spectacle,
judging by the description in the official Mariavite weekly. It consisted of
two parts: the twelve chosen Sisters were first consecrated deaconesses,
then fully ordained as 'priestesses of Christ'. The Archbishop recited a set
of questions which the Sisters answered with 'Amen'. Prayers followed, and
then, seated on a stool, with Isabel's assistance he put an alb on each of the
Sisters (a sign of purification). After the alb came the engirdling (for courage),
then the Archbishop rose and, as each Sister approached him, placed both
hands on her head, saying: 'Who at Pentecost gave this grace to men and
women alike that the Holy Spirit descended upon them.'

The placing of the deacon's stole on the left arm provides a possible clue
to the kissing of the left breast in the ceremony of initiation as described at
the trial. The next two symbolic acts concerned the sacramental power of
baptism and communion, the Sisters taking in turn the plate with the cup
and the ciborium with consecrated hosts. The ordination itself followed.
The Archbishop summoned each Sister by name; each answered 'I am
present' and approached. When they were all kneeling, Kowalski delivered
a long oration in which he again castigated the male priests for having in
the past abused the sacrament as often as their souls were soiled. Now, he
said, 'the Holy Spirit calls upon the second half of human kind to this
highest of honours. . . . You, most beloved Sisters, will keep your hearts
in purity to obtain His Mercy for the world.'

Solemnly, he intoned the Polish version of the hymn *Veni Creator
Spiritus* and began placing chasubles on the ordained priestesses. 'Light is the
burden of Christ.' To which they replied, 'Amen'. Then he proceeded to
attach a diadem to the wimple of each of the twelve. The embroidered
design represented the chalice with the host, the letter J (for Jesus), and the
initials of the Temple of Mercy and Love. Kowalski, of course, devised the
whole thing. After passing the chalice with wine and the consecrated wafers
he once more put both his hands on the head of each priestess. The most
impressive sight came with the Mass celebrated jointly by the Archbishop

and all the priestesses. They were twelve, the new apostles of womanhood, and he the thirteenth, the only male at the altar of Love.

On Holy Saturday sixty-two Sisters were made deaconesses. This was a revival of an early Christian practice, and complied with the wishes of the Little Mother. In his pastoral letter 'On the New Priesthood of the Holy Virgins' (dated 14 March 1929) Kowalski mentions the deaconesses who were active at the time of the apostles (e.g. Feba, Evodia). He also emphasizes women's share in the work of redemption. For, apart from the Virgin Mary and Mary Magdalene 'who preached the gospel', there were also 'the sister wives' of the apostles (thus called by St. Paul). But 'until now', he writes, 'women were not ordained to be priests or made bishops.' He trusts God's mercy that in this decision too his will was guided by the Holy Spirit. 'I make all things new,' said Christ in the Apocalypse, 'and new they are becoming in the Mariavite Temple of Love.' The admission of women to priesthood is 'an epoch-making event in the life of the Christian Church'.

In terms of propaganda—and one cannot ignore this factor—Kowalski's novelty paid off at once. On Easter Day, 31 March, Bishopess Isabel celebrated a three-hour Mass, assisted by the new priestesses, their chasubles and diadems glittering against the candlelight. The Archbishop himself received communion from Isabel and the fully packed Temple watched every detail of the ceremony with fascination. This was a grand spectacle followed by a traditional procession inside the Temple, in which Isabel carried a monstrance and the younger girls of the convent school threw flowers before her. The older girls marched with Mariavite banners while the priests and nuns held lighted candles and sang the Easter hymn, 'A joyous day has come to us'. A new church of mankind in a procession towards heaven, as the Mariavite reporter put it enthusiastically.

After the Mass, Bishopess Isabel gave a blessing to the crowd, which included many curious Catholics. They had come expecting to see a female circus and left the Temple visibly impressed. What we heard and saw, some of them said, was far too deep to be a comedy. It seemed that in a simple language they expressed the voice of their collective unconscious, yearning for the revelation of the feminine. On 31 March 1929 they witnessed 'the first Mass celebrated by a woman'. Was it in fact the first? From a canonical point of view, yes. For Archbishop Kowalski was no Vintras or Towianski: he had apostolic succession, therefore his act of ordination was valid, even though the Roman Church did not allow women to be priests.

Kowalski set a dangerous example, and the Catholic hierarchy was aware of this, however hard it tried to dismiss him as a pervert and a blasphemer. The town of Plock, accustomed to strange news leaking from the Mariavite Temple, was this time taken by surprise. Only five months after his trial that crazy Archbishop was daring them to admire his pluck. And they responded. Now the Archbishop saw his chances of fighting back doubled. He had his women apostles plus robes, ritual, and their physical radiance. And so, like a travelling player, he began a tour of the Mariavite centres, all the priestesses packed in a bus, and he directing the whole show.

At Lodz, the biggest industrial centre, the church was full, many Catholics present and watching in respectful silence. The press, considering Kowalski's notoriety, reported the Mass of the priestesses accurately, without any sniggering asides directed at him. A priestess reading the Mass delivered a sermon as well: this innovation had been in progress since Easter.[1]

The Archbishop received his due in praise for establishing the new priesthood, and he also had some prophetic backing from the past. The Romantic bards supplied the words. Mickiewicz, for instance, was quoted in Isabel's sermon: 'If it were not for the presence of the Most Holy Sacrament on our earth, the Lord would have destroyed it.' A sound apocalyptic reminder. Moreover, the same Mickiewicz predicted the presence of the priestesses (*kapłanki*) on earth.[2]

The tour continued. On the whole, the diademed and chasubled Sisters made a favourable impression. They looked so attractive to begin with. But those who remembered the Little Mother would ask: 'Why all that silk? She never wore such things.' They were right; she didn't. Aside from the grudges, however, even the practical peasants loved the pageantry. Their lingering nostalgia for the Earth Goddess found at last a pious outlet. The reports in the Mariavite periodicals hinted at some rebel priests who didn't like what they saw and felt threatened. Others, however, bent over backwards to convince the Archbishop that they adored his innovation. 'Welcome' in large letters on streamers, panegyrical greetings, and processions awaited the bus in loyal parishes. Even a poor community, buried deep in the forest, knew how to receive them. Outside a small church they gathered. An old peasant, his eyes fixed on the visitors, addressed them in a lofty manner:

[1] The sermons are printed in *The Kingdom of God on Earth*, but most of them are poor, padded with quotations and straining to be meaningful.
[2] This, incidentally, the Mariavites learnt from the late Professor Pigoń, a Catholic of Vilna and a great scholar, who discussed Towianski's teaching with learned fairness in his volume of essays, *Zepoki Mickiewicza*. It is reported that when the Professor's wife heard of the priestesses as foretold by the poet, she interrupted a discussion about it with the comment: 'Sheer nonsense.' So much for feminine loyalty.

'We welcome you, Beautiful Crown composed of the twelve daughters of our most beloved Little Mother. It was you that Saint John saw made up of twelve stars.'

The conceit of the twelve delighted the Archbishop, and the priestesses were moved by this proof of divine inspiration.

But a few unpleasant incidents marred the triumphant tour. At Latowicz they went to see the house where their leader was born. On returning to the bus they met some local women, who spat in their direction. A prophet is never honoured in his native place. In another village they somehow avoided falling into a trap. Their bus was to be garaged for the night in a barn, but Kowalski changed plans. Later they learnt that a group of Catholic youths had broken into the barn after dark and were surprised to find it empty. Elsewhere a mob smashed windows and threw stones into a house where a Mariavite altar was prepared. The priestesses celebrated Mass there just the same.

Kowalski had everything under control. Like a head of state on a foreign visit he kept in touch with his capital in Plock. When he heard, for instance, of a certain Sister Celina's 'treachery', his reaction was swift. He suspended her by telegram. A Pope wouldn't have put that much trust in the postal services. The Mariavite Archbishop wired his wrath and it worked.

The priestesses scored a considerable success in Silesia and in the Lodz area. During their visit the newly consecrated Bishop Bartholomew preached in the town of Pabianice, extolling the Woman who in the divine plans was meant to be the crown of the creation. The first archpriestess, he said, was the Virgin Mary, then the Little Mother, and now at the start of Christ's reign on earth, the sacramental equality of the sexes had become a reality. 'Indeed, women have shown more virtues necessary for priesthood than men.' Thus spake Bartholomew, while in some parishes the Mariavite priests found the female competition intolerable. Many more people came to church when they heard that a priestess was to celebrate Mass. Doubters and waverers returned home strengthened in their Mariavite faith. As the revivalist mood was catching fire, the jealousy of the priests increased. The tour spelt trouble for them at some point in the future.

Again, Kowalski overreacted by sending the priestesses to weak parishes where the spirit was low. They were told to do pastoral work on their own. Soon a rumour went round that the Archbishop would eventually replace all parish priests with women. This wasn't so far-fetched, since he kept talking about the past sins of the clergy, and quoted the message of La Salette in his periodicals. He couldn't help being reminded of his former subordinates who turned against him at the trial. In the religious profession, it would seem, men are more treacherous than women. And Kowalski demanded total loyalty.

Seeing that the new priesthood worked in his favour, he ordained more nuns and created bishopesses who, as it happened, were also bound to him with the mystical seal of marriage.[1] A touch of cunning and caution could perhaps be detected in his choice of nuns for these high honours. Some of them were neither very bright nor particularly interested in self-education. By placing a diadem on their heads, the Archbishop had their gratitude and devotion secured for ever. He was right in his foresight. When the split occurred in 1935, the women did not fail him.

3

Isabel Wiłucka was not only beautiful, she also photographed well. The white wimple over her eyes emphasized their size and the innocent look. One is not surprised that her mouth, so generous in shape, made Kowalski think of Solomon's kiss of kisses. Not much 'understanding' was needed to fill such a thought with desire.

In a photograph which shows her in full splendour, wearing the robe and diadem of the Archpriestess, she looks somewhat wistful, the pout on her lips asking for sympathy rather than a kiss. The gold-yellow robe was probably too stiff; with one hand she had to clutch a missal, with the other a crozier as tall as herself. Instead of the nun's wimple she displayed Eucharistic sun-rays spread out like a fan, with an elaborate cross at the top and a pair of wings below. This was a crown embroidered in silk and covered with imitation pearls. Isabel must have been too much aware of her apparel to feel relaxed before the camera. But looking now at the wimple, now at the diadem, one gets a flickering impression that the character of this woman could never opt for the crown alone: it wanted the shade from the wimple as well. Back to the maiden innocence of a nun. She was the sort of girl who provokes her parents to say with exasperation: 'You'll end in a nunnery.'

She had received her secondary education at a typical *pension* for genteel young ladies and, judging by her matriculation certificate, she did well in all her twenty-three subjects, which included four languages and music.[2] Later, when she accompanied the Archbishop on his travels abroad (a big journey to the Holy Land in 1926), her knowledge of German and French

[1] They were the twelve 'Nazirites' of the inner church, and they could wear their hair long, in accordance with the vows described in the Old Testament (Samson, Samuel, and John the Baptist, for instance, were Nazirites), cf. Numbers 6; Judges 13; Luke 1.
[2] Born on 28 October 1890, she finished school in 1909. I saw the original certificate in Felicjanów and photographed it.

proved useful. Her family background was comfortably middle-class and she could have found a prosperous husband. Her looks were, of course, a great asset. She had black hair, dark eyes, olive complexion, her high cheekbones made her face appear narrow; she was tall and carried herself with natural grace. Everybody who met her commented on the beauty of her smile.

But Antonina (as she was called then) suffered from a phobia: she was afraid of men and rejected all her suitors. 'You'll end in a nunnery,' said the parents. And she did at the age of twenty-eight after a visit to Plock in 1918. The Little Mother tipped her as a very promising novice. Besides, educated nuns were needed in the growing organization. She worked as a teacher in a convent school and was excellent at her job, though her perfectionism made her both over-anxious and over-pious. She developed psychosomatic ailments. When Kowalski bestowed on her his Solomonic kiss and more, she was over thirty, an old maid by the standards of her milieu. In three years she rose from the novitiate to the office of Mother Superior, a progress so quick that it caused resentment. But once she became Kowalski's wife Number One, the Abishag of the inner church, the Sisters recognized her loving nature and sympathized with her marital problems when David-cum-Solomon started his permutation tables. More and more nuns were invited to enter the Kingdom via the mediator's sacred sofa, and she as Mother Superior had to give them her blessing and deal with their scruples.

Undoubtedly, Isabel suffered much during those seven years before the diadem of bishopess crowned her meekness and patience. She had become by then the pliable instrument of the Archbishop's will[1] and seemed to possess none of her own, whereas he exploited to the full the masochistic streak in her, until in the end her whole being was an open target for his whims, fantasies, and bouts of foul temper. Highly strung, she found relief in tears and sometimes, one hopes, in sex. Occasionally, she had hysterical fits.[2] They told each other dreams as a matter of course since the Archbishop was always on the lookout for prophetic messages. One morning he declared hers to be an inspired dream and asked her to repeat it when all the nuns gathered in the afternoon. Isabel tried and soon muddled things up; the Archbishop stopped her abruptly with a loud 'Stupid!' He did that often, and she would only bow her head; so good for her humility, so good

---

[1] Kowalski, it must be remembered, called himself 'the passive instrument of God's Will' (*martwe narzędzie*).

[2] She became an expert on weeping when it came to spiritual advice. She warned the nuns against anxieties which result from hysteria and not from love, e.g. in an article of 1929, 'On the Love of Our Beloved Little Mother'.

for the others to see. The Sisters who are still alive recall those scenes with admiration.

Children were being born. A young priestess proud to have a child showed Isabel her first-born and the Mother Superior, aloof as she could afford to be, found it impossible to hide her true emotions. Her whole face contorted with envy as she peered into the cot.[1] Was she sterile? If so, her suffering must have been great when Sister Dilecta bore Kowalski's child and he (after some hesitation) acknowledged him. The more submissive she became, the more outrageous were Kowalski's demands on her. Would she take this? and if this, why not a stronger shock? Only the pure, it would seem, are unshockable. An orgy to them is an exercise in spiritual liberation. Père Enfantin and the Abbé Boullan knew this type only too well.

According to the evidence at the trial Isabel collaborated with Kowalski in his erotic excesses. But was she capable of helping him to rupture the virginity of girls under age? His belly, it was said, made things awkward.[2] I asked one of the uninhibited ex-priestesses who had no reason to speak ill of Isabel.

'Yes,' she answered. 'It's not the question of her liking or disliking it. She even might have liked it without knowing why. What matters is that she would have done anything; yes, anything that he wanted her to do. Her will was entirely at his disposal.'

'A case of possession, you might say.'

She hesitated. 'No, Isabel would have thought it all part of a perfect union.'

I was reminded of Boullan's *union de vie* and probed no further.

The transformation of Isabel from a male-fearing creature to a constantly abused instrument of one male seems to me psychologically coherent. For endless is the erotic humiliation of a body offered to the pure demon of perfection. A crown on her head, the Mariavite Abishag could look back on her years of tribulation with that innocent look that belonged to the wimple.

In 1934 Archpriestess Isabel greeted an English visitor with these words: 'In the past it was the time of the male. Now it is the age of the women. We have been slaves until now.' She echoed Mickiewicz's address to the female disciples of Towianski, and obviously believed in what she said. As

---

[1] I heard this story twice in conversation with Mariavite nuns. One of them confided to me that, being liable to conceive easily, she and another nun risked going to a chemist's shop in a big town to ask what was the best way of avoiding pregnancy. They both wore secular clothes and pretended that this information was needed for someone else.

[2] Z. Deczyński remembers an incident during the cross-examination of a girl who maintained that she was deflowered by Kowalski aided by his wife.

'Describe the expression on his face,' said the prosecution.

'I didn't see his face. He was behind me all the time.'

The priestesses:
Celestina, centre,
with her two
sisters.

Bishopess Desideria

Bishopess Dilecta

Bishopesses at the altar of the Temple, celebrating Mass.

The male Mariavite hierarchy in the garden of the Temple, with the French Mariavite Marc Fatôme (extreme right); the Archbishop second from left, with Philip and Jacob to his left.

she believed, whole-heartedly, in Kowalski's polygamy. In her wimple-white innocence she went to the villages and preached polygamy to Mariavite peasants, telling the men how useful it would be to have a few women around for work and for pleasure. The men puzzled over it in silence, but their wives spoke up and ridiculed the Archpriestess. 'Just put two wives in the same kitchen and you'll see. As for the bed, with all the kids in it, well . . .' Sweet, genteel Isabel had no idea how cramped families were in their one-room cottages. The cloister had large kitchens and the 'God-minded' were up in their choir, contemplating the altar and not a table with a pile of unpeeled potatoes.

The contrast between the two sisters of Bethany applied to the Temple of Mercy and Love, revealing now its merciful, now its ironic facet. The contemplative Marys, elected to mystical marriage, were by virtue of their spiritual advance enjoying the lower pleasures of the body as well, while the hard-working Marthas (*służebne*), who belonged to 'the serving choir', the lowest one spiritually, were in practice too tired physically to sanctify their flesh on Kowalski's sofa. They overheard this and that, sensed the injustice, and so they complained, usually in the confessional, and sometimes to the Most Reverend Father. But he would dismiss such grumbling with the wave of a hand. Work harder still and seek the will of God in humility. Again they trusted him. He was so learned, so pious. The serving Sisters rarely left the cloister for good.

Manically active, Kowalski appreciated good work and praised those who deserved praise. In this he was just. Every nun I spoke to mentioned his basic fairness. But he hated grumpy faces around. Smile, smile, he would say. 'Don't make yourself uglier than you are. The ugly ones will not be admitted to heaven.' Did he mean the Third Heaven? A cruel remark by any account. However, it occurs to me now that in the apocalyptic aura of the Temple, statements like this might have been taken literally by the busy Marthas. They probably thought: Well, the Most Reverend Father must have heard that in one of his understandings.

Kowalski was prone to sudden outbursts. The nuns recognized the violence of his temper by the sound of his steps and, like mice, would run into corners to avoid meeting him face to face, and the poor uglies ran fastest.[1] He could be crude and utter the first word that came to his head. Once he barked at a group of nuns: 'What are you doing here? Farting in unison?'

Yet the economic truth was, as usual, simple. The Marthas kept the whole establishment going. I often asked which of the many businesses

[1] The phrases about the ugly ones and the running are quoted exactly as I heard them.

attached to the Plock cloister brought most income. And the answer was the same: the cheap restaurant in town, the bakery (excellent cakes for one-tenth of a zloty), the soda water factory, and also the embroidery workshop which, though less profitable, was famous all over the country. If you want a splendid banner, people said, order it from the Mariavites in Plock. Since the Little Mother began this particular workshop, even the 'God-minded' Sisters lent their spiritual fingers to marry silk thread with needles.

Apart from commercial ventures (big parishes outside Plock had them too), there was the maintenance of the whole cloister to be looked after. So the good Marthas made underwear, habits, and chasubles, they produced shoes and stockings, not to mention the work in the vegetable gardens, the cooking for the community of over five hundred, and the usual domestic chores. In the bakery alone nearly two hundred loaves of bread (weight one kilo each) had to be made for consumption at the cloister, not counting rolls and special bread for the elderly and the sick. As for the other services that were needed, their sheer size impressed most witnesses. And the visitors were welcome.

The Archbishop knew that the best propaganda came from eye-witnesses, so he wanted them to see the Mariavites at their home, especially after the trial of 1928, when he himself needed a new public image.[1] He instructed the Sisters to show the charitable works at the cloister and in Felicjanów where a nursery for illegitimate babies[2] was run by Dr. Kopystyński, one of the most admirable Mariavites, who gave up the directorship of a military hospital to work for the destitute and the outcasts.[3]

People commented on the model cleanliness of each Mariavite institution and workshop. Hygiene was to the Little Mother a spiritual thing. If your soul is in order, she would say, you will keep everything else in order. The pure in spirit use soap. Clean from the sandal to the wimple; from the nun sweeping the floor to the priestess at the altar.

4

In the past the Archbishop had been liable to change his mind when sorting out the live embodiments of his Song of Songs. Now this wife now that

---

[1] In 1934 a well-illustrated pamphlet was published in Plock, *At the Mariavites* (*U Mariawitów*). It purports to be the work of a visiting reporter, but is clearly the Archbishop's own trumpet blowing.

[2] In a pastoral letter (12 April 1929) Kowalski urged the Mariavites to accept any illegitimate child into care without payment.

[3] His conversion was typical. During a psychic crisis he entered a small chapel—he didn't know what denomination it was—and suddenly he felt the presence of God. When he learnt it was a Mariavite church, he chucked his career and came to Plock with his wife.

wife would take precedence over the others, with the exception of Abishag-Isabel who stayed fixed and accepted all. It is amusing to read some of Kowalski's Biblical footnotes, in which his female galaxy appears rearranged in his own mystical sky. Probably the Archbishop got tired of these adjustments after the final escape of Sister Love, and opted for a hierarchical order.

This he achieved by raising twelve of his priestesses to the rank of bishop. More chasubles, more diadems, and more croziers had to be made by the patient Marthas. The number of priestesses was to increase—in fact he ordained over a hundred (including the deaconesses)—while the apostolic twelve was to comprise the bishopesses only. Isabel was their Archpriestess. Since Kowalski rushed things and loved liturgical display, there was soon some overcrowding at the altar. Celebrating Mass in a group is applying ritual to traffic regulations, and the touchy among the bishopesses jostled for positions near the altar. There were apparently scenes of sacerdotal peevishness punctuated with catty asides. Look at the way she waddles; then a sisterly whisper: Your lisp is getting worse, dear. But there must be, after all, thousands of clerical jokes in this vein.

The Archbishop beamed with confidence and told tales of supernatural wonder. The Temple was only a beginning, a mere antechamber to the Temple of Temples, which they would eventually build. He drew plans in his head, pushing the Vistula back and extending the gardens. Angels would walk in them. And you—he would turn to the bishopesses—you are the twelve stars of the new heaven which is unfolding. He improvised fantastic names for them and gave them queendoms within the Kingdom. She who loved him most—he was still testing them—would possess a realm of such great beauty that Solomon in all his splendour had never seen the like of it; and so forth. For there are many mansions and palaces in the Little Mother's Third Heaven, and after the purging of the world by fire every one of them will be brought down to earth.

At this point Kowalski would spin yarns of terror, and they shuddered, listening to him. When I heard about them from the witnesses—for like frightened children they remembered every detail—I began to wonder how the Archbishop managed to keep the Demon of Noon at bay, with all those diadems catching sparks from the luminosity of the arch-tempter. Ah! Let's have a preventive measure—and he thought one up. The Archbishop introduced prayers for the conversion of the devils. A special Mass with this intention was celebrated by the priestesses in October 1929. Kowalski's mind was already attuned to Lermontov's 'Demon' and, no doubt, he must have heard of Victor Hugo's poetic plea in *La fin de Satan*.[1]

---

[1] Several years ago Giovanni Papini got in trouble with the Vatican for arguing, in *Il Diavolo*

But most important of all, the peasant in him understood the rural mentality. The prayers for the devils delighted the simple Mariavites. Good, they said, this should keep the rascals out of mischief for a bit. Kowalski recorded with approval a little folk story which was sent to Plock from a village:

> When God was about to throw the devil into the pit, he said: 'Off with you, Satan! into the eternal fire you go, for ever and ever', but he didn't finish it with *Amen*. So Satan said to himself: 'Well, I am not yet lost, since the Creator didn't say his *Amen*.' And he's still hoping, the devil is.

Sapientia rustica. The Archbishop had a proof that his instinct was right. He connected the idea of conversion with the priesthood of women. Didn't the demon of Lermontov's poem seek redemption through the woman he loved? And wasn't the hell-bound Faust saved at the crucial moment through the intercession of Gretchen?

More and more the Archbishop was turning his volatile mind to the feminine force in the cosmos. Through the sacrament of priesthood it could be transformed into a new redemptive energy. In the early 1930s, despite his troubles with the law, Kowalski had constant brain waves, bringing him fresh ideas and connecting them with those he had outlined in *The Work of Great Mercy*. Now, a sort of system was emerging from his trials and errors. The cloister at Plock was his experimental station: there he tested his ideas in the mystical marriages, in polygamy, and in the sacerdotal innovations. Equally important was the release of his own sexual energies which (if we are to believe his autobiographical confessions) had been suppressed by the vow of chastity until he was fifty. It seems that sexual experience liberated his mind as much as his genitals. And if we want to see Freudian symbolism in the writer's tool, Kowalski's pen became a very busy organ as well. He finished the translation of the whole Bible, a gigantic task even though he relied much on the early Polish versions; he translated the *Divine Comedy* and supplied it with extensive notes (again using and acknowledging other authorities); he produced a commentary on the Apocalypse, a book his followers regard as essential reading. Besides that, he wrote a few sets of consecutive articles for his periodicals, not to mention polemical pieces and short pamphlets.

Isabel was from the beginning involved in his intellectual activities. Like Tolstoy's wife she copied her husband's work in progress, seated in the room next to his. He liked having a companion nearby. And what was written

---

(1954), that the devil would finally be redeemed. Had Kowalski lived at that time, he would have defended Papini with passion.

went down to the cellars beneath his office, where the printing machines were installed and the trained nuns set up the manuscripts in type, read the proofs, and finally bound the printed pages.[1] Nothing could be more inducive to a compulsive writer (and the Archbishop was one) than to have the printing facilities so conveniently placed. He grew fat, his belly obtruding, so he preferred to write at a pulpit, standing. He covered narrow strips of paper with straight lines in a clear hand. Now and again he descended into the cellar, discussed the layout and other technical matters. The proofreaders suffered from damp, but they put up with it. Marthas always did.[2]

Sex stimulated scribbling, and after scribbling came sex for relaxation, with the mandolinists' music or without, with one of the wives or with a girl being initiated. I don't think the Archbishop let all this interfere too much with his mental gymnastics. He searched, unconsciously perhaps, for an over-all symbol, a universal premise from which everything else could be deduced. He found it in Beatrice, the eternal feminine, who before the creation of man existed as a she-angel, equal to the spirit of Mary.[3] She was finally incarnated in the Little Mother. Dante saw her on earth in Beatrice Portinari, but, when she reappeared in his celestial vision, she was a pure spirit again.

As a result of his work on the *Divine Comedy*, for which he studied Italian, Kowalski embarked on a poem in three parts (naturally) and called it *Beatrycze* in honour of the Little Mother who was born Feliksa. He linked the meaning of her name with that of Beatrice. Unfortunately, he stuck to the *terza rima*, a metre ill suited to Polish since it lacks a variety of masculine rhymes. Hard as he tried, the Archbishop could not produce verse of any distinction, and too often sacrificed sense to metre. The only interest the poem has lies in its Marian content.

By a mystical coincidence Teilhard de Chardin wrote a prose poem in March 1918 which he entitled 'The Eternal Feminine'. In form it is 'a very free paraphrase of the Book of Wisdom',[4] and the character who speaks is the enigmatic Béatrix representing the very force which 'brought the Word down to earth'. As in Kowalski's poem she is not Dante's Beatrice; Teilhard's spelling makes it clear—she is the cosmic love: 'Lying between God

[1] One usually finds the name of J. Rżysko, a priest, on Mariavite publications (he was responsible before the law), or this phrase: 'Printed at the Temple of Mercy and Love'. Kowalski, however, liked variety, so he would sometimes have his wife's name as publisher: for example, on the title-page of his version of the *Divine Comedy*.
[2] I owe most of these facts to one of the proofreaders, who has since died.
[3] Vintras, too, taught that the spirit of Mary existed before her immaculate conception. Kowalski believed in the trinity of spirits (Christ was once an angel) to which Beatrice belonged.
[4] I quote from comments by Father Henri de Lubac, S.J., in *The Eternal Feminine* (1971).

and the earth, as a zone of mutual attraction, I draw them both together in a passionate union.'

Allowing for the differences in temperament and learning, one recognizes a common concern in Teilhard's and Kowalski's concept of Beatrice.[1] Without the eternal feminine, transforming the sexual instinct, the world would be demonized into a loveless desert. At this point Kowalski parts company with Teilhard's hopeful trust in Mary the Church, his eyes flashing signals: he is all set to welcome the apocalyptic riders. The poem *Beatrycze* ends with a Mass celebrated by himself and the new priestess of the Little Mother in a place which was once his own parish. In my beginning is my end.

I had apocalyptic feelings when I first saw a Mariavite priestess consecrate the host. The year was 1971; the scene, a room in a tenement house in Plock, not far from the Temple. To reach it I had to climb a dilapidated staircase along cracked walls, passed the usual smells of cooked cabbage on the way, and bumped into a pram on a landing. Here it was, the door behind which the priestess lived, one of the oldest nuns in the movement.[2] A charming wrinkled face, her voice cultured and strong. True Franciscan poverty around her, and on the wall a portrait of her dead husband. We talked for a while. Through the window I saw the street with people going to a nearby parish church. It was Sunday. Could I attend her Mass? I asked hesitantly. Yes, of course. Soon a few women arrived and I was led into the next room. It was a chapel, spotlessly clean, in the best Mariavite tradition, with an almost gay altar. The Virgin of Perpetual Succour on one side and the Little Mother on the other, looking at the wicked world sideways. The priestess pronounced the words of liturgy beautifully with a lilt in her Polish that reminded one of the language spoken by the gentry before the First World War.

I began to imagine I was hearing the last Mass on earth, the hooves of the four riders piercing the sky above my head. The flowers on the altar could not appease the invisible threat. But I was also at a beginning, one of the beginnings not yet comprehended. Behind the monstrance there was another photograph: the Little Mother on her death-bed, with a belly like a mound threatening to explode. A birth in death. In my end is my beginning.

---

[1] Kowalski cannot have been acquainted with Teilhard's work, which became known only after his death in 1955. What seems fascinating in both is the unconscious yearning after the ancient sources of worship. By marrying his priestesses Kowalski re-enacted (without knowing it) the Sumerian ceremony of the 'divine marriage', in which the king took a chosen priestess as his bride, she representing the goddess Inanna.

[2] She was one of those who remained faithful to the teaching of Kowalski after the split in the movement.

If this woman before me, breaking the wafer over the chalice, was like one of the apostles, would I perhaps meet her on the road to Emmaus?

> There is always another one walking beside you,
> Gliding wrapt in a brown mantle, hooded.
> I do not know whether a man or a woman.

A man or a woman. Should one identify the sex of a sacramental sacrifice? And is one always supposed to divide in order to know? The priestess gave her blessing: Go in peace.

And so I went.

9
Adam after the Fall

I

AMBITION was Kowalski's driving force, propelled by his sexual curiosity. Both augmented his fantasies until he dreamt up a vast glass cupola over his Plock kingdom, which would cover paradisiacal gardens, vineyards, a new big temple, new cloisters, nurseries, schools for those born without original sin, and so forth. Sometimes the way he talked, especially in the presence of his priestesses, seemed to bring the dream close to reality. Yes, he could do it all: a gesture, a sudden understanding, and behold! the new Kubla Khan did 'a stately pleasure-dome decree'.

Like all obsessional men who have absolute power—be it Napoleon, Mussolini, or Stalin—Kowalski acted out his fantasies in public and aloud. He was good at monologues, and after years of this, he could hardly distinguish between what was plausibly grandiose and gigantically impossible. Within the Mariavite domain dreams were treated as the realizable property of the Holy Ghost, and who knew better what was going on in the upper kingdom than the diviner of dreams, John Maria Michael? Kowalski admired strong men—absolutists always do—and the 1930s, his potential decade, was also the decade of dictators. Contagious ideas were in the air. More and more Kowalski lapped up the language of adulation. The Mariavites called him 'Our Leader' (*Wódz*), 'Who-like-God Michael', 'the beloved Son'; they showered his inexhaustible vanity with epithets in speeches of welcome and in print. Those who were soon to vote him out of office, Bishop Philip among them, excelled in panegyrics.

There were other signs of the times in the movement: a Mariavite youth organization, the Templarians (*Templariusze*), which was modelled on similar ventures of the Pilsudski regime and elsewhere (Soviet Russia and Italy included). The Templarians were drilled, wore uniforms, and marched in a military fashion.[1] The organization was Bishop Philip's personal

---

[1] Their units included boys and girls, had bands and banners. Special periodicals were published for them. The Templarian as a chosen name suggested a hidden link with the Knights Templars who brought the knowledge of the oriental rites to medieval Europe.

success. Tall and handsome, he looked splendid in a Templarian blue cap.

The children of the mystical marriages created a special educational problem, for the Archbishop wanted them brought up as a group apart. They were the guinea pigs of the new Apocalypse, kept in isolation so that they would not be contaminated by the world which was doomed to perdition. In another sense they represented a curious experiment, something between a kibbutz, a kindergarten, and a Soviet orphanage, with communal virtues impressed on their minds day after day.

The Archbishop's decade it certainly was, if we consider the boldness of his reforms. One might speculate whether he would have produced so many surprises out of his mitre, had it not been for the court cases which had bedevilled him. But the desire to astound and provoke was part of his nature. During her life the Little Mother had checked his impulses, those ones especially which aimed at building a provisional theology around her person. But once she was gone, Kowalski the reformer took over, a St. Paul combined with a Boullan. He sent out epistles to his parishes as if he had the seven churches of Asia under his pastoral care.[1] One of them, the Philadelphic Church, he soon restored in spirit and in flesh, the flesh being provided by the mystical couples. One day his policy was to reconstitute what was ancient and forgotten, the next to abolish what seemed to him a mere vestige of papal domination.

Towards the end of 1921 he had begun giving communion in two kinds, first to the elect whom he was preparing for the nuptials of the Lamb, then, on the anniversary of Kozlowska's death, to all. He solved the question of hygiene (always important to the Mariavites) by designing a chalice with a glass container inside it for the sacral wine. The hosts were placed round the container and could easily be taken out, dipped in the wine, and given to a considerable number of people. In the summer of 1973 I witnessed communion in two kinds administered at San Damiano in Assisi, but the same cup was passed from person to person. Half a century earlier Kowalski solved the question intelligently.

His next reforms were linked with one another. He gave communion to infants at baptism. Weren't they at their purest then?—why not reinforce one sacrament with the other. That was what the followers of Hus did in the fifteenth century.[2] But he abolished the sacrament of extreme unction. Holy oils? he asked. There is no evidence for them in the New Testament.

---

[1] Between 1909 and 1935 he issued 40 pastoral letters.

[2] The communion of infants was urged in the Eucharist hymns of the Taborites ('let us not deny it to little children'). In the diary of a Mariavite priestess I found a moving description of a Mass celebrated by her, at the end of which she gave communion to her three-year-old daughter, whose name day it was.

No sprinkling with holy water either. And since the Eucharist came before the Crucifixion, he abolished the gloom of Holy Week, and told the Mariavites to ring the bells even on Good Friday. For in his Passion, Christ triumphed over evil and pain; you should rejoice, and not put on hypocritical expressions of sorrow. Neither should you indulge in any *pompes funèbres* by dressing up Christ's tombs in churches. Who told you to adore his grave? He is life. Glorify his open tomb instead: the meaning of Easter is rebirth.

There was a good deal of innate intelligence in Kowalski's ruthless pruning of Christian appendages, for which he usually blamed the money-grubbing clergy. Statues, miracles, and sprinkling with holy water—he would have none of that. He had come a long way since his own pious exercises during the early crises. When, however, he decided to make the oral confession a matter of choice he was looking ahead towards the sin-free Kingdom of God. For the pure all things will be pure. The children born of the mystical marriages will inherit the earth cleansed by fire, all sinners gone and finished with. So no more spiritual accountancy for a thousand years.

Yet there was still a genuine need of individual confessions now that the Mariavite women could go to the priestesses.[1] Reports to this effect came from the parishes where priestesses had replaced priests. A direct woman-to-woman unburdening of souls had an obvious therapeutic value. After all, that was how the 'self-accusations' worked, and the Archbishop had used them as a psychological weapon in the big clash of consciences over the marriages in 1922.

And the Mariavite Kubla Khan did decree. The glass dome was somewhere in the sky ready to descend on the New Jerusalem at Plock. In preparation for this third reign Kowalski announced his last great innovation, universal priesthood (*powszechne kapłaństwo*). This he did in 1930, only a few months after launching the priesthood of women. To some of his critics it appeared to be a contradictory action. Why have both? The Archbishop argued in his pastoral letter that once again the Mariavites were going back to the practice of the early Christians. Every apostle was a priest then. Did Christ ever consecrate any bishops? A good democratic sentiment, no doubt, although Kowalski himself had no intention of relinquishing his title of Archbishop. Like a dictator wearing a peasant's cap outside his palace he wanted to be identified with the common lot.

'The People's Mass' was the result of the priesthood for all. Any Mariavite could celebrate it provided he received permission from his bishop and

[1] As a rule the priestesses could not confess men, except those who were seriously ill.

was instructed in the liturgical form of the Mass. The prayers were brief and built around consecration, the central act. The whole sequence was meant to take no more than ten minutes. Of course, the People's Mass was bound to be abused and, indeed, before long worried priests began to send their warnings. The Archbishop took them as another proof that his male priests could not keep up with the pace of the Holy Spirit.

After the split in his church in 1935, the Archbishop encouraged individuals to make use of universal priesthood, dispatched his permissions by letter to those 'who were worthy' and printed enthusiastic reports about the new Mass in his official periodical. Today, seeing how a crisis is affecting all the churches, one is inclined to admire Kowalski for his foresight. In some Communist countries (in China, for instance) the Christians are left to themselves while their priests are either in prison or deported. The time of the catacombs may yet return and the prophecy of *religio depopulata* prove true. A hunted or an isolated Christian may have to become his own priest. The mad Archbishop, as some Catholics called him, had a madman's vision which the sane were unable to admit as a possibility out of fear or narrow-mindedness.

One side of Kowalski's character was earth-bound and practical despite his fantasies and increasing paranoia; he saw that the Mariavite holdings were shrinking, there were no new parishes (he confirmed that in print in 1934), and the immense costs of the trial forced him to sell some property in the provinces and a few churches (in Warsaw, for example). The Roman Catholic hierarchy paid well for the churches (according to Kowalski)—the fewer they were, the sooner the sect would disperse. The People's Mass then might one day become a remedy for the Mariavites in diaspora. This, too, must have crossed his mind, an icy flash across his euphoria.

Much as he hated the papal supremacy, he made a gesture of reconciliation in October 1929, a year after his trial. In an open letter to the Catholic bishops he implied that the Mariavites would be willing to discuss their return to the fold. From a tactical point of view he chose an awkward moment: he was still waiting for the decision of the Court of Appeal. But perhaps he wanted to appear helpless. The exiled Archbishop Edward Ropp,[1] attached to the Clerical Court in Warsaw, replied and a correspondence ensued (published by Kowalski in 1930). It is a fascinating exchange of letters, although the Catholic side must have wondered whether Kowalski was in earnest. If so, he should first admit his theological errors, eat a big humble pie, and then a solution might be found. Prompted by a few questions, tactfully worded, Kowalski wrote a sequence of epistolary tracts,

[1] Ropp was the Archbishop Metropolitan of Mogilev and had had to leave Soviet Russia.

seething with impassionate learning, and sent them off to Warsaw at short
intervals. Archbishop Ropp sat tight and pondered. When in December the
Court of Appeal upheld the verdict of 1928, he replied from a position of
strength, but tediously. He was no match for Kowalski.

The Mariavite leader scored point after point, whether quoting examples
of papal mistakes in the past or querying the grounds for celibacy. The
Fathers of the Church, he writes, tell us that

> the apostles had wives, lived with them, conceived children, therefore they
> knew best whether the state of virginity was advisable to the servants of
> God. . . . Not only the soul but also the body with all its inclinations,
> senses, and reproductive functions God created pure, holy, and perfect.
> Therefore the sensual awareness of the bodily pleasure is in no way worse
> than the sincere pleasure derived from the spirit—it is almost impossible in
> any case to separate the one from the other. . . . God created marriage
> perfect and put its perfection above the solitude of Adam, saying: 'It is not
> good that the man should be alone.' Let us not say that it is good and even
> better for a man to stay alone than to be married, since God said otherwise.

Certainly, this is morality infused with common sense: the long letter to
Ropp of 8 December 1929 is one of the best things Kowalski wrote. If
Mariavitism managed to remove some odour of death from religion, it was
thanks to the Archbishop's belief in the undivided human nature.

A more intimate tone characterizes the exchange of letters between
Kowalski and his former colleague at St. Petersburg Academy, Z. Łoziński,
now the Catholic Bishop of Pinsk.[1] Łoziński was a Mariavite at the beginning of the movement, so he knew the theological issues involved. Perhaps
out of this knowledge he addressed Kowalski in his first letter as 'My poor
John'. And the poor John took it well. He was most anxious to have a
dialogue. And again he didn't meet his match. Łoziński waffled and sighed
piously, while Kowalski hammered his points relentlessly. You tell me to
beg forgiveness—why should I? It was Rome and your bishops who 'threw
us out by force'. If we come now towards you, we come with our flock,
our wives and our children. Kowalski implied they were equal parties and
ticked Łoziński off for thinking otherwise. No Canossa for the Mariavites.

Of course, Kowalski cheated over polygamy, saying nothing about it and
suggesting that the trial was only lies, lies, lies.[2] Maybe he thought: these

[1] Which meant that his pastoral work was done in a predominantly Greek Orthodox area; he
had fewer souls to look after than the Mariavite Archbishop. The published volume includes
one letter from Bishop Jacob and one from Bishop Andrew, who were also Łoziński's colleagues at St. Petersburg. But the correspondence is dominated by Kowalski.
[2] He accuses the Papal Nuncio and the bishops of responsibility for his prosecution. Rome
always protects her own culprits. Here his love of numerology comes into play: 'If the
evidence of my immortality was written not on 666 pages in folio, as it is now, but on 6666

two stuffed owls—how could they ever comprehend the secret of the multipliable Three? But the correspondence is much to the Archbishop's credit. If only he had been born later and could have attended the Vatican Council. What an agile polemicist he would have made. The conservative Catholics accused him of rocking the boat. In a letter to Ropp (24 November 1929) he quotes Pius IX who, on hearing *ad nauseam* the confident dictum that the boat of Peter could never sink, is reported to have answered: 'It won't sink, but all those in the boat may have to jump into the water.'

Kowalski must have copied this *risposta* with a splendid apocalyptic grin on his face.

But the demons of the Apocalypse were catching up with him. The higher you climb the lower we will push you. The Archbishop had to grow a thicker skin (his own was tough enough) to get used to the mockery of the mob. Vendors outside the central station in Warsaw waved broadsheets with the latest song, 'How Bishop Kowalski amused himself with the mandolinists'. They shouted the title with relish.[1] Tellers of jokes recited dirty verses about him. One of these listed famous Poles. A popular tenor was coupled with a discus-throwing Olympic lady, a famous pianist with the Mariavite Archbishop, in answer to the question, What are they famous for?

> Konopacka for her discus,
> Kiepura for his mouth,
> Paderewski for his fingers,
> Father Kowalski for his balls.[2]

On 22 October 1929 the Archbishop had to face another trial, held again at the County Court in Plock and presided over by the same judge, Momentowicz. The prosecution had taken a few months to prepare the evidence, which concerned the 'blasphemous' character of Kowalski's version of the Bible. The Catholic Church and the Pope were the chief targets of his blasphemy, it was charged. The case was heard *in camera* and the Archbishop was sentenced to a year's imprisonment, later reduced to six months.[3] The Mariavite press reported the verdict with a touch of understandable weariness.

After the Court of Appeal upheld the verdict of the original trial for

---

pages . . . and collected from all over Poland during 33 years I would not have been condemned at the trial' (meaning, had he remained a Catholic priest).

[1] The Students' Association of the University of Poznan invited Kowalski to a ball on 23 January 1932. The invitation was addressed to 'Bishop Kowalski and his orchestra'.
[2] In the original: 'Konopacka dyskiem,/Kiepura pyskiem,/Paderewski palcami,/Ksiądz Kowalski jajcami.' The list ended with the old Marshal, as usual.
[3] A first appeal against this verdict failed in 1930, and a second in 1931. Meanwhile Kowalski's translation of the Old Testament was banned after 1929.

sexual offenses, Catholic opinion clamoured for Kowalski's imprisonment. Why is he still in Plock? Who is protecting this pervert? Among the Mariavites, too, voices of dissent were louder and coming from different quarters. But when a second appeal was tried, on 15 February 1931, one of the judges exercised his *votum separatum*—a fact of which the Mariavites make much to this day. The High Court, however, on 22 October 1931 confirmed the verdict of guilty against the Archbishop.

2

As months and then years passed without his being required to serve his sentence, Kowalski was lulled by preparations for the twenty-fifth anniversary of his consecration in Utrecht. Two Englishmen who were to become Mariavites saw Kowalski in Plock a few weeks before the jubilee, and had no doubt that he was in full control as he appeared to them, surrounded by his bishopesses.

On the eve of his anniversary, 4 October 1934, the General Chapter met and Kowalski faced some criticism. He answered questions in a subdued voice, offering amends. In fact, neither he nor the priests gathered for the jubilee wanted to spoil the festive mood. Moreover, the priests renewed their vows before Kowalski in the Temple. The plotters behaved like the assassins of Caesar, flattering him to excess before the final blow. And they had every opportunity to do so. For the jubilee became a continous eulogy in honour of John Maria Kowalski winged with the Archangel's name. All his appellations were declined in the seven cases of his native tongue. Michael 'Who-like-God', Our Leader, Our Dearest Brother Archbishop; of whom the Lord said to the Little Mother, 'This is my beloved Son', and so on.

The jubilee number of *The Kingdom of God on Earth* is a sixteen-page-long panegyric with a few dreadful poems besides: signatures follow each tribute and though the praises are tedious to read, the full list of names represents a documentary record of some value, especially as this particular issue is hard to obtain. (I possess a battered copy.) On the front page a stern photograph of the Archbishop shows him with a crozier, his right hand touching his heart under the monstrance embroidered on the heavy chasuble he was wearing for the occasion. The protruding fleshy lips look like a double seal over the secrets of the elect. Indeed, the man embodied the history of Mariavitism from its beginnings in 1900. Even those who plotted against him couldn't help feeling proud on the day of his jubilee. He was in each of them. The faithful Marthas of the Temple declared their loyalty in these words: 'Even though the whole world abandons you we shall stand by you always.'

There were special prayers, speeches, music, banquets, and gifts. A car, for instance, worth 15,000 zloty, was bought with the money collected from all parishioners. The Templarians marched with banners unfurled and saluted the Archbishop who stood outside the Temple with the whole Mariavite hierarchy assembled: the bishops, leaders from the provinces, priestesses, and, above all, his wives. There is a photograph showing them all, Kowalski in the middle as benevolent as a Pope, Archpriestess Isabel next to him, and Bishop Philip towering over the crowd with his Templarian cap on. In a few months he would drive a spiritual dagger into his Leader's back. *Et tu, Jonatha?*

Philip Feldman was born into a middle-class family (his father supplied building material to a railway company). At the age of four he lost his father and was later brought up by a priest who had aristocratic connections and introduced the young man to provincial high life. Philip acquired social graces as well as friends, at the Polytechnic in Tallin enjoyed the *Kameraden-schaft* of a posh student club, looked and behaved like a Heidelberg *Bursche*, making more friends in the process (some of whom proved useful in his later contacts with the government). His foster father joined the clandestine Mariavite congregation and through him again the young man was put in touch with the high-ups in Plock when the movement had already broken away from Rome. The Little Mother took to him at once, she recognized his potential, and before long Philip was a novice, having abandoned his engineering studies for good.

From the start he was the blue-eyed boy of the new movement, in which his versatile talents found many different outlets, both social and spiritual. During the First World War the Little Mother entrusted him with an important job: he ran the Mariavite hospital in the cloister. A hundred beds were provided for the wounded soldiers, mainly German, but owing to Feldman's humanitarian fervour, Russian casualties were also looked after. His knowledge of foreign languages was an asset in dealing with the military authorities.

After the Little Mother's death he came closer to Kowalski and the big crisis over the mystical marriages sealed their bond of friendship. David discovered his Jonathan. From that time on Bishop Philip was regarded as Kowalski's second-in-command, polygamy included. The Archbishop could be whimsical in the choices of partners, now and again coupling the quick with the dead, but Philip was too alive, too handsome, and the nuns dreamt of having him rather than some venerable Mariavite from the other side of the grave. Sister Love, Kowalski's *femme fatale* if ever there was one in his polygamous set-up, preferred the willowy Philip to the Most Reverend Father with his powerful paunch. Her two escapes from the cloister were apparently due to this conflict; her return, one may assume, was due to the same reason, i.e. the magnetic attraction of the best-looking Mariavite. Did the old man recognize his potential rival?

There was a curious incident when the two pillars of the Temple, Jacob and Philip, went on a missionary expedition to the United States to win the wicked land for the Slavonic Pope. Neither knew any English. Philadelphically bound at home, they went to Philadelphia abroad. The Archbishop didn't seem all that enthusiastic, so instead of allowing the bishops to travel with their official wives, he attached two of his to this quixotic venture, no doubt to keep two pairs of eyes on the absent pillars. For he took as much pleasure in coupling as in separating people. The mission was, judging by Philip's own diary, a mixture of pathetic incidents (they preached in Polish to baffled Negroes) and misguided hopes. Still, they bumped into the inevitable millionaire who could have solved their problem with one fat cheque, but didn't. And, the oddest encounter of all, they met Eugene O'Neill who must have scrutinized the priestesses with a playwright's curiosity. But Philip, despite his literary pretence, had no inkling that he had met a great writer. He was toying with the idea of bringing a poor Negro boy to Plock, the first black apostle for the future. The boy was keen, and they bathed him thoroughly (Mariavite hygiene above all), but somehow the plan petered out.

The Archbishop on the other side of the Atlantic got suspicious, though they kept sending him a dollar a day as required (he expected such offerings). He thought his women were being enticed by Philip and Jacob, had slept with them and obviously had no desire to return. He became possessive and ordered them to come back.[1] Kowalski the polygamist didn't enjoy offering his concubines to the greater glory of universal love.

There were two distinct streaks in Philip's character. The first—let's call it Jonathanian—was poetic, with a touch of sentimentality. He identified himself with the romantic poet Slowacki, fashionable among his contemporaries. When the ashes of the poet were brought from Paris to Poland in 1927, Marshal Pilsudski ordered that the coffin be transported up the river by boat, all the way from Gdansk to Warsaw. Philip Feldman stood on the

---

[1] The whole crazy venture was set off by the invitation of a Polish priest once attached to the Polish National Church in America. The Mariavites co-operated with that church for a time but Kowalski soon quarrelled with Bishop Hodur, his opposite number in America, who like himself was a very ambitious man.

bank of the Vistula in the cloister gardens at Plock and watched the coffin pass, his hand romantically placed on his heart.[1] That was the moment of spiritual identification, but alas! it didn't improve his versification. During a convalescence after his critical illness in 1922, he compiled a 63-page theatrical medley, bits and pieces of mainly Messianic poetry (Slowacki being the favourite source), and this *Mysterium*[2] was soon staged with the young girls of the Temple school reciting the parts and the mandolinists providing the musical illustrations. The thing went on tour, was performed in halls or outside Mariavite churches, and everybody loved the children for being so gifted and charming. Philip travelled with his successful show and enjoyed every minute of it. Did he object to the Archbishop exceeding in his adoration of the performing girls? I have found no evidence that he did. They were David and Jonathan then, bound with the seal of the elect.

The second streak in Philip's character—let's call it Absalomian—was practical, perhaps a little envious. Those who didn't like his suave manners would have described him as 'a smooth operator', but I think his idealistic fervour was genuine and pushed him to do a great deal of intelligent planning for the Mariavite establishment. While Kowalski was devoting more time to his publishing schemes, Bishop Philip became a kind of general manager, responsible for different sections of commercial work in the cloister as well as for the affairs of the young. The boarding school, for instance, and the blue-capped Templarians were under his direct supervision. He acquitted himself admirably in each of his duties: he grew in strength, and when the time was ripe for action in 1935 Absalom turned against David—and won.

Philip Feldman has left a personal account, based on the diaries he had kept, but written after the Second World War, of the deposition and the events which followed it. For obvious reasons it is a somewhat biased account, though Philip tries to appear impartial by quoting his correspondence with Kowalski. He enumerates the reasons for Kowalski's downfall:

(1) Parish priests were gradually being replaced with priestesses. Apparently Kowalski confided to Philip that he no longer trusted the Fathers and intended to recall them all to Plock. Women alone would do pastoral work.

(2) Many parishes objected to this procedure. Some found the priestesses undignified and tactless. Philip Feldman comments that out of the twelve bishopesses only very few had sufficient schooling. Some were hardly literate.

(3) In spite of Kowalski's reassurances, his moral behaviour did cause

---

[1] This I heard from a witness who prefers to remain anonymous.
[2] See p. 102.

much concern among the Mariavite people, especially when the big trial was followed by others in which the Archbishop was charged with blasphemy for his attacks on Catholic dogma and the Pope. There were many rumours afloat and ordinary parishioners recalled odd incidents in the past, such as Kowalski's way of picking out the prettiest girls during his pastoral visits to the villages. He would invariably stop the cart in which he was being driven, talk to the girl he fancied about her vocation, and then persuade her parents to send her to the Płock cloister.

(4) Philip Feldman had contacts in Marshal Piłsudski's circle and claims that those in the know informed him of the government's intention to disband the Mariavite organization unless something radical was done about its leadership. Meanwhile Bishop Jacob (Próchniewski) reported after a tour of the Mariavite centres that the people were perturbed by what they heard about their Archbishop.

Kowalski realized the danger and, as usual, wanted to take counter-measures quickly. He summoned all the Sisters and Fathers to the refectory and announced that Bishop Philip would be in charge of the cloister under his direct supervision. To this Philip objected: he preferred to be responsible to the General Chapter alone. Kowalski lost patience and asked the Sisters to declare their allegiance openly. A great commotion took place and the majority stepped over to Philip's side. This time Isabel lost her temper and rudely told the Sisters what she thought of them. The Bishop Philip group moved to the school building and a house near the cloister, the Temple and the cloister itself remaining under the Archbishop's control.

The split was now a fact. Bishop Philip visited the Archbishop every day to discuss the new arrangement, and Kowalski seemed anxious to remain on amicable terms with him. But whatever he agreed to, he was likely to change the next day. This was due to the influence of his female entourage.

In the end Philip gave up his attempts at a compromise acceptable to both parties. The final decision lay in the hands of the General Chapter. An extraordinary meeting of the Chapter was called for 29 January 1935.[1] Thirty-nine out of the fifty members assembled in a house next to the cloister; the Archbishop was not asked to attend. (The bishopesses, including the Archpriestess, were not members of the Chapter: male supremacy was still upheld at the top, perhaps in keeping with St. Paul's advice that women should be silent in church councils.)[2] The proceedings were routine: every-

[1] I have seen the official minutes of this historic meeting.
[2] For such is Kowalski's interpretation of St. Paul's phrase, 'As in all the churches of the saints the women should keep silence' (I Corinthians 14.34). It is interesting that this very quotation should have appeared in the correspondence columns of *The Times* (London), 21 May 1973.

thing had already been decided. Kowalski was deposed. The Chapter elected Philip Feldman as his successor. The title of Archbishop was to be abolished once and for all.

The Chapter sent their demands to Kowalski: he was to return the Temple and the buildings together with all church utensils and the printing press to the new administration. The Mariavite organization considered itself relieved of all moral responsibility for the Archbishop's publications between 1921 and 1935. The last decision sounded both pompous and impracticable. To renounce such a large body of work meant to deprive the Mariavites of a great part of their heritage. What were they going to be left with, if even Kowalski's translations were to be rejected? The rebel bishops had nothing to offer instead.

The Archbishop reacted swiftly. The day after the Chapter's meeting (30 January 1935) he dispatched his own pastoral letter to the Mariavites, stating the facts. Eighty conventual Sisters, he writes, have remained with him, but nearly a hundred Sisters sided with Feldman. He admits that except for a handful all the priests have turned against him. Then the apocalyptic sound and fury take over: the rebels have no right to say Mass, for their offering is invalid (Kowalski uses the same weapon as the one he used against the Catholics), they have become blasphemers and Pharisees. Moreover, they drink vodka, smoke cigarettes, and, of course, fornicate.[1] Refuse to go to their churches, pray at home, and ask for a priestess to be sent.

The whole business had to be cleared up. A government commission came from Warsaw and ordered Kowalski to leave the Temple with his followers. The ex-Archbishop and his wife had to sign a document at the district office (*starostwo*) ceding their leadership to Bishop Philip, who assumed full powers on 13 March 1935. Late at night they were taken by car to the estate in Felicjanów which was put at Kowalski's disposal until his death. The following day eighty Sisters (the bishopesses among them) began their exodus in cars. A lorry was loaded with their belongings.

The removal itself caused much resentment on both sides. The Feldman-ites accused the Kowalskiites of stripping the cloister and the Temple.[2] The cells were abandoned in disorder as if a foreign army had ransacked them. Photographs were taken to prove this. Kowalski in turn accused the

---

[1] The last accusation is typical of the Mariavite squabbles and reveals Kowalski's obsession with sex. He didn't like imitators.

[2] The Archbishop did take with him some Mariavite treasures, the Book of Life among them. Out of curiosity I asked in 1973 what happened to the names of those who forced the Archbishop to cede power in Plock. Were they still in the Book? I didn't see any names crossed out. The reply was brief. Whichever page contained the name of a traitor, he tore it out. A true gesture of wrath. No record to be left for the angel unfolding the scroll.

Feldmanites of burning his books. Some certainly were destroyed, the Old Testament in particular; in many copies offensive pages were torn out.[1] Spiritual defumigation was on.

But those who truly suffered were the innocent ones, the good ugly Marthas, for ever busy cleaning, baking, mending shoes. They believed all that the Archbishop chose to tell them; now they heard from the new leaders that what the press had said was partly true. The effect was like that of Khrushchev's speech at the Twentieth Party Congress about the crimes of his former boss. The conventual Sisters were in a state of shock.[2] Worse victims, however, were children born of the mystical marriages. Their group was now broken up. Some of them were too small to comprehend to which parents they belonged as they were being taken away from Plock. Polygamy was over and the tragedy of the innocent about to begin.

3

So at the age of sixty-four 'Our Leader' became a Napoleon exiled to a rural island, and like Napoleon almost at once began to plot his comeback.

All the features characterizing a schism emerged in the quarrels between the two factions. The Archbishop who, like the Emperor of the French, never abdicated his title, started a paranoiac counter-campaign, more papal in his anathemas than the medieval pronouncements of the Bishops of Rome.[3] According to him Christ slammed the doors of the Plock Temple in disgust and was gone, but also the Little Mother wanted to have nothing to do with the three 'spiritual pillars' still propping up the shameful building. No salvation then outside the church of the rightful successor, i.e. himself. I agree with those defending Kowalski, who say that his apostolic wives and concubines encouraged the mean streak in his character. At times he acted without a trace of charity. No room for you, traitor, in the Book of Life, you have condemned yourself to the fire of hell. This is how he abuses the new leader of the Mariavites (in a letter written before the exodus) after addressing him as 'Dearest Brother':

> I call you Brother, although you have become the worst enemy and traitor, such as the world had not yet seen or the history of the Church

[1] When I asked a nun to show me one of Kowalski's pastoral letters which was included in his version of the New Testament, she became indignant. 'I tore the pages out years ago,' she said. Similarly, in my copy of the Old Testament in Kowalski's translation some names in footnotes are crossed out. Anathema in retrospect.

[2] I talked to a Sister in Warsaw who was a cobbler in the time of Kowalski's dominance and had no idea what was going on in the cloister.

[3] Among the notes in his version of the *Divine Comedy*, vilification of the Popes occupies much space.

known. . . . Towards me your friend who wanted to give you everything, you have become worse than Absalom, worse than the greatest of criminals. What else can I tell you? Only that a terrible fate awaits you. You are dead in the spirit and will die a despicable death in the flesh. Your name will be the symbol of a traitor worse than Judas because Judas repented and out of sorrow hanged himself. You won't do this but God will hang you and bring eternal shame on you. . . . In my eyes all of you are traitors, liars, thieves, and the usurpers of property which is not yours. . . . You have surpassed Lucifer in treachery, and sooner will he receive mercy from God than you. Therefore we shall never enter into any reconciliations or agreements with you.

Philip Feldman's answer was almost too subdued to sound sincere, but one phrase in it must have infuriated the Archbishop. 'You have become so pathetic in your anger and hatred.' Which was, unfortunately, true.

Once Kowalski moved to Felicjanów he felt even freer to pour scorn on his former lieutenants. However, he no longer had the printing presses to absorb the venom of his pen. No more cellars to which to dispatch strips of paper covered with his small handwriting. On 10 July 1935, six months after the deposition, he managed to publish a special number of the *Mariavite News* and there at last he could vent the fumes of frustration in exile. He proudly refers to his previous pastoral letters, one 'On the Abolition of the Clergy' (7 August 1930), the other 'On Universal Priesthood' (21 August 1930). Now he encourages the Mariavites to take full advantage of those harbingers of the Third Reign. Every Mariavite home should be a home of God. 'You can do without churches and chapels.'[1] The bishopesses added their own pastoral letter, in which 'Our Beloved Leader' is praised and the Mariavites resident in Plock are called Feldman's sect. As with every schism the process of separation seems to demand proofs of superiority, and a sect is a name for an inferior organism which is doomed to perish.

Alas, the position of Kowalski was far from superior. In his enforced exile he ruled over a minority with great difficulty since he was not allowed to visit the parishes. Therefore he had to adopt a schismatic pattern of self-aggrandisement through anathemas delivered against the apostates. Some prophetic backing was needed as well. Soon Kowalski had a collection of dreams remembered by his followers which, they said, had prophesied the split in Plock a few years before the event. This dreamy proof gratified him no end and he printed the tedious accounts (mainly from women) in his *Mariavite News*.

---

[1] In the *Mariavite News* of 15 September 1935 the Archbishop made it plain: 'A good Maria-vite', he wrote, 'should every day celebrate the People's Mass, receive the Lord Jesus into his entrails, walk with Jesus in his heart and adore Him.'

While the fallen Adam was neurotically raving in rural seclusion, once his own demi-paradise, Philip the angelic protector of the Philadelphic Church quietly accumulated power, mended the cracks after the split, reorganized the work in the main centres. Good on foreign relations under Kowalski, the well-travelled, urbane Philip, who spoke excellent German, could now fully exploit his talents. With some diplomatic skill, he put forward a new image of the Mariavites. They were now so clean, so good, that the anti-Papists outside Poland would have to embrace them once again. For a time he busily ordained priests and priestesses to restore the balance in the Temple, but soon the priesthood of women had to be abandoned in the hope of winning re-admission to the Union of the Old Catholics. The women regretted the loss, since they regarded priesthood as their greatest glory. The news and gossip of these developments had not far to travel to Felicjanów, and the Archbishop claimed to have his sources of information in the enemy camp. The apocalyptic Big Brother was watching them, and from time to time breathed fire in their direction.

I have collected some facts which bring to life the daily routine of the fallen Adam. He had still his galaxy of Eves, and they tried their best, in every way, to make his exile tolerable for him. They certainly wanted to reach his heart through the stomach, but he lost appetite without losing the tendency to put on weight. The maniacal desire for work remained with him. If anything, he worked harder, getting up very early. Sometimes he wrote an article before Mass which he and Isabel celebrated in turn at eight or nine o'clock. After Mass he polished the tercets of his *Divine Comedy*, translated other things, and saw those who wanted to see him. He became even more accessible than in Plock. Anyway, he had to stay put: a newly consecrated bishop, Titus (Siedlecki), did the visiting.[1]

At midday he lunched and between 1 and 2 p.m. observed an hour of recreation, walking in the park and talking with his faithful. He loved the peripatetic method of teaching and the Sisters who accompanied him on the walks remember those conversations vividly. He was convinced that he would, sooner or later, return in triumph to the Temple. Perhaps the conviction was put on for the sake of the others. The later hours of the afternoon he spent on his literary projects. Supper was at 6 p.m., and at half-past six the evening service was held. He rested afterwards, and one presumes dispensed love to the elect.

The Felicjanów estate offered simple country pleasures and he needed them, too, in order to forget his humiliations. Isabel's loyalty to him was

---

[1] Bishop Titus, resident in Lowicz, was the first to be consecrated by the bishopesses alone, in May 1935. One of the few priests who stayed with Kowalski, he died in 1946.

deeper now that his bullying fits had become less frequent. Without realizing it she was preparing herself for greater responsibilities in the near future. The Church of the Little Mother had been broken and only a spiritual miracle could put it together again.[1]

Kowalski had not much time to adjust himself to the new situation, for in the second year of his exile he had to serve his reduced prison sentence. The law was enforced partly to appease the Opposition: after the old Marshal's death the government, mainly composed of mediocrities, sought popularity in the country, and Kowalski had nobody to plead for him. Moreover, he was still harrassed by the outstanding costs of the trial.

The police took him by train to Poznan in western Poland (the first brief letter to Isabel is from Poznan, dated Thursday, 9 July 1936), then to the Rawicz prison where long-term sentences were served. To spare the Archbishop any embarrassment his guard on the train was unarmed. But the journalists knew the whole itinerary.[2] He arrived at half-past ten in the evening, was given a clean cell which reminded him of other cells ('It seems to me that I have come to a cloister for a retreat,' he writes to Isabel). He soon learnt that the building was once a Franciscan monastery. They locked him up in the right place, after all. He slept very little the first night, prayed and found peace. In the morning he said Mass in his cell, ate a prison breakfast, and started getting used to his daily routine.

Throughout his stay in Rawicz he was treated with courtesy and consideration—Poles are full of respect for priests of all denominations. He was allowed to wear the Mariavite habit. The governor of the prison was glad to have someone so unusual to talk to and found the Archbishop most amiable. Even the Catholic chaplain asked Kowalski's advice about the spiritual welfare of the prisoners. The Archbishop obliged: Give them the Scriptures to read. And copies were duly provided, though not in his translation.

Judging by the ordeals of prisoners during the occupation, Kowalski had it almost easy, except for the length of his sentence. He served eighteen months, and in fact, came expecting to serve two years.[3] There was a small restaurant, owned by a man named Falkiewicz, not far from the prison and three times a day meals were taken to him by a Mariavite nun who stayed

---

[1] The Kowalskiites were grouped in Felicjanów and on the farms nearby, which belonged to Mariavite peasants. Elsewhere Kowalski had few followers: only two families, for instance, in Cegłów, a big parish. In another place, Gozd, a minute cloister for six Sisters was maintained.
[2] Photographs from his journey to prison appeared in the *Poznan Courier*, a conservative daily which represented Catholic interests.
[3] The original (1928) sentence of two years and eight months for sexual offences had been reduced by half, but the sentence for blasphemy (1929), six months, might have been added to that time instead of being allowed to run concurrently.

for this purpose alone in a room attached to the restaurant. She carried the metal containers with food to a gate with a small window, then to the first courtyard where the guard on duty would take them and deliver them to the Archbishop's cell. The containers were never opened and examined.

At first one of Kowalski's wives (Melania) and Sister Leonia stayed in Rawicz, then Leonia was in charge of the meals for over a year, until his release.[1] Nobody from the outside, of course, could see the Archbishop in his cell, but he had visitors, sometimes once a week. He worried about their travel expenses (Plock was 200 km. away) and very probably shunned emotional disruptions. Isabel was a visitor he really wanted to see. The unhappy events had brought them close together. In her letters she called Kowalski 'Our Dearest Treasure on Earth after God'. And she was busy on his behalf trying to gain an audience with the Prime Minister and the chief prosecutor of the Court of Appeal. She still hoped that the sentence would be quashed, and telephoned every influential person she knew in Warsaw.

Kowalski found the prison routine tolerable. He rose at a quarter to six, enjoyed his daily walks which lasted half an hour, liked his fellow prisoners and they seemed to like him. He worked on his literary projects,[2] meditated, and went to bed at nine in the evening. Above all, in Sister Leonia's words, 'he got used to the silence of his cell.' His chief ambition was to finish Dante's *Paradiso* (so far he had published two parts of the *Divine Comedy*), but he also composed much bad verse in the *terza rima*. He read books and newspapers—and, what is important as a biographical source, he dispatched long letters to Isabel and his flock. He was allowed to receive and write four letters a month.[3] Some of them read like Pauline epistles, meant to be perused with devotional care by the faithful.

They have a certain theological interest, particularly in his comments on the invisible church, since he knew after the split that he could hardly afford to built 'new houses of worship'. So 'let our Temple be founded in human hearts'. In the altered circumstances he encouraged the propagation of the People's Mass ('*głoście że dla wszystkich jest to łaska*') among his scattered followers and gave practical advice on the juice from grapes to be used instead of wine. He instructed Isabel how to grant permission to those who

---

[1] I owe much of my information about Rawicz to this remarkable lady, now nearly eighty years old and still a Mariavite priestess in Warsaw. Her excellent memory, dry wit, and common sense were of great assistance to me, for which I am grateful.

[2] Kowalski must have intended to continue his memoirs which he had dictated to Isabel, for the exercise book was sent to him in prison. But it was confiscated as 'anti-religious, anti-state, immoral and critical of authority' (written in red ink at the back of the book and signed by the prison chaplain).

[3] Both his letters and those he received were censored. A letter from Isabel to him, dated 10 July 1937, bears the stamp 'Looked through'.

Letter from Kowalski, in prison at Rawicz, to Archpriestess Isabel (1936)

would not abuse the sacrament. Anyway, the Holy Spirit will show who has grace.[1] He felt inspired by the Book of Wisdom which he carefully re-read, composed psalms and variations on the Lord's Prayer (this, no doubt, under the influence of Cieszkowski's book),[2] but unfortunately, as months passed and the threat of boredom increased, he flogged the dreadful *terza rima* to death, producing reams of poetic rubbish, from cantos of his anti-Miltonic *Paradise Restored*[3] and a poem on the Lamb's nuptials,[4] to

[1] Curiously enough, a few Vintrasian miracles occurred in 1937. Peasants saying Mass saw Christ holding the host. But it didn't bleed. Kowalski distrusted miracles (Vatican-approved), though he accepted visions and dreams, from the simple souls in particular.

[2] See p. 66.

[3] He objected to Milton for making Lucifer fight God, which Kowalski said was impossible (it was a war of angels); also for denying Christ's divinity and, above all, for ignoring the Virgin Mary.

[4] A passage from this poem, called 'God's Metropolis', is typical of his manner and style:

> Cieszcie się tedy wszystkie tu narody,
> A wy najwięcej, Dziewice wybrane,
> Które Baranek wezwał na Swe Gody.

vitriolic pieces on 'the fallen Stars' of the Mariavite church, culminating in an effort called 'The Treachery of Feldman', in which he spells out his apocalyptic curses.

The whole collection of his letters from Rawicz (unpublished) amounts to three hundred foolscap pages. As a mirror of Kowalski's mind, undergoing a process of purification (his phrase) in accordance with the Will of God, the letters are indeed revealing. His vulnerable pride and humility are there, also his desire to dominate, even at a distance.[1] But a curious weakness can be detected as well; he wants to be pampered and adored.

Certainly his women missed no opportunity to flatter him in print. The periodical *The Kingdom of God on Earth*, now appearing at Felicjanów, became the Archbishop's trumpet and the priestesses were blowing it on St. Michael's day, on Christmas (his birthday), and on other anniversaries. They turned him into a martyr, their great Leader enchained and suffering for the sins of others. 'Don't praise me too much,' he protested in a letter. It looks 'as if you were already writing my obituary'. But later he reports that he showed the number in question to some visiting journalists. Let them see who I am.

The loving Sisters kept sending him food, and again he protested it was too much. But he liked dry sausage, butter, and honey. A jar with honey broke in a parcel. He told them to be more careful. When they asked his advice on practical matters, he answered briefly and to the point. 'Yes, thrash the corn', or 'Sell oats and clover if you have a surplus'. He remembered the Mariavite farmers in the neighbourhood of Felicjanów and mentioned them by name; he always knew how to respect the dignity of peasants.

Two of his priestesses tried apostolic work among men and were shocked to hear their indecent suggestions. Kowalski reprimanded them in his next epistle. Don't you remember what the press was saying about us? Those men think you practise free love. Go and preach to your own sex. No men. But without him the women were at times getting on one another's nerves. The inner circle, too, suffered from the oldest monastic vice: jealousy. Celestina and Dilecta, Dilecta and Celestina, not to mention Emma,

---

Będzie was pieścił i będzie całował
Wiecznie prześliczny i wiecznie Pan-młody.
Żadnej nie będzie objęć Swych żałował,
Lecz będzie z każdą, jak w Komunii świętej
W pokoju Swoim z miłością obcował.

('Rejoice then all you nations/ and most of all you chosen Virgins/ Whom the Lamb has called to His Nuptials./ He will caress you and will kiss you/ He for ever beautiful, for ever a young Bridegroom./ He will not begrudge one of you His embraces,/ But lovingly make each of you stay/ In His room as in the Holy Communion.')

[1] The women he left behind vied for his attention. Those on the lower rungs felt neglected in his letters so he ticks them off for being petty.

Eufemia, and the second Sister Love.[1] Like Solomon, the Archbishop pronounced: 'What Sister Celestina has, Sister Dilecta hasn't got, and vice versa'. And the old man knew what he was talking about.

In a similar way he pacified the Sisters who were not yet fully fledged nuns. Tell them, he writes to his first wife, 'that I love Sister Marynia without the veil as much as Sister Flora with the veil.' One does believe him: a Freudian comment would be too obvious. He had special words for Sisters who were working hard in the garden, the kitchen, the laundry, in the fields and tending the cows.

Every letter, however contained special praise and tender endearments for Isabel his Abishag, as if he wanted during his absence to reaffirm that she was his successor.[2] 'My most beloved little Isabel [*Izabelko*]. You are most dear to me because in you I see the portrait of the Little Mother.' He would sign his letter: 'With all my heart your Husband and thine in particular.' 'Your' (*wasz*) refers to the other mystical wives. Now and again he had to scold her, otherwise she might not have believed it was her super-spouse writing. The most beloved little Isabel should not 'in her letters jot down gossip from the Plock Masons' (meaning the Feldman group) 'because here in the Poznan district they take us for Masons too.' Poor Catholics were now so confused about the Mariavites, and the Mariavites themselves after the split didn't quite know who was who.[3]

They had Sister Secrecy and Sister Suspicion in their midst, both veiled.

4

'War is approaching,' Kowalski wrote from prison almost with prophetic relief. In 1937, contrary to the signs, most people didn't believe it would come, and the colonels in the post-Pilsudski government pretended all was well along the German frontier. Unconsciously, the Archbishop wanted his misery to end with a bang. In all apocalyptic thinking calamities precede Christ's kingdom on earth.

Ah! that's it!—he exclaimed when he read about Mussolini restoring the Imperium Romanum—the end is nigh.[4] Splendid. With Blake-like simplicity he felt his visionary powers were back. He had his great moment of

---

[1] Sending his greetings from Rawicz he seems to observe the following order: Celestina, Dilecta, Honorata, Melania, Desideria, Eufemia, Emma.
[2] Celestina and Dilecta came after Isabel. Now they are in the Council of Three with the present Archbishop who succeeded Isabel as leader.
[3] Meanwhile Philip Feldman announced that Kowalski was no longer a Mariavite. This reminded the Archbishop of the priest possessed by the Demon of Noon who 'removed the Little Mother from the Mariavite church'. (See p. 44.)
[4] The restoration of the Roman Empire was among apocalyptic prophecies.

illumination when the whole cell was bathed in light and he understood beyond understanding the feminine mystery in the Three. The experience seemed so intense that it filled him with gratitude and he 'kissed the walls of the cell'.[1] He returned from Rawicz more Mariavite than ever, convinced that the Little Mother was with God at the creation of the world.

The return itself was described in raptures for the readers of *The Kingdom of God on Earth*. He was released on 9 January 1938.[2] About twenty people greeted him in a guest room at Falkiewicz's restaurant near the prison from which Sister Leonia used to carry his meals. Archpriestess Isabel, tense with emotion, was there. A car arrived to take them to the station, and some local people, Sister Leonia remembers, asked Kowalski to bless them. On the train he and his party had a separate compartment. Kowalski was in excellent mood all the way, chatting, cracking jokes, and despite tiredness looking almost triumphant. 'Who-like-God' Michael was spreading his wings again. At Felicjanów the whole community and the Mariavites from the neighbouring farms had to wait patiently since the train was delayed.

Snow fell and the flat landscape began to glow in the evening, a good sign of welcome. When the clock struck ten, someone shouted with excitement: 'They're coming, they're coming!' And a taxi-cab appeared in the drive. Lamps were brought to the windows. 'Our beloved Leader, prophesied by the poet Slowacki, has arrived.' He entered, said the Mariavite greeting, 'Let us praise the Most Holy Sacrament', and without exchanging a word with anyone walked into the chapel. A thanksgiving Mass was celebrated until midnight, then he took off his chasuble and accepted the homage of his faithful. They all kissed his hands, visibly moved; many sisters cried. Though it was late, a ceremonial supper began and lasted two hours.

John Maria Michael seeing so much love around him could well have thought that his purification had ended his troubles. But he had aged in prison and his belly protruded in the likeness of the Little Mother on her death-bed. A photograph taken on the day of his release and reproduced in his periodical shows a barrel of a man. It could have been a caricature of a fat vicar waddling towards his next meal. His obesity was, in fact, an illness. He had a bad liver condition. The prison doctor had put him in a hospital cell for a time and placed a card with '*Obesitas*' over his bed. Seeing

---

[1] If we accept this mystical phenomenon—and why shouldn't we?—two facts are worth recording: Kowalski meditated in prison on the Book of Wisdom which to Teilhard de Chardin was the voice of the Eternal Feminine; then he saw Wisdom, Sophia's glory, a parallel to Solovyov's illumination.

[2] The press reported that Kowalski was released early, because of his 'impeccable behaviour' in prison. This was not true. He served the full sentence.

it day after day Kowalski became morose, thought of death, and sent appropriate admonitions to his sisterly wives and sisterly concubines.

Those who suffer from the liver are prone to be irritable and bellicose. After his return from Rawicz, the Archbishop allowed his bilious temper to get the better of his judgement. Instead of letting things quieten down, he engaged in unnecessary squabbles with Bishop Philip's group, printed silly rumours about their reforms, often resorted to insinuations and sometimes to lies.[1] The issues of his periodical *The Kingdom of God on Earth* for the year 1939 are filled with anonymous accusations, gossip, dream reports, and trifles. He and his female assistants turned an idiosyncratic but lively periodical into a sectarian rag, petty, parochial, and portentous.

A Sister X, a veiled Mata Hari, writes from the occupied Temple in this manner: 'I apologize for writing in pencil, but I fear that someone might spy on me. . . . The person who will deliver this can be trusted', etc. The dream of a certain Kurek is reported five years after his prophetic slumbers. He saw an emissary on horseback bringing a blessing for the Archbishop while the street in which the Temple stands was covered with evil-smelling corpses. For corpses read the rebel Mariavites, and always trust dream messengers, Amen.

Among the personal attacks on Philip Feldman which are printed in practically every number throughout 1939, one was to cause serious repercussions after the German invasion of Poland. Kowalski asserted that his arch-traitor was the illegitimate child of a Jewess and the priest who brought him up. The charges of his Masonic affiliations were mild by comparison. It is perhaps ironic that the last issue of *The Kingdom of God on Earth*, published on 1 September, the day Hitler invaded Poland, should have proclaimed the removal of the fallen angels of Plock from the Book of Life.[2] Thus spake the fallen Adam, and soon the sky above him was filled with the roar of bombers. As he looked up, he apparently sensed fate closing in on him. No vineyards under the glass cupola. Only the dome of death.

The Germans entered Plock on the eighth day of the war, and the Mariavite schism, like most schisms in the past, was faced with a new political authority, to which they could appeal for protection. In the fourth century the Arians nearly won because they had the Emperor Constantine on their side. They triumphed at the Council of Sirmium. But the Mariavites were good Poles, their church was a Messianic concept reflecting the

---

[1] His periodical reported in 1939 that 'the reformed priest Skrzypiciel hanged himself on his Mariavite belt', which wasn't true.

[2] See p. 167. In the same issue Kowalski printed his version of Lermontov's 'Demon', about a fallen angel of yore.

nation's destiny.[1] That's how the Little Mother saw it, as did Kowalski who together with Feldman divined the future from the chiliastic writing of the nineteenth-century bards. It was just round the corner of the Temple.

Now the Demon of Noon, whoever he was in Kowalski's interpretations, had a tempter's golden opportunity. The Apocalypse is here, he whispered into Kowalski's 'understanding': the fire burns in the open sky; those who sinned against the Holy Ghost will be destroyed, you are a passive instrument of His Will, let yourself be used by the Will which wills destruction.

This is how I would try to explain Kowalski's behaviour after September 1939. Whether he and his top wives wrote letters to the German authorities denouncing Philip Feldman or not is hard to say with absolute certainty— and only absolute proof would do in this unpleasant case. After the war Philip Feldman produced copies of these letters and, if authentic, they are certainly ugly documents.[2] But the whole problem is darkened by clouds of suspicion, some of them, I am sure, wilfully produced *post factum*.

I will merely state here the facts which resulted from the animosity between the deposed Archbishop and Bishop Philip, leader of the Mariavite reform in Plock. Philip's surname was German, but could also have been Jewish. Accused of hiding his Jewish origin he had to produce documents going two generations back: this wasn't a joke, the Gestapo men were after him, but fortunately for Feldman his cousin from Königsberg, a German citizen, came to his rescue. The next step was almost inevitable. Feldman had to take the papers of the *Volksdeutsche* thinking this would also save the Mariavite organization.

On hearing in April 1941 that the whole Temple might be taken over by the Germans, Philip decided to open the tomb of the Little Mother. This was done in great secrecy at night. They found only a few bones, some loose beads of her rosary, and part of the embroidered monstrance. The wood of the coffin was used for making crosses, small and large; the bones were placed in a casket and hidden under the altar of the Mariavite church in Lodz.

When finally the Germans decided to use the cloister buildings for their own purposes and removed the Sisters from the Temple, Feldman accepted the post of pastor in a parish in Germany and stayed there from 1942 throughout the war with his youngest wife and their children.

[1] 'Danzig and East Prussia should be returned to Poland', Kowalski's paper wrote a few months before war began.

[2] I have read the copies, but I must stress that I haven't seen the originals. Philip Feldman claims in his memoir that the copies were found in a stove at Felicjanów after the deportation of the entire commune in March 1941. I talked to a Sister who was then under Bishop Philip's jurisdiction, who confirmed that the documents were discovered in a stove. It is puzzling, however, that Philip should have arrived so soon after the deportation of the Kowalski group.

Kowalski was arrested on 25 January 1940 and put in prison in Plock which now belonged to the Reich.[1] Why should the Gestapo have wanted him, a sick old man? One of the reasons given is his crazy letter addressed to Hitler via the *Landrat* of Plock, in which among other things he suggested that the Führer should adopt Mariavitism and save the world, otherwise he was certain to lose the war. Thus said the prophet and the prophet went to jail. I am inclined to accept the fact that Kowalski wrote such a letter. It was very much in his style.

A strange confrontation took place between the two Mariavite leaders in the presence of the Gestapo officers. Kowalski was brought out of his cell. His denunciations of Philip Feldman were taken point by point. Apparently he accused him also of living with twelve wives. The interrogating officer called Kowalski a liar and hit him in the face. The Philadelphic brother Jonathan saw the old king David smitten by the enemy and could do nothing.[2] The pincers of fate closed on the Archbishop: his destination was a concentration camp.

Today his followers blame Bishop Philip for almost everything in the final scenes of the Mariavite drama. True, Philip survived the war and others didn't. True, he knew German like a German and therefore could use it persuasively. But had he been a compromised collaborator, would he have dared to return to Poland in 1957? He did return with his family, was neither tried by a court of law nor attacked in the press.[3] No matter what one thinks of Bishop Philip's role in the downfall of Kowalski, he was not born to be a martyr. People of his adaptable resilience usually live very long. Feldman died peacefully in his flat at the Temple in 1971, aged eighty-six.

On 9 March 1941 the entire Felicjanów community—158 persons, including 110 Sisters, 15 Brothers, 13 children from the boarding school, and 20 other inhabitants—was deported to a transit camp near the former frontier with East Prussia. There all the best qualities of Archpriestess Isabel, now spiritual leader of the group, came out. The sanitary conditions at Dzialdowo were appalling, but with the help of her industrious Sisters, she brought some order and cleanliness to the part of the camp occupied by the Mariavites. Her influence on the morale of the deportees was soon noticeable.

---

[1] Fearing his arrest, the priestesses had hidden him by day in a barrel of oats.

[2] We have only Feldman's version of this incident; one would like to know how Kowalski remembered the encounter.

[3] He used all his money to buy the church bells and some equipment for the impoverished cloister in Plock. I have read his pamphlet on the Mariavites, *Die altkatholische Kirche der Mariaviten* (Plock, 1940), published in German at the beginning of the occupation, and found nothing in it that could offend Polish sentiments.

She radiated that delicate angelic beauty which drew everybody towards God. All the prisoners who met her were under her spell, and the Germans, too, felt the impact of her personality. She spoke excellent German. . . . and said what she wanted to say regardless of the consequences. She would explain the prophecies and the directives coming from God which were to guide people back to God. The Archpriestess often intervened when she saw prisoners being beaten. The Germans became less violent in her presence and some stopped inflicting pain on their victims. The worst of them, who was nicknamed 'The Flogger', gave up beating Poles altogether, and would come to the Archpriestess to have spiritual conversations with her.[1]

This was probably the reason why, when the community was moved later to another camp at Plonsk, the Germans decided to employ some of the Mariavite Sisters, including the Archpriestess, as hospital nurses—and why they survived the camps. Isabel died at Felicjanów in 1946.

Archbishop Kowalski spent more than a year in the Plock prison before he was taken to the concentration camp at Dachau on 25 April 1941. He arrived with a transport of priests, mainly Catholic. Against their black cassocks he looked most conspicuous in his light-coloured habit with the embroidered monstrance, and his fatness made his movements awkward. The guards had the technique of applying immediate shock on arrival, and they pounced on Kowalski who seemed the easiest target for mockery. They treated him like a grotesque balloon, passed him from hand to hand, kicking and pummelling the flabby flesh.[2] This was *aber gut*, a good example to the rest of them.

The prisoner No. 24542 became from the start a special case, an oddity among the Roman Catholic priests, a heretic in this moribund synod of the condemned. By the end of 1941 nearly two thousand priests had been brought to Dachau.[3]

The Archbishop passed his seventieth birthday in the camp: it would have been an occasion for a great celebration at home. He felt his age, walked with difficulty, had no glasses (they were broken on his arrival), and the lack of proper nourishment blew him out. The inmates were mainly fed on bread and carrot soup with one or two potatoes added, or on soup made from blue cabbage which caused flatulence and wind. Kowalski wore the prisoner's garb of white and blue stripes, walked in wooden clogs which he noisily shuffled on the gravel. One day when the priests were lined up for

---

[1] This is how the present Archbishop of Felicjanów remembers Isabel in the camp, to which he was taken at the age of twenty-five.

[2] As related by Father F. Korszyński (a Catholic) in his *Jasne promienie w Dachau* (Poznan, 1957).

[3] Jan Domagała's book, *Ci, którzy przeszli przez Dachau* (Warsaw, 1957), ends with a comprehensive list of names. The author notes that on 29 April 1945, eight hundred priests were still alive in Dachau.

The Archbishop's jubilee, October 1934: Kowalski in the centre, with
Philip on his right in the Templarian cap.

The Mariavite community entertaining their guests at the jubilee, with
some of the mystical children; Sister Melania, far right.

The Archbishop and the Archpriestess in their ceremonial robes.

Kowalski receiving homage from the Felicjanów parishioners after his
return from prison, 1938.

inspection an SS man found fault with Kowalski's posture—it could have been his legs or his stomach which he pushed too much forward. He was dragged out of the line, thrown to the ground and beaten up. The boots of the German over his face, the blood gushing—and Kowalski crawling on all fours, his belly hanging down like a sack. Then the whole column marched back to their block. A Catholic bishop, of peasant origin like Kowalski, came up to the old man who was leaning against the wall, and gasping.

'My brother, my poor brother . . .'
'It's all right.' Kowalski's voice sounded throttled. 'Go away, Bishop, away from a heretic.'
'Brother, if only you wanted—'
'I have no need of you. The Little Mother, the Most Holy Little Mother . . .'
'Don't—'
'Oh, never mind.'[1]

They were drawn to each other despite the Archbishop's reluctance. And he had good reason to keep aloof, for the majority of priests expected him to be converted. But converted to what? His Mariavite faith was never stronger than now on the point of death. This is how his end is described in the semi-fictional account from which I have quoted:

Kowalski's face looks like a puffed-up pumpkin, swollen from hunger. His skin is yellow and sagging, black rings under his eyes. He doesn't recognize people.
'*Laudetur Jesus Christus.*' The same Catholic bishop bends over his bunk. 'Make peace with the Church. If you cannot speak, make a sign.'
A faint voice answers. 'You've come to convert . . . me?'
'No, I am begging you on my knees. Have mercy on your own soul.'
'Bishop, I am in constant union with Him. It's you, you should convert yourselves. I see Him every day. He comes to me.'
The bishop is rejected again. The younger priests are annoyed by this heretical obstinacy, but the bishop ignores them and remains on his knees by the dying Mariavite. While he is praying someone tosses out a remark: 'It's sheer stupidity to be so obstinate.'
The bishop lifts up his head.
'And if it is sainthood?'

This happens to be a reconstructed dialogue, nevertheless it rings true.[2] Certainly Kowalski had no wish to go over to Rome. He was comforted

[1] Here and in what follows, I am quoting from Teresa Bojarska's *Cierniowa mitra* (The Mitre of Thorn) (Warsaw, 1969), which is a semi-documentary account of Bishop Kozal's martyrdom in Dachau. Kozal had a great sympathy for Kowalski but I want to stress that the conversations in Bojarska's book, though based on reported facts, are imagined.
[2] As soon as the war was over someone from Poland mentioned Kowalski's death to me. 'He didn't recant.' I was moved when I heard this.

by his visions, he believed he saw Christ and the Little Mother, the illumination which he had experienced at Rawicz did return to bathe the sores of his spirit. That he occasionally shocked some conventional priests is also true.

At Dachau the priests kept bits of bread for consecration in case one of them was allowed to say Mass and they could join him. But Kowalski took communion in two kinds, and there was no wine. One day they saw him bless a mug of ersatz coffee. He whispered the words of consecration over it. This is the blood of Christ. And he drank it with reverence.[1] How strange that anyone in the conditions of Dachau should have been shocked by an act of such direct simplicity. The Archbishop was beyond all conventions of religion. He thought God, he acted as a passive instrument of His Will. He could have been mistaken, but who is to judge the mistakes of faith?

Father Murat was forty when he met Kowalski in Dachau during the terrible winter of 1941–2. He remembered well the dignity of his bearing, the straight thick neck, the strong jaw. 'Yes, the strength was there, in the lower part of his face. But he didn't look into your eyes. Strange, our eyes never met. Kowalski was often seen in the company of two Mariavites. One of them was youngish and kept silent. The other, I remember, told me he was an artisan by profession, and the Archbishop ordained him. A simple, honest man.'

'Father, did you talk to the Archbishop?' I asked.

'No, he wouldn't talk. Said Good morning and then Thank you.'

'Thank you for what?'

'Every morning I helped him to get to the place where we gathered for the roll-call. Each *Blockführer* counted the prisoners. Sometimes we stood an hour in the biting frost, until the *Lagerführer* received all the reports.'

'Did Kowalski complain?'

'Never. But he couldn't manage on his own to walk on the frozen surface of the main road through the camp. It became slippery, and he had to be present at each roll-call. We would assemble outside our block in groups of ten. Kowalski was in my group. I held him by the arm, he shuffled his feet and slipped now and again. Somehow we made it each morning, I mean we got there in time for the roll-call.'

'And no conversation?'

'None. When we were forming a line he always sought me out, then would lean on me as if I were his son. Kept silent all the time. Maybe he prayed.'

[1] This incident was reported to me by two ex-prisoners who were in Dachau at the same time as Kowalski.

'What did you think of him?'

'I liked him. He had dignity. A determined man.'

I saw a letter written in German from Dachau, addressed to Archpriestess Isabel. Gef. Nr. 24542. Dachau K 3 Bl. 30/4. The letter is brief and begins with this greeting:

'*Geliebte Gemahlin! Gelobt sei die Allerheiligste Trinität in Allerheiligste Sakramente.*' Kowalski's teaching about the presence of the Trinity in the Eucharist. The mystery of the Three. Then he speaks of himself, he is '*wie immer getröstet durch die unsere Allerheiligste Mütterchen*'. The Little Mother is his comforter. The letter bears the stamp of *Konzentrationslager Dachau 3 K* and is dated 21 February 1942.

Letter from the Archbishop in Dachau, addressed to his wife Isabel (1941)

Unfit for any work he was taken from Dachau with a transport of invalids, probably in the direction of Mauthausen or Linz.[1] He was gassed on 18 May 1942. No ashes were sent to his wife.

---

[1] A Protestant pastor, W. Gastpary, talked to Kowalski 'as he was standing in a file ready to be marched off. I had the impression that he knew where he was being taken. He asked me to look after another Mariavite priest in Dachau (prisoner No. 3793).'

In the Mariavite Temple at Plock I looked for a plaque in Kowalski's memory. There is none. No body, no tomb. It makes sense: he was supposed to be the reincarnation of Archangel Michael. No particle of matter will claim him on the Day of Judgement.

10

The Survivors

BY their fruit you will judge them. This chapter is mainly about the children of the mystical marriages. I have left it on purpose towards the end of the book because I felt that their problem is unique. Each of them embodies the Mariavite experiment and each of them has the right to judge it. The first of the children were born in 1924 to the Archbishop's surprise and horror;[1] their very existence forced him to issue a pastoral letter and face a strong public reaction. His enemies still think it was the beginning of his end.

Altogether some forty children were born at the cloister and about twenty outside, after the split. Ten have since died. Of those alive today the oldest is fifty, the average age of the others being over forty. They are in a critical decade in man's life. Those who were born after the split in 1935 do not, strictly speaking, belong to the same group, although they share some psychological difficulties with them.

I have the strongest sympathy for the ones who became the guinea pigs in Kowalski's mystical laboratory. They were isolated from the start. The room in which the married nuns were bringing them into the world faced the gardens and few inhabitants came near it. Discretion befitted the mystery, and at first the arrangements were such as to suggest some divine intervention. The nursing Sisters who assisted at each delivery had a strong sense of witnessing a birth unlike any other birth.[2]

The Mariavite regard for hygiene extended to the spiritual care of the children. They were hygienically protected from the psychic bacteria of their parents. No parent, in fact, had any say in their upbringing. Once the Archbishop had an idea (and he produced one quickly in this case), he flogged it down to the smallest detail. The priestly babies (called *dzieci kapłańskie* by the Mariavites) were conceived without original sin—a clean

---

[1] When Father (later Bishop) Francis (Rostworowski) reported the pregnancy of his wife, Kowalski collapsed into the chair and the shock made him speechless. When he heard of the second pregnancy he laughed.

[2] This was confirmed to me by a nun who with Dr. Kopystyński, the resident physician, was present at the deliveries.

beginning—so why not treat them as a new chain of spiritual cells, linked only with one another. In order to do this, they had to be severed from their progenitors and brought up as a unit: they were dressed alike, ate the same food, had special Sisters to look after them day and night, and were always together. A kindergarten for future saints, motherless and fatherless. The still-born babies were buried without any trace in a pine grove near the Vistula, where the cloister children would often play.

How did the mothers react to the whole experiment? They suffered greatly, because they could not feed their babies. 'My breasts ached, they longed to be suckled. Oh, how they ached!' an old nun told me with tears in her eyes. Was she allowed to see her baby? I asked. Yes, once a week for ten minutes. 'That was the ruling for all of us.' But those who worked in parishes outside couldn't even do that. Those terrible partings; the babies cried and cried. When a child was ill, the mother could come and see it through the window. There were two rooms for the newly-born.

The Archbishop seemed quite adamant about this communal upbringing without any emotional interruptions. No attachments should be formed. Parents should not inflict their possessive love on the cloister babies. He wanted to break the obvious relationship pattern. Some said he did that because he resented the existence of these children. They spoilt the mystical fun. Maybe it was true. He certainly kept away from his own son. But the third Adam in the Archbishop liked bestowing names. So he chose them for the priestly babies as well, and in each case the parents had to accept his decision. He would stride into the room, point at a newly-born in a cot and say, 'His name is John.' That was final, and off he would go.

The process of conditioning went on and did produce results. The children were so accustomed to seeing the Sisters only that they reacted with fear to other people, including their parents. A little boy of five would hide in a corner of the nursery whenever his father came from the provinces to visit him.[1] The children, it was said, appeared to be happy in their own company, they played together and were on the whole well-behaved, but to the outside world they were wild. Perhaps it was the smell of sin like the odour of unwashed bodies that put them off ordinary human beings. One has to argue from Kowalski's premises in order to grasp the whole system imposed by him on the innocent. The full detachment, he thought, would be achieved once the children grew up. As soon as they were able to talk they had to address their parents, using the Mariavite form: 'Brother priest' to the father, and 'Sister' to the mother, but no diminutives, no endearments. After all the children stood on a higher rung of the spiritual ladder than

[1] So I was told by his mother.

their parents, according to Kowalski's teaching, even on the day they were born. The Abbé Boullan would have nodded with approval to this reversal of roles. No original sin, no weight on the soul: you go straight up into the sphere of perfection and stay there.

I was understandably curious about the strange human products of Kowalski's blueprint for redemption. Tracing them was not an easy task thirty-seven years after the great disruption at Plock when Kowalski's experiments were wound up and the children dispersed. However, I managed to trace fifteen, a good proportion of the surviving fifty. I soon found out that almost every one of them preferred to remain anonymous. They had already moulded their lives, though a few struck me as ill-adjusted to their professions (Kowalski expected they would all become priests or priestesses). Some left Poland during or after the war and tried to succeed in a foreign environment. For one reason or another they did not wish to be known as Mariavites, still less as the offspring of a notorious experiment. How can one say with ease, 'My mother was a nun, I was born in a cloister'? Unless you treat it all as a joke. But the Mariavite children suffered far too much, even if they remember little of the Kowalski kindergarten.

The oldest were only ten when the whole organization broke asunder and they were meted out to the parents they hardly knew. Worse still was the fate of those who were part of the polygamous set-up. Some were not even registered under their father's name. After the reform of 1935, wives had to be discarded in a hurry. And the reformer himself, Bishop Philip, had three to drop. He stayed with the youngest who fortunately for him proved a very loyal wife during the difficult years.[1] Kowalski sneered at the reformers economizing on older wives, for they invariably 'retained the younger'. The confusion resulting from the polygamous kinships added to the children's insecurity.

What could I do but respect their desire for discretion? I have solved the problem here by altering the names but not the circumstances. In each case, however, the choice of a particular name will be understood by the person in question. A private code for secrecy's sake, in the best Mariavite tradition.

I met Judith in a genteel tea-room off Piccadilly Circus. She had come from South Africa to stay, her children were at school in London, and presto! she materialized on a drizzly afternoon in a red coat, as if the whole arrangement were a meeting of ex-lovers. I had known her married name for years, but the way my inquiries meandered to establish her Mariavite identity would have pleased a writer of thrillers. She herself, while vehemently denying any Mariavite connections, couldn't fail to sense the

[1] Altogether Philip had nine children by four wives. Some of them were born after 1935.

thriller atmosphere, and suddenly remarked out of the blue: 'Are you a spy or something?' But later it turned out that she had also read one of my novels in which the main character is a spy on holiday.

Between cups of Ceylon tea I found myself explaining to Judith who the Mariavites were—I produced names and dates out of my learned sleeve to keep up the pretence. Now I was curious to see where all this would lead. I showed her the photograph of Archpriestess Isabel in her ceremonial robes —she didn't bat an eyelid, only her voice faltered for a second.

I began to talk about her father, an admirable Mariavite priest who, incidentally, objected to the mystical marriages and nearly left the church.[1] As I described his work—a silly thing to do before a daughter—Judith broke down and started crying. Now we did look like ex-lovers or lovers about to part, and the waitresses in the tea-room observed us from a distance with mixed feelings. I could almost hear them say: Poor dear crying her heart out. And he, just look at him, isn't he playing it cool? Those men!

'So you are his daughter. What was it like to be in Plock in those days? Tell me, please. It may help you, I mean talking about it.'

Judith still denied ever being near Plock. Yes, her father was a priest, but he soon left the Mariavites and sent her to a school in eastern Poland. She was a good Catholic. Her children were too. She had never heard of Kowalski's trial. Who did you say Kowalski was? And so on, until I drank my seventh cup of tea to comply with the Archbishop's art of numerology. Meanwhile, we changed the subject. Judith was interested in faith healing, in second sight, telepathy, knew a woman who worked extraordinary cures but never took a penny from her patients. In fact, Judith, the daughter of a priest, was still a nurse at heart.[2] She had loved her father with a possessive passion, she still does, probably because she was deprived of his company in the first years of her life. She tended him in illness day and night, he was exclusively hers then, and when they laid him in a coffin, she held his cold hand and kissed his fingers.

A grief of this intensity stays in the mind unresolved either by marriage or children. When I saw her she was in the middle of a deep crisis, a woman at a critical turn in her life, no longer a healer herself, but searching for healers, anybody who would administer the priest's power. Thy will be done, Father, my father, mine alone. 'Once a Mariavite, always a Mariavite. It's God's choosing, you see,' a wise old nun told me in her poor room surrounded by photographs of the past glory.

---

[1] Though he consented to marriage in the end, he did not produce a 'Testimony' for Kowalski's book. He was given one of the poorest parishes as a punishment for his mystical doubt.
[2] It was she who nursed Sister Dilecta during her illness after the war.

We arranged to meet again: the same tea-room, the same day of the week, the same hour—women like a repeated pattern of this sort—but Judith did not turn up. I rang her the next morning. Apparently she had confused the rooms, waited an hour for me and left. I believe her now; it was a psychological evasion acted out to appease the demon of guilt. And when I thought she wouldn't come the week after, she appeared on the dot of three o'clock and we talked amiably. With a pedant's lack of sensitivity I mentioned the wretched kindergarten, and again Judith shook her head and her dark eyes calmly scrutinized my stupid curiosity. No, no kindergarten; she was in a posh school for young ladies. Her family helped. At our first meeting, however, talking between tears, she didn't hide the nastiness of her family who had treated her father as a leper, ashamed of his association with Kowalski, pushing the good man towards his grave.

But unpredictable as women are in their disturbed years, Judith gave me a few addresses. 'See them, they will talk.' And she obviously meant talk. In my pocket that afternoon I had a group photograph of the mystical children with Judith, one of the tallest, prominently visible in the second row. But the pleasure of any investigation is not to show your trump card. Scoring an easy point leads nowhere. Besides, she might have cried again, and with the playboy's outfit I was wearing to cheer myself up, I would have got no sympathy from the blond waitress. She was grumpy, so visibly anti-male, and had lots of war-paint on her eyelids.

From a tea-room in London to a French observatory on a hill where Beata works as a technical assistant, was indeed a jump on the wings of the Holy Ghost. I felt inspired as I drove on a hot July day, the road climbing towards a cupola as large as a science fiction fantasy. I passed a gate, identified myself, drove past the barrier and stopped at a group of white buildings. In one of them she worked. The first impression of a person, provided it is precise, acts as a beam of light. I could almost see Beata's future as we shook hands and exchanged greetings. There in front of me stood a tall handsome girl carrying her pregnancy with a natural grace.

Her story interested me because she was a priest's daughter but not born at the Temple. During the war she spent her childhood outside Poland, returned to Plock at the age of twelve, attended a secondary school there, and five years later was abroad again, first in America, then in France where she bravely studied at the Sorbonne, got her degree and married.

What does she think of religion now in her essentially non-religious milieu? Oh, she said, my father used to say, If God wants your faith, you can do nothing to stop Him. My husband heard this and it worries him still. Does she go to church? Yes, any Christian church. And what about the sacrament? Would she confess to a priest? 'No, only within myself.' There was a Greek Orthodox church which she liked and where she once took communion. But the second time the priest noticed her and asked whether she was Greek Orthodox. No more communion. 'You can't do that,' the priest said. 'You are not one of us.'

This shocked Beata. How can anyone deny Christ to a hungry soul? I made no comment and studied her face while we talked. There was so much generosity in her features. Had she been a priestess she wouldn't have been capable of refusing the food of mystery to any sinner. An indelible Mariavite trait was stamped on her personality. Again, like Judith, she cherished the memory of her father, but seemed not to know much about his practice of polygamy. She heard rumours when they returned to Plock but was too young to understand or to want to.

'You are supposed to have been born without original sin. What do you feel about it?'

'Original sin?' Her eyes widened. Oh yes, she knew what original sin meant, but the whole expression of her face denied the acceptance of sin. Was this innocence there since her birth or was it the coming birth of her child that lighted it up within her body? For the first time I began to question my own disbelief in Kowalski's dogma concerning the mystical children. Supposing the maniac was right, supposing he was right just in one case?

2

It would be foolish, I think, to use a code name for Kowalski's only son, Michael, born in 1930. He shares with most children of famous men the painful experience of being treated as his father's mirror, and the curious will stare into it. Fortunately for him, the name is common; there are thousands of Kowalskis.[1] I had some doubts whether he would be willing to talk to me, and I wouldn't have blamed him had he said no. But during my second visit to the Felicjanów commune in January 1973 the present head of the Kowalski group promised to arrange a meeting, and it took place outside the commune, in Plock itself. When a Sister brought the message to the hotel where I was staying, the receptionist thought she was a Catholic nun. How times had changed if even in Plock a Mariavite could pass unrecognized.

Michael was probably recognized because he was talking to a visitor from abroad, and hotel lounges have a pair of observant eyes somewhere.

---

[1] The present Chief Bishop of the Mariavites at Plock, for instance, is called Kowalski and is in no way connected with the Archbishop's family.

When he entered he wore a lambskin cap which suited his rugged features. I was reminded of his mother as soon as his wide mouth stretched in a smile. That generous Mariavite greeting: he couldn't help showing his friendliness to a stranger. And a childlike trust. But he was nervous. We sat in a cafeteria, one of those plastic attempts at modernity in eastern Europe which look shabby from the first day they are opened to the public. Now and again Michael would glance sideways as though he expected someone to enter. It is a precaution people adopt in this part of the world, it becomes automatic like a facial tic.

We started, of course, with his father. Yes, there was always a distance between them. A severe man but just. As a child Michael hardly saw him. Too busy, too important. Later I was told by two Sisters, one pro- and one anti-Kowalski, that Michael had indeed had a difficult childhood. A solitary, withdrawn boy, and Archpriestess Isabel was to a certain extent responsible for this. She always blamed him for one thing or another—what an impossible child—and said all this to his father. Why did she do it? Was it a real dislike of the child who was formally registered as her own but wasn't? Or perhaps she envied every married Sister who could bear children when she couldn't.

Michael was starved of paternal love. Sometimes Bishop Philip or Bishop Jacob would come to the children's quarters and play with him. They assumed the role of godfather to him. Jacob especially, who was married to Honorata and had no children of his own, showed much love to the little creatures isolated in the mystical hot-house for the sake of some ultimate redemption. He was an elderly man, puzzled by it all, both frightened and jealous of Kowalski's power, and his kindness as well as his guilt found an emotional outlet in the warmth he gave to the offspring of a vision he himself thought dubious.

I asked Michael whether he had any grudge against the way he was brought up. No—he hesitated—not really. We were treated as one family. Sister Illuminata he remembered with affection: 'She gave us so much love.' He spent five years in the kindergarten, less than others, and after the split was moved to the boarding school at Felicjanów. 'You know, of course, that my mother wasn't the Archpriestess.' I said I knew and in a flash the face of Bishopess Dilecta superimposed itself on his sharp features.

Did he think the marriages were right? Oh yes, the best thing my father did was to persuade the women to be truly free. Some achievement, he said, to push it through in a convent. Some courage too, I added. Still—Michael glanced sideways as if he were about to reveal a secret—still, the marriages had to happen. There was such a large number of men and women grouped together in one place. But the Sisters were separated, I said, especially the 'God-minded' in their choir. True, true, but in the Temple and at various functions the priests couldn't help noticing the faces under the wimples. And most Sisters were attractive and young. But Michael's own marriage proved a failure. A civil marriage, he added. Now he and his three children were staying at Felicjanów. Back at the Mariavite home.[1] He began to tell me the story of his marriage in detail—he obviously needed a sympathetic listener and I was touched by the trust he showed me.

Then we returned to the war years, a nightmare that nobody in Poland who experienced it is capable of forgetting. Michael was nine when the Gestapo came to arrest the Archbishop in January 1940. 'Early in the morning it was; two cars pulled up—we all knew what it meant. Father was wearing his habit and they took him as he stood, no time for any practical arrangements.' A year later, with the whole community at Felicjanów, the boy was deported to the transit camp at Dzialdowo.

How could Michael ever adjust to the relationship of marriage? Kept in seclusion as a baby, ill at ease with his authoritative father, deprived even of that presence after his arrest, he found himself at the age of eleven in a concentration camp. After their release he moved with his real mother from parish to parish, saw the butchery during the retreat of the Germans, and, finally, returned to the devastated Felicjanów. Is the dead Archbishop to be blamed much for his neglect of the boy? He occasionally mentions him in his letters from the prison in Rawicz. 'Little Michael mustn't be too sad' ('*Niech Michaś mi się nie smuci*'), he wrote in August 1936,[2] but the letters were composed as epistles and read by the whole flock. Moreover, in addressing Isabel he kept up the pretence that Michael was their son. The Mariavites expected their Archbishop's heir to be a priest and were disappointed when he refused to become one.

Now there are the grandchildren still attached to the Mariavite commune. Will they be entirely free from the burden of the Kowalski myth? I met the younger first, a good-looking boy, then when I was back in Felicjanów, seated between the two bishopesses, a boy with glasses was shown in and we shook hands. 'Doesn't he look like his grandfather?' said Bishopess Dilecta. The stamp of that formidable personality was there, unmistakable. Unto the second and the third generation, as the prophets of the Bible used to say.

I had arranged with Michael Kowalski to continue our conversation, this

[1] The Felicjanów commune feels obliged to help the Archbishop's son when he is in trouble. The curious legal situation arose after Kowalski's death, when the Felicjanów property was to have passed to his son. (See p. 56n.)
[2] In the same letter he mentions Dilecta who should encourage the child to eat more.

time in Warsaw, but he didn't turn up. It was a bitterly cold night. This alone could have put one off travelling. Besides, his younger boy was unwell on the day of our first meeting; perhaps he got worse. But, most likely, with all the trust and sympathy on both sides, he had had enough of being the Archbishop's son in my company.

Paul would come fairly high in the hierarchy of the mystical children, if such a hierarchy were to be established, for his father had a considerable influence on the development of the movement and within Kowalski's inner circle practised polygamy. We met in New York outside the building in which Paul works. I recognized him at once. Tall, blue-eyed, with bird-like features, he emanated an aura of separateness which no crowd could ever absorb. There he stood, waiting for me, and straightaway I imagined him in a grey habit, even taller and more detached.

'You must be the only Mariavite on Madison Avenue.' A good beginning to a conversation, I thought.

'In this city you can never be sure.' And as he said it, I knew that he hated New York.

We talked for hours in his flat overlooking the Hudson River. The view liberated the mind from the urban claustrophobia. On the walls opposite the panoramic view there were enlarged photographs: thatched cottages, puddles, wispy willows, the Chopin-like melancholy of the Polish plains. He had taken them during his last visit to the Plock region.

'So you like going back there.'

'One day I will return. For good.'

'After this?' I made a circular gesture with my hand. 'What would you do in Poland?'

'Work in a parish, with the people. The ordinary Mariavites. They were so badly, so very badly let down.'

'You still consider yourself a priest?'

'My father ordained me a deacon. We were still abroad. I am a priest.'

'But you work in an office, you have no chapel, no congregation.'

'True, I am a useless priest. That's why I would like eventually to go there.' We both looked at the wispy willows. So resilient.

Paul's story is a story of contrasts: failure, success, and failure again. Now he is happily married and proud of his Mediterranean wife. The first caused him a great deal of suffering.

'When did you come to America?' I asked.

'Nearly twenty years ago. I went to school in West Germany, got into trouble with some neo-Nazi Jesuits, was chucked out, tried odd jobs, then school again. My father didn't want me to return to Poland.'

Back to the Mariavite fold. Inevitable, the compelling force behind the desire. I made quick calculations in my head: Paul was only three when the split occurred, so the kindergarten hardly touched him. What was his childhood like, I wondered.

'Praying, always praying. Three minutes every hour. And we said the rosary together, the whole family. Father gave the example: he would fast for a few days and observe silence in preparation for his episcopal meditations. I think he wanted me to see what it really meant to be a priest. And I had to confess once a week, every Saturday. It was a torture.'

'How did you address him? I mean, did you say Father, Papa, or *tato*?'

'Good heavens, no! Always Brother Bishop. He was strict and kept his distance. Once when he saw me playing with a girl he punished me with a rubber rod. He had that idea, you see, about my virginity.'

'And when did you lose it?'

'At twenty-three. He was furious. You won't be a priest, he said. I threatened to appeal to the Mariavite Council.'

Paul had no interpretation for this incident. It puzzled him still. And I didn't realize at the time that the Bishop's insistence on his son's virginity must have been connected with the Mariavite concept of the mystical union. The elect must be pure when they enter such a union. Afterwards the flesh is sanctified and remains in this state even in polygamy. What the Bishop in fact wanted from his son was that he be eligible for the mystical mystery, the priesthood of the chosen. Had Paul any idea of the polygamous set-up at the Temple before the split? Yes, he knew of it when he clashed with his father, but Brother Bishop seemed singularly reluctant to talk about this aspect of Mariavitism.

'I never heard him speak of the opposite sex otherwise than in disparaging terms. Those women, those dreadful girls, and so on. I think he despised them.'

Was it the result of the polygamous experiment or the guilt over its disastrous consequences? Perhaps he even hated the physical act?

Paul certainly saw some of the consequences when he visited Plock. Suddenly a girl came up to him at the Temple and said in a hushed voice: 'My name is Aldona. You don't know me, I am your half-sister.' It was like a clandestine meeting, but what shocked Paul later were the obstacles put up to prevent the girl from seeing her own father. It was then that she felt being a concubine's daughter. 'We go on erring until we find ourselves,' Paul's father used to say—his favourite *sententia*, based, it would seem, on experience.

I don't think Paul has resolved his parental problem. His mother was too much enwrapped in Brother Bishop, she had won him for herself alone in a polygamous contest, therefore she always wanted to prove that he came before everything else. Not all the children felt it, but Paul did. She also screened them from the secret side of the Mariavite story (she altered her maiden name, for instance). Maybe she was right.

Paul became a full priest in the United States when he worked under appalling conditions for the Polish National Church, an institution he doesn't remember with affection.[1] 'After four years I was used up. A burnt-out case.'

So now in his beautiful New York apartment Paul is a priest waiting for Godot. Will he ever get a clear message from him? The Little Mother claimed that she did.

'Do you still believe in the Little Mother's Revelation?' I asked him the following day after having read some of his father's notes on the conversations he had had with the foundress.

'Certainly I do. I wouldn't be a Mariavite otherwise. And look, I have translated her Revelations into German.' He showed me a typescript. 'Yes, God did speak to her.'

'And do you speak to God?'

'Yes—it's a monologue.'

'But is it heard?'

'It's heard even if it is unanswered.'

I liked his reply.

Now that Paul has studied some of the Mariavite documents, he is inclined to believe that the system of the elect operated within the church, and that his parental Brother Bishop was part of it. 'Yes, there were nights of love in Felicjanów, with coloured lamps shining among the trees. And those nuns gliding by the pond, dressed up like dolls—Kowalski had a cloister and a theatrical show as well. And he certainly loved the Lolitas from the convent school.'

I didn't ask Paul whether he thought his father had liked some of them, too. We understood each other well enough. Finally, we got back to the clan of the mystical children, now broken up, dispersed, and hidden under anonymity. But they keep in touch and seem to know what each of them is doing and where. Grapevine and telepathy, you might say.

'Whenever we meet there are long silences. We just look at one another. And we never talk about the Mariavites.'

---

[1] Nor did Archbishop Kowalski, who shared with the National Church their hatred of the Pope but ended by himself hating Bishop Hodur, their tough boss.

Paul's half-sister Aldona did talk about the Mariavites. But we were alone at a table in a Warsaw café, and nothing intruded, not even my oblique questions about her father. She knew that I knew and that made the conversation direct and sincere. Aldona said I reminded her of Paul. Soon his telepathic presence began to work on me, so I too had a brotherly feeling for her. Intelligent and self-assured, perhaps domineering in her marriage, Aldona has managed to rise above the bitterness of her childhood. She was one of those children who were not officially acknowledged by their fathers when the polygamous unions were breaking up. One would have to be well informed about Mariavite affairs to guess her real parent from her maiden name. Did she mind this? Occasionally. But some children had to be rejected during the big clean-up at the Temple. 'I happened to be one of them, that's all.'

I liked her acceptance of fate. This was the voice of sanity and courage. But she also remembered insults, people sneering at the Mariavites even after the common experience of the war and the occupation. Tolerance? No, she said firmly, there is little of it in the world. Those who are ignorant or those who couldn't care less pass for being tolerant.

The same evening, when I met her family at home, she gave me an embroidered monstrance from a habit once worn by her father who is now dead. I was deeply touched and hesitated as to whether I should accept such a gift.

'There were two habits left,' she said simply. 'You have it. I want you to have the Mariavite emblem. I know you will respect it.'

Sudden shyness came over me, and I didn't wish to use a mere polite phrase to thank Aldona for her spontaneous gesture. I think she understood my silence.

3

I was beginning to experience the sensation of being their silence-breaker, a visitor who had to stir the memories and touch the wounds still unhealed. There was no other way. I surprised Felix by ringing him up: something vulnerable was touched at once though I didn't mention why I wanted to see him. If he becomes aggressive, I thought, I will get nowhere. But on acquaintance he proved to be most willing to help me. I knew his family background, and since he was very proud of his lineage, our conversation started off well. Soon we were racing along the bumpy Mariavite track.

Like Paul, Felix had faint recollections of the kindergarten for the priestly babies, although he stayed there until he was five. He was born outside

Plock in a poor Mariavite parish to which his father had been demoted by Kowalski for daring to oppose the mystical marriages. With a rope around his neck and ashes on his head he implored the Archbishop to change his mind. But the will of Our Leader crushed his and soon he found himself with a wife, a nun from a good middle-class family. Their children were in a sense unwanted, and the poverty inflicted on them during the later years marked them all for life as victims of perpetual insecurity.[1]

Felix's tough looks seemed to belie this at first sight, but he didn't try to hide his almost feminine sensitivity. His restlessness seemed to add a sharp flavour to his intelligence. One frosty afternoon he turned up dressed for the season, with a splendid fur cap after the fashion of those worn by the Polish nobles a century ago. I praised his outfit and this pleased him. Felix has an unmistakable aristocratic bearing and would like the drab world to acknowledge it from time to time. The misery of his Mariavite childhood lies buried under the glory that is the past, and very remote at that. How he would have enjoyed wearing hussar's armour with a pair of wings and leading a charge against the Turks.

He is still puzzled why his father should have joined the Mariavite movement, and thinks it was due to his uncle's persuasion. About poverty he says nothing. Too painful for his pride to bear. No, he did not believe his birth had a special mystical significance. His harrassed father reacted strongly against some of Kowalski's instructions. When little Felix once addressed him as 'Brother priest' he lost his temper and shouted at the boy: 'You'll get a whacking brother for that!'[2]

The boy couldn't understand where his affections should go. There was an angel of a nun at the kindergarten called Sister Amata. A loving name for a giver of love, for she was that to the children. Felix corresponded with her and after some years met her again. Yes, women like Amata justified Mariavitism in his eyes. The movement attracted extraordinary people and brought out the best in them. Kowalski?—well, he was a character apart.

'Would you call yourself a Mariavite now?'

'Yes and no. I am still involved. I tried to do some work for them after the war. One expected the old enthusiasm would return.' His pause implied that it hadn't.

'Is your religion essentially a thing of childhood?'

'If you mean the emotional side of it, yes. It goes back to my early years.

---

1 Most children born of the mystical marriages inherited hardly anything from their parents who, in the best tradition of Mariavitism, had no possessions to pass on, only letters and photographs. Brought up in such holy poverty, the children developed an instinct for sharing and a carefree attitude towards money. Their generosity is, I feel, as natural as it is profoundly moral.

2 *Ja ci dam brata*: the phrase is more effective in Polish.

I remember the Temple illuminated—it must have been soon after Kowal-ski's fall. How old was I then? About five. "We praise Thee, Lord", they sang—all those lights above me, I stared and stared and stared. This surely must be heaven, I thought.'

And where is that heaven now? Where is Kowalski's promised King-dom? He smiled. And I suddenly remembered the shadow of sadness crossing the faces of the old nuns when I asked the same question. They had outlived a beautiful dream. A catty ex-priestess told me how she had bumped into one of the bishopesses for whom Kowalski had a realm in store: She looked so confused, poor thing, her wimple all crooked, wisps of hair sticking out. And she used to love the diadem on her head. Poor old thing, what could one say to her?

Felix took me to see one of his friends from the Plock days, a priest's daughter too. Maria works in a big state firm, has a university degree, and for a woman approaching forty looks remarkably young and attractive. She promised to show me some Mariavite pamphlets and an album of photographs. 'Only the priestly children,' she said. And a few days later I saw them. If ever Kowalski wanted visible proof that his experiment worked and produced a *genus mysticum*, there it was, page after page, eyes reflecting the mystery of each unpolluted soul. It was a married nun who decided to keep this photographic file. Each child is recorded there. I was struck by one face in particular. Its beauty had the wisdom of ages.

'That must be you,' I said to Maria.

'Yes, it is me. Taken after my first communion. I felt on that day as if I were looking at the world for the first time.'

But Maria's life was anything but happy. She was only two at the time of the Mariavite break-up, moved with her parents from parish to parish, then the occupation came, and afterwards the most difficult adjustment of all, facing her contemporaries at school away from the close family circle. Whenever Maria's mother visited her she wore her Mariavite habit and this created problems. Maria never denied her religious identity, she was proud of her parents. 'I felt it was an honour to be the daughter of a priest and a nun.' But intolerance can hurt. Walking with her mother in Warsaw, she noticed how her acquaintances reacted to the veil. Some recognized the emblem. A Mariavite, fancy that! 'Now we have learnt to compromise. Ordinary dress for the streets, a habit at home.'

Maria's older sister Ivona was in the kindergarten nine years, and later took the veil to please her parents, but left the convent soon. All this affected her character. She is more detached and has difficulty in expressing affection. They trained her to call her father 'Brother Bishop' and her mother 'Sister', and she did.[1] Both girls helped their parents in church, they swept the floors, dressed the altar, and did small errands. The true priestly daughters, conscious of their duty.

When I asked my usual question about being born without original sin —did this knowledge penetrate their minds?—Maria shrugged her shoulders. 'I suppose I appeared to be better, but that's artificial, don't you agree? Children adopt angelic poses until their wings are soiled by life. At eighteen I broke away from the Mariavite cocoon. Then I learnt how hard it was to have relationships with others. It's still hard for me. Who on earth can understand my psychological block?'

'We all have them,' I said.

'So they keep asking me, why aren't you married? My boss asked that in someone's presence. Then he apologized. But what is one to say? I am all too conscious now that I will never find a partner.'

Her dark eyes glistened as she turned towards the lamp.

How could she say such a thing with a face radiating so much gentleness and beauty? But true solitude is like drug addiction. You want to get out of it and cannot on your own. Yet you resent a rescuer. Too much probing.

Maria continued: 'You are at a party in a very good mood, liking the company. Then a drunk voice says aggressively: I know who you are. You are the daughter of a Mariavite bishop. And the others begin to titter around you. Oh, yes, those bishops and their convent girls. Wasn't there a big trial before the war at—? And so on behind your back, sniggering. I understand why Bishop Bartholomew's daughter wants to forget that the Mariavites ever existed.'

'But forgetting doesn't obliterate facts.'

'You're right. One has to live on, my mother says, with that hump on your back.'

'Surely it would be better to marry a person with exactly the same experience?'

'You mean one of our lot? There has been only one marriage between the priestly children.'

'Does it work, Maria?'

'It seems to. Some half-Mariavite couples, though, cut themselves off completely. No reminders. You mix with the people who take you for what you are.'

---

1 Ivona remembers well Kowalski's visits to the kindergarten and his talks with the children. 'Your mama is the Little Mother', he would say, 'and your father Christ.' Sometimes instead of Christ he said the Heavenly Father, but 'heavenly' in Polish means also blue. So one clever boy got confused and to the question: Who is your father, answered: 'The Green Father, of course.' Kowalski laughed. They all remember how gaily he laughed.

I detected a note of sadness in her voice.

'Tell me frankly, is this conversation painful to you?'

'No, oh no! On the contrary, it soothes my nerves. It's so good to talk without any inhibitions about a taboo subject.'

And to prove she was at ease with her past, Maria sang me a plaintive song about the Mariavite peasant. The words dated from the beginning of the movement, the music was composed later by her own father. She sang naturally as she must have done in those early days when her eyes reflected the deep innocence of faith.

There were a few reunions of the priestly children, the last organized discreetly in the bleak years after the war, in 1950. About thirty of them came to the Plock cloister and they all stood in a queue before the aged figure of the nun they regarded as their true mother in the kindergarten days. One after another they kissed Sister Amata's hand in gratitude, and she kissed their bent heads, and cried. There was to have been another reunion later, but somehow they didn't succeed in organizing it.

My presence in Warsaw led to a small gathering improvised in a casual Polish way. A few telephone calls and within two hours they started to arrive. At a table in a fashionable café I was surrounded by the priestly children. They talked and laughed and shared reminiscences.

'Do you remember that old Mariavite church at M——, infested with mice? Old Father Augustine was celebrating Mass and the mice kept scuttling over the altar. He tried to frighten them with his sleeve, with his missal—no use, so he beckoned to a Sister to do something. She, poor thing, was as baffled as he was. So, in exasperation the priest whispered: "Bring the cat," then louder, "The cat! The cat!" And we children loved the scene when a fat brown puss took over.'

Casimir spent most of his childhood in a Mariavite parish and lost much of his reverence for the priestly authority. Was he still a believing Mariavite? 'No,' he said. 'I want my children to have a normal adolescence. Sometimes I envy them.'

'What does Kowalski represent for you now?'

'He is the drama of my life.' And then he smiled mischievously. 'But if it hadn't been for him, we wouldn't be here at this reunion, would we now?'

Then we talked about the tricks of memory and about guilt.

'At least you have none,' I said to all of them. 'Kowalski may have imposed a burden on you, but what he did releases you from any bond of guilt.' I felt like adding that such a release could be understood as the absence of original sin. For guilt lies at its centre. But I didn't want to put any more labels on the priestly children.

At the tables around us people talked, and from time to time looked in our direction. Our laughter made the café even gayer than it looked. Who there could possibly guess that ours was a Mariavite reunion? But in Poland life is nourished by surprises.

The Archbishop's plans for the mystical generation went awry. No priests or priestesses came out of it. Only one man worked as a priest for a short time and then left the church altogether. Neither Kowalski's son nor the sons of his rival wanted to commit themselves to apostolic work.

What happened instead was a subtle transformation. As they grew up and apart, the priestly children became the bearers of an invisible Mariavitism. They don't find an alternative to the religion of their parents, though some reacted strongly against the parents themselves. At their most eclectic they practise what Beata does, a kind of Christian *laissez-faire*: a Greek Orthodox communion one day, a pious self-confession in a Catholic church another day. Will Paul ever shepherd a flock of Mariavite lambs in a melancholy landscape of willows and ponds? I wonder.

By stirring their memories I hope that I performed a useful psychological task. Perhaps I made the child in them look straight into the mystery of their origin. Sin-free or sin-bound, what were they born for? Whenever I parted with one of them I had a feeling that the person I had met was almost reconciled with his or her Mariavite identity. Even the one who wanted to deny everything and cried over the loss. For all I know Judith may be praying to the Little Mother again.

4

By their fruit you will judge them. Archbishop Kowalski was responsible for about fifty mystical marriages. A cynic would say that he was also responsible for all the children born from these unions, especially since he claimed access to each wife whether directly his or not. The mediator's seed then might have mingled with that of others, and apparently some priests enjoyed coitus after the Archbishop had done his bit of mediating.

The catalogue of sexual pleasures lists this sort of perversion. The innocent are easily pervertible, and those provincial priests brought up in the fear of the flesh had no chance of resisting Kowalski's *démon de midi*. However, it would seem that mysticism alone could not guarantee the happiness of these strange unions. To some it brought much misery, other marriages simply broke down as the ordinary ones do.

How many of them were really successful? I asked Sister Leonia who is pro-Kowalski and whose evidence I found, on the whole, reliable.

'Nine,' she said.

'Nine out of fifty. Eighteen per cent. Not bad. Would you think it offensive, Sister, if I said that there were spiritual divorces among your mystics? As on earth so in heaven. A parallel in reverse.'

She smiled: 'It's your way of looking at it. Who knows what's in heaven.'

Especially in the Third Heaven, I wanted to add, but didn't.

The supposedly immaculate conception of the children didn't seem to worry Sister Leonia. It's a promise for the future. It will come. 'There is something different in all those children.'

Brother Raphael, the present Archbishop of Felicjanów, eagerly confirmed this. As a boy of fourteen at the Temple boarding school he often saw the priestly children whose average age at that time was eight. 'They were unlike any other children I knew then and know now.'

I said something about the hothouse atmosphere in which most of them spent their formative years. Their lives contradict the expectations vested in them. None of them likes communal life. They are a strange family, composed of outsiders. They either don't want to marry or have difficulty in adjusting themselves to marriage. Similar surprises occurred among the human products of the *kibbutz* system, so hopefully devised to solve the psychological hang-ups of adult life.[1]

With all their contrariness I found the priestly children easy to communicate with. Most of them are strikingly handsome, have charm, spontaneity, and a kind of generosity that singles them out in a country which has the reputation of being hospitable. Are they withdrawn perhaps because they are in constant touch with ultimate reality? If so, the adjective mystical, however misused otherwise, does apply to them.

They made me feel a great deal of affection for them. What is the world's give to the world, and to the children of the Temple of Love you can only return love.

There is a postwar generation of the Mariavites and they want to have a modern image for their church. Keen on returning to the Union of the Old Catholics, they expect to get rid of the last vestiges of sectarian isolationism.[2] For this reason, too, they are sceptical about winning over the small group of the Kowalskiites entrenched in Felicjanów. How can one accept their peculiar theology, a young priest told me, since they will insist that God the Father is, in fact, the Virgin Mary. I could have replied that 'peculiar'

[1] See Bruno Bettelheim, *The Children of the Dream: Communal Child-Rearing and its Implications for Society* (1969).

[2] The new Chief Bishop of Plock is to be consecrated in Utrecht. But the real issue lies elsewhere. Originally, the Mariavites were a congregation, a movement within the Church; they did not want to replace that Church but to redeem it. An independent organization representing a religious minority is, strictly speaking, a concept alien to Mariavitism as revealed to Mother Kozlowska.

has a relative meaning in theological speculations, but there was no time to speculate.

In *Mariawita*, the official organ of the Plock group, which was revived after the last war, I read the history of the movement in monthly instalments. They continued for ten years, from April 1959 (no. 2 of that year) to June 1969 (no. 6 of that year), but the story broke off when it reached Kowalski's trial. In 1971 I made inquiries and received a detailed reply from the then Chief Bishop of the Old Catholic Church of the Mariavites (Starokatolicki Kościół Mariawitów), as the Plock group is known.

He confirmed that the serialized history of their church was discontinued quite consciously and for a purpose.

> Because we would have had to make our position clear as regards Archbishop Kowalski's trial and give a number of comments on it. We decided to abandon printing the history in order not to touch on matters painful to us all, and especially to the Felicjanów group. Archbishop Kowalski went the way of martyrdom in Dachau and he died there. This fact demands that we should forget and forgive many things. We do not want to distort history, yet to write it objectively would be painful and would bring no benefit to our church at this moment. We realize, of course, that the majority of public opinion is still formed by the sensational information from the past, which was much exaggerated and hostile.

In the opinion of the Chief Bishop the trial was an attack on Mariavitism as a whole. During the trial 'our Church should have been defended far more than Archbishop Kowalski'. Two years after my inquiry Kowalski's trial was briefly discussed in *Mariawita* (March 1973), but I found the account both misleading and evasive.

Brother Luke is in charge of a Mariavite parish in a large suburb of Warsaw. Their church, destroyed during the war, was rebuilt by the parishioners themselves. Luke is a third-generation Mariavite; he was the youngest priest to be ordained (at twenty-one). With five years of pastoral work behind him he is only twenty-six. His age stands for the new image and he talks young. In his opinion the Catholic Church is turning Mariavite and not the other way round ('hence the interest in our movement'). Yes, the Roman Catholics come to his church and some of them take communion.[1] 'No serious Catholic would now question the validity of our Mass. The ideas of Mother Maria Frances [Kozlowska] may still win the people over.'

Did he himself believe in her?

---

[1] The reason for this could be the strict observance of oral confession in the Catholic Church. The Mariavites do not require it after the age of eighteen.

'She is my spiritual mother,' he answered with sincerity.

I remarked that the Revelations of the Little Mother could be a serious obstacle to some sympathizers.

'Well,' Brother Luke said, 'someone who had great difficulty in accepting them expressed his doubts to the Little Mother. "Do you adore the Eucharist? Do you ask Mary for help?" To both he answered yes. "This is what matters," the Little Mother replied.'

As for the heritage of Kowalski, Brother Luke has many reservations. He introduced the personality cult (his own), he thought he was the Slavonic Pope, he threw good nuns out because they dared to question his arbitrary decisions. And he kept many things secret. Brother Luke spoke with passion in defence of the hard-working Sisters in Plock who had no idea what was going on. No, you cannot whitewash Kowalski knowing the damage he had done. But he died bravely, a Mariavite to the end.[1]

So back I was with the archdiviner John Maria Michael, a bad versifier but a very inventive poet in theological matters. *Wer den Dichter will verstehen, muss ins Dichters Lande gehen.* On a crisp morning, 18 January 1973, I hired a taxi and went in search of Kowalski's childhood. From Warsaw we drove north-east via Minsk Mazowiecki to the place called Latowicz where he was born over a hundred years ago. The sky was low. Patches of snow lay on the fields. Between the villages we passed horse-driven carts on ugly rubber wheels.

A windmill on a hillock cheered me on entering Latowicz, then I spotted a few isolated farms against a grey sky. Someone directed me to the farm of a Kowalski. He was not even related to the Archbishop's ancestors. The name, as I have said, is common. Did he know the Kowalskis in Holy Ghost Street? No. He took me to his neighbour, a courteous old peasant: 'Cousin,' he said, 'here's a gentleman looking for Kowalski's house in the village.' I explained as best I could that it was a family whose son became a bishop. I did not mention the Mariavites. The old man had a dignified presence and a thoughtful wrinkled face, he kept touching his moustache to help his memory. He didn't mention the Mariavites either. Yes, he knew where the old house used to be. 'You go to the village proper, straight to Burial Street.[2] We call it Burial because every funeral passes that way to the cemetery.'

'Was it ever called the Street of the Holy Ghost?'

'Could be, could be. But to us it's always been Burial Street.'

---

[1] According to Brother Luke, the Catholic priests in Dachau did not offer communion to Kowalski, but I had no confirmation of this from any other source.
[2] In Polish *Grzebalna*, from *grzebać*, to bury.

Latowicz proper is an old settlement with a marketplace. One-storey wooden houses on both sides of a long street, all painted yellow and peeling, the provincial inertia on human faces. I look for some indication. None. Where the hell is that Burial Street? A puzzled woman points vaguely to the right.

'Well—they say it's Warynski Street now, or maybe Dzierzynski.' She gets the Communist heroes mixed up.

It turns out to be a crooked continuation of Dzierzynski Street, and it has a different name as well. Finally, there it is, a house with a greenish verandah and a sign above it saying it is the Co-operative Bank. It was built on the site of the original house which belonged to the Archbishop's father. Nothing of it is left. I walk behind and spot a burly man pottering about in a courtyard.

'Perhaps you remember John Kowalski, the Mariavite Archbishop?'

'A Mariavite?' Something dawns on him. 'With the monstrance here?' He touches his chest and grins. 'Yes, yes, I remember. A tall fat man. He came once and talked to the people in the marketplace. Explaining like, you might say. They didn't care much for him. Some women shrieked as women do, you know.'

'I know. How old were you then?'

'A small boy. I am fifty-eight now, you see.'

So at last one person in Kowalski's native place acknowledged his existence. The recollections were hazy. Posterity, why are you that indifferent to your prophets?

As I returned to the car, the driver said we had to wait a little and pointed towards the end of the street. A crowd of people moved slowly in a funeral procession, a shining cross at the head, and a few black banners swaying above. I was acutely conscious of being in a country where nobody is ashamed of death and grief. Both are displayed in public and with dignity. This is what the boy Kowalski must have seen quite often. For it was Burial Street, true to its name, whatever else the officials chose to call it from time to time.

11

Without Secrets there is no Mystery

I

THOSE who talk about the death of God should rather talk about the death of the mysteries. Veils are being removed, the splendours of liturgy are thought superfluous or offensive ('while there are so many poor in the world', runs the argument). The bare functional churches look dead and hardly anybody is seen inside. Who indeed would want to pray to a moribund mystery? Jesus the unknown in Merezhkovsky's search, the hidden God of Shabbetai Zevi, *ignotum per ignotius*, approachable only through a daring act of redemption. All this is nearly gone. Offered in a hygienic wrapper as a useful commodity, religion cannot breathe. It makes you feel good to do good, I heard a preacher say. A stifling squeeze of the wrapper.

Transfiguration and transformation act on the nucleus of a religious pattern. Without them there would be no change in the pattern. The transfigured Christ on Mount Tabor is dramatically different from the Christ who delivers the sermon of the blessings on that other mountain. On Tabor he appears clothed in light, a sun-like figure in the sky, the cosmic Christ. Throughout the three years of his public life he wears the clothes of common men, he is one of them. What distinguishes him from anxious humanity is the way he talks, the way he looks, the way he touches the frightened and the sick, the way he imparts love by being always in the present, in the eternal Now.[1] Outwardly then he is ordinary, inwardly unlike any other human being.

And they put on Christ a purple garment and crowned his head with thorns. They dressed him for the occasion. It was a mocking dress-rehearsal before the ceremony of death, nevertheless this enforced transformation projected an unforgettable image of Christ, which is still haunting man. In

[1] The nearest example of this kind of spiritual emanation in our times was the late Pope John XXIII. It didn't matter what reforms he introduced, his presence mattered more. And people in distant places felt it as a *presence*.

South American countries or in Spain where church statues are lavishly dressed and carried in processions, the act of transformation is part of the ritual. The initial mockery is still in the pattern, but reversed. Reversals of this kind bring in pathos, and liturgy has made ample use of them.

Put a real cloak on a statue and it comes to life, transforming its previous expression, carry it along the street and it is further transformed into a theatrical scene.[1] You mock the object by treating it as if it were alive, but you also create the illusion that a sequence from the Passion is happening again as the folds of the cloak open out and the colour invokes blood. The early Passion plays draw on this suggestive quality whenever the familiar figures of Christ and the Virgin Mary speak directly to the congregation. For the sense of the present is in the participation and it can involve a whole community. The inhabitants of Oberammergau, for instance, live within the pattern of transformation. A peasant who for the rest of his life is to represent John the apostle willingly accepts another continuity for the sake of a ritual: he is an embodied mystery, not a performer.

The cult of the Eucharist evolved over the centuries an ornate ritual which gave the Mariavites a model for their subsequent innovations. The incense, the hymns, the monstrance carried under the baldachin, the Corpus Christi altars—every ritualistic detail has a strong sensual appeal, and not visual alone. Even the sense of touch receives pleasure from the texture of brocade and silk. It is indeed the mystery of the body celebrated by all the senses. When the Mariavites put the emblem of the monstrance on their habits, it was an instinctive choice. I don't think they realized how archetypal their symbol was.[2] For it showed the transformation of the sun image into the cosmic symbol of the body of Christ.

My own experience of religion goes back to summer processions round a country church, in which the monstrance was carried by the priest, his arms supported by two village elders. The yellow of the baldachin and the gold of the monstrance echoed the light in the sky: the rays of the cosmic Christ in the communion of the two suns. The pagan sun god was still shining within the Christian emblem, transfigured by the mystery of incarnation. The power of this archetypal memory was so strong that it drew thousands of peasants to the Mariavite monstrance. They saw the old and the new within the same golden circle, and it was not an abstraction but a body. The body meant birth and rebirth. In a country which worshipped

---

[1] In medieval times a statue of Christ on a donkey was fixed to a platform which had wheels. The illusion of motion was thus enhanced.

[2] The monstrance upside-down resembles the sign of Venus, the female symbol used by alchemists and astrologers.

the Mother in the Virgin, physical attributes dominated the religious imagination.

And the Mother was crowned Queen of Poland in 1656. Throughout the seventeenth and the eighteenth centuries her images were decorated with silver and brocade. Votive emblems and jewels completed each transformation. A wooden statue, for example, representing the Virgin as a child, became the triangular figure of a young Mother goddess, her enigmatic smile still visible amidst the distracting richness of her robes.[1] A little mother-to-be but unaware of the secret that would come with the Annunciation. One begins to grasp the psychological juxtaposition which is reflected in the concept of the Little Mother. The Revelation of 1893 was to Kozlowska a direct Annunciation. No angel delivered the message but the Lord himself. In the presence of Christ she was little, in the likeness of a child, whereas to the priests under her guidance she had to be a mother. Spiritual girlhood transfigured in motherhood, and both contained in the affectionate diminutive: the Little Mother. Just like an icon under the load of glittering adornments which is made to look eternally youthful and eternally old.

Once Archbishop Kowalski stepped on to the slippery path of secrets, a grand religious masquerade was inevitable, so he enriched the Mariavite ritual and appealed to the people through the senses. This, he believed, would prepare the chosen among them for the mysteries beyond the outward splendour. He placed an ivory necklace with an ivory cross on Sister Love whom he would have made Archpriestess had she not rejected him. He designed the diadems and robes for his bishopesses. Their transformative function was obvious as soon as the priestesses appeared at the altar. They evoked ambivalent longings in those who watched them, eroticism mixed with filial piety. Archpriestess Isabel in her stiff attire looked as though she were a statue covered with adornments and ready to be carried in a procession, a Mother figure come to life.[2] The convent children, too, were dressed like dolls. They wore regional costumes—two for each child, and Kowalski chose which ones.[3] Also the theatricals in which the children acted created a fantasy world parallel to the paradisiac dreams of the third Adam.

As the secrecy increased, the masquerade had to be more elaborate, and in the end the Temple of Mercy and Love became a stage on which the same

[1] This is the statue of Our Lady of Skempe in the district of Dobrin, a place of pilgrimages. The striking image of the young girl came into full view when the art specialists examined the statue in 1953. Now it is dressed up again.
[2] A form of religious fervour gripped the whole population of Great Britain at the coronation of Queen Elizabeth II in 1953. Millions watched a live statue on the throne and in a procession and had pious tears in their eyes.
[3] The Dobra and the Lowicz costumes were his choice.

characters performed a number of roles, passing from one reality into another. Archbishop Kowalski was at the same time a conjurer of fantasies and a pedantic stage manager; he directed the whole liturgical show besides playing the best parts: he was now the benevolent father, now the spiritual son, now Michael the Archangel, now Michael the Archbishop. He demanded total obedience and worship from his nuns as he veiled and unveiled them, as he summoned them to the altar and to his bed.

All masquerades are potentially incestuous. The Little Mother created a big family of religious, and when she was gone, they started playing a continuous game of transformations. Their marriages could be described as a justification of mystical incest since in coitus each pair embraced the spirit of the Little Mother. Kowalski the lover challenged the paternal authority which was vested in him. His virile *alter ego* rebelled against the Most Reverend Father, his outward self. Hence the ruthless manner with which he pushed through his reforms. From now on he had to live his contradictions in all his *personae*. Kowalski is a character out of a Genet play.

In *The Balcony* and *The Blacks* Genet exposes the obsessive theatricals of man. Each of his characters dresses up to attack his identity through a fantasy, and in doing so each performs a religious act. For clothes stimulate man's desire to worship and they also attract worship to the person behind the apparel. All over the world now the young parade dressed up as for some fancy-dress ball which will end with a general swap of identities. The Bishop in *The Balcony* is not a real bishop, but the robes make him act like a bishop while the transformation itself gives an outlet to his sexual energy.

Similarly, the character in Pirandello's drama who thinks he is the Emperor Henry IV derives strength from his madness. By acting it out he revitalizes his personality. The return to sanity is a return to weakness, so unbearable that only the crazy costume can protect him from complete disintegration. No human being, it would seem, is spiritually equipped to see his naked psyche. As soon as he glimpses the denuded self, his or anybody else's, he dresses it up in a hurry.[1] The history of every religion consists of wardrobes, and a musty air hangs over them which some people confuse with the odour of piety.

2

Religious language, too, belongs to the historic wardrobes. That's why it smells of mothballs with occasional whiffs of incense to prevent nausea. Alas! the Mariavite movement happened at a bad time in church devotional

---

[1] 'It is impossible for a finite being to stand naked anxiety for more than a flash of time.' Paul Tillich, *The Shaking of the Foundations* (1962).

writing. The sonorous verbiage of nineteenth-century hymns conditioned the mood of public worship and from the start dampened the revivalist passion. There was much to choose from in the Polish vernacular as regards the cult of the Virgin Mary. The Mariavites had no problem there. They also adapted songs, especially later when the Little Mother was given a status equal to that of the Virgin.[1] But whenever they tried to express the new mysteries in their own manner, the results were not impressive. In each text the writer fell back on an accepted formula and kept within its range both in vocabulary and tone.[2] The Little Mother deserved a more original treatment than this, modelled on the Litany of Loreto:

> Spouse of the Very God,
> Spouse of the Heavenly Jerusalem,
> Spouse without blemish,
>> Pray for us.
> Angel nourishing Christ in Gethsemane,
> Angel taking away the cup of the Passion from Christ in Gethsemane,
>> Pray for us.
> Divine Saint [*Święta Boża*], united with the Body of Christ,
> Divine Saint, filled with the blood of the Lamb,
> Divine Saint, united with the Mother of God,
> Divine Saint, sitting beside the Son of God,
> Divine Saint, equal to Him in all things,
>> Pray for us.
> Queen of the Virgins,
> Queen of the priests and the bishops,
> Queen of the priestesses and the bishopesses,
> Queen of all the Saints,
> Queen of the Mariavites,
>> Pray for us.

Even 'Queen of the Mariavites' which sounds euphonious in the original (*Królowo Mariawitów*) is a calk. The pompous phraseology of litanies weighs heavily on this attempt at the deification of the Little Mother. Other prayers and songs addressed to her bear a similar stamp of adaptation. As for versified texts they fare even worse. Grammatical rhymes abound and determine the word order. For example:

> Hail, Lady of the Sun, upon Patmos seen,
> With the crown of twelve stars dressed, and with the moon.

[1] The Lent songs addressed to the Little Mother, for example, are the same as the Catholic ones, except for a few changes. After the opening lines of '*Gorzkie żale*' (Bitter Laments) we get this sort of couplet:

> Ból Mateczki, Jej cierpienie
> Wzrusza serce i sumienie.

(The Little Mother's pain and suffering/Moves the heart and conscience.)
[2] Although Archbishop Kowalski was a prolific writer, he took no interest in devotional songs.

or:

> Holy Archpriestess of the new priesthood,
> you are the guiding star of mystical life.[1]

What creates the interest here is the Mariavite deviation from Christian theology.[2] The literary expression has no aesthetic value, or very little. Curiously enough, Kowalski's person transfigured by a sanctifying process comes out more vividly:

> O Heavenly Prince, Saint Michael,
> Who balances the affairs of men in the scales;
> On Judgement Day at God's tribunal,
> Be my Defence, Saint Michael![3]

The words here have greater literary power because they operate on two levels of meaning: one refers to the Archangel in the signs of the scales,[4] the other alludes to Kowalski without naming him explicitly. Something shadowy moves between the lines and suggests a hidden area of mystery. This, in my opinion, is essential to a religious text if it wants to reawaken a longing for the unknown.

In the Litany to Saint Michael, printed in the Mariavite breviary, the same effect is obtained by hinting at the millenarian fulfilment:

> O Saint Michael, Patron given to men for ultimate times,
> Saint Michael whose coming in ultimate times was
> foretold by Daniel, St. John, and other Prophets,
> Pray for us.
>
> Saint Michael, Patriarch of the Eternal Covenant and
> Archpriest of the new priesthood,
> Pray for us.
>
> Saint Michael, first to adore the Most Holy Trinity
> in the Mysteries of Incarnation, Redemption, and the
> Holy Sacrament,
> Saint Michael, Shepherd of the Johannine Church,
> Pray for us.[5]

[1] In the original:
> Święta Arcykapłanko kapłaństwa nowego,
> Tyś gwiazdą jest przewodnią życia mistycznego.

[2] One hymn speaks of the Little Mother as the 'Redeemer of the Eternal Church and the promised Eve of the new Paradise'.

[3] In the original:
> Książe niebieski, święty Michale,
> Ty sprawy ludzkie kładziesz na szale;
> W dzień Sądu Boga, w Jego trybunale,
> Bądź mym Obrońcą, święty Michale.

[4] His feast day falls on 29 September under the zodiacal sign of Libra.

[5] As far as I could ascertain this litany was composed by Bishop Titus (Siedlecki) and Archpriestess Isabel.

A believer uttering such lines may bring his devotion to a point of ecstasy through the mantra-like repetition of a refrain, whether it be 'Pray for us', 'Hear us', or 'Have mercy on us'. Prayer depends on reiterated sounds rather than on the meaning of words. The great Hindu mantra *Om namo Narayanaya* was originally a secret imparted only to those who were ready for it. Sound acts quicker than meaning, it can seal off the mind from the interference of verbal associations.

The choir of the 'God-minded' nuns in the Mariavite Temple minded God's business which meant a descent into silence. The Little Mother, according to those who observed her at prayer, never moved her lips or made pious gestures.[1] The Curé of Ars noticed a peasant in his church, who would sit there for hours without any visible signs of praying. The curé asked him what he was doing and the peasant answered: 'I look at Him, and He looks at me.' What the peasant described was an eye-to-eye dialogue, a language of light and not of words.

Why is it then that devotional literature goes on being produced despite the fact that most verbal prayers fail miserably to achieve their purpose? The language of religion dissipates its energy too soon and becomes fossilized through constant and passive usage. Yet all churches persist in verbalizing the approach to the unknown. They rush to name the ground which the angels fear to tread. Perhaps the Hebrews were right in keeping the name of Jehovah away from utterance therefore unsoiled by speech; perhaps the shamans did protect the sacred alliance with animals by not naming them directly but in a roundabout way.

But should one be so harsh on the inadequacies of verbal adoration? True, it is irritating to hear the superlatives vying with one another: 'the most holy', 'the purest', 'the highest', and so on. Is the Almighty in need of this kind of reassurance?[2] The language of political science and of modern economics is as irritating as that of religion. However, it is accepted without much protest because it seems to be relevant to some sort of reality or social necessity. The whole problem, as I see it, rests on the built-in hypocrisy in most abstractions. A fanciful term is invested with authority and becomes a kind of god. Statistics, in particular, need such a watchful god above the figures toted up in columns. As for the inflated language of psychology, it has become intolerably presumptuous. Two centuries from now it will make

---

[1] I was told this by both Sister Felicita and the late Sister Mieczysława.
[2] In his *Lettre ouverte à Jésus-Christ* (Paris, 1973), R. L. Bruckberger writes: '. . . un certain langage qui retentit aujourdhui un peu partout dans vos églises et jusque dans certains mandements épiscopaux pue à plein nez le faux témoignage! Nous en avons assez. Assez de l'équivoque! . . . Assez surtout qu'on vous prenne pour un minable!' Alas, the author is often self-indulgent in his use of rhetorical devices.

A Mariavite priestess celebrating Mass in Warsaw, January 1973.

(*Above left*) The Book of Life. (*Above right*) Philip in old age. (*Left*) Bishop Francis in adoration before the altar, on his return to the Temple after the war.

The People's Mass, photographed for the first time in 1974. (*Left*) The table used as an altar, with the picture of the Little Mother. The sequence (*below and on facing page*) shows consecration; communion; and final prayers (the Litany to the Holy Spirit).

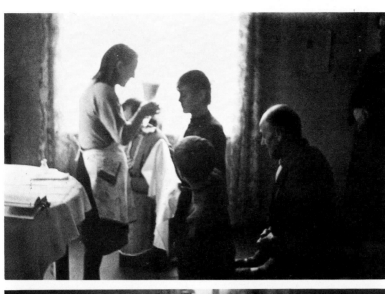

(*Left above*) The Archbishop's birthplace; (*left below*) farmyard at the Felicjanów commune, with an old Sister, 1971.

(*Above*) The English Mariavite, Walter Wilman.
(*Below*) The second and third Mariavite generation: Michael Kowalski with his son, 1973.

us look a gullible lot. Yet the pious invocations to the Virgin or the saints are thought outmoded or rhetorical while the religious reverence accorded to Freud or Jung, with the same prayerful sighs for help, is regarded as a proper relief from our modern anxieties. In other words, it is a matter of what is socially acceptable, a conditioning of attitudes within a given environment.

If we stop regarding religion as a set of fossilized beliefs and instead look for a changing pattern in which man's perception of the perennial mystery is reflected with all its failures and misconceptions, then we have to adjust our view of religious language. The question is not whether it sounds sonorous or whether its message is elevating, but whether it has the ability to bring man closer to the unmapped area of secrets. The question is indeed wide open. St. John of the Cross came to the conclusion that the language of discourse was inadequate to express mystical experience, and yet as a poet he was singularly endowed with a sense of verbal precision.

Jorge Luis Borges shows a similar distrust of the medium when he says (in 'A New Refutation of Time') that 'all language is of a successive nature; it does not lend itself to a reasoning of the eternal, the intemporal'. This is perhaps too discouraging from a poet who is preoccupied with time ('the substance I am made of'). After all, religious experience is, so to speak, time-soiled, despite the longings for another dimension that accompany the experience.

Science no longer boasts that it is superior in exactitude, for it now faces 'a crisis of objectivity'. Scientific experience, like any other experience, cannot be divorced from the observer. In the last analysis, everything we observe is only a sensory illusion. Time, mass, space, are illusions, and so is temperature. The body receives messages, some of which may be misleading—our perception has to act on the evidence it gets, even when it is contradictory. If the universe, according to Jeans, is a great thought rather than a great machine, a thought as big as that may well contain illusions that contradict it. We are close to Shabbetai Zevi's 'thoughtless light'.

Yet, however imperfectly expressed, cabbalistic and Gnostic speculations dared the language to meet the contradictions of mystery. *In principio erat Verbum.* What was the mystery of that primordial word? Why have we gained speech and lost the word so that we cannot cope with secrets? They elude our vocabulary and syntax.

The apostate Messiah from Poland, Jacob Frank, guarded his *Da'ath*, a great secret. Whoever believes in it will gain eternal life. But the second great secret he revealed on 9 November 1788, when he had been brought down by illness. Thus he said: 'The Lord is the royal prince from the womb of the Mother.' Is the language of his revelation satisfactory? Was it clear enough for him? Three years later he died.

Archbishop Kowalski had his 'understandings'—each was like an electric current trilling the brain—but on the level of language his imagination struggled hopelessly to find the right words. With all its leaps and bounds, his theological thought was bold enough to invigorate the language about which he cared. But it didn't. At his best he used Voltairean snarls in polemics and had a flair for journalistic topics. In *The Work of Great Mercy*, which was meant to be a monument to the Little Mother, Kowalski indulged in the pious idiom of his day, plastering her image with too many adjectives and diminutives; he failed to project the mystery of her Revelations, leaving the Little Mother's own text to speak for itself.[1] His poems exhibited the worst features of post-Romantic verse, distorted further by his maniacal use of the *terza rima*.

The Mariavites under Kowalski found themselves in possession of a mystery. They dressed it up in robes and diadems, and kept the secrets of the elect hidden from the eye. But neither Kowalski nor any of his disciples had the poetic power to project the mystery on to the language. They accepted the fossilized phraseology of the devotional writing on which they had been brought up and tried to impose their pattern on it. But the pattern didn't fit and fell out into the morass of verbiage.

3

'The truth of the myth is in the mystery.' Merezhkovsky used a poetic key to open *The Secret of the Three*. But mystery is always set against meaning, if by meaning we understand any attempt at definition or categorization. That's why the lavish praises of the Trinity or Jesus the Unknown sound so hollow in the official language of worship. Kowalski couldn't cope with the secrets he had unleashed from the Christian dogmas any more than he could protect them from vulgarization, including his own. His grief and guilt after the Little Mother's death made him see her shadow in a primordial archetype. This brought out the fear and fascination of the unknown in the sexual act.

Scratch the peasant and you'll find a pagan. Quite unaware of being so close to the pagan mysteries, Kowalski attracted the sun god to the monstrance on his habit, and the sun god heated up his body for the nuptials of the Earth Goddess. Did he know what truth he was hoping to find in the

---

[1] Kozlowska's language is plain with a touch of coyness. But at least she manages to convey the sense of her own helplessness in being the instrument of God's action. On the whole she avoids rhetorical chanting.

paradisiac myth of bodily innocence which he linked with the mystical marriages? The truth as seen by others rebounded against his worldly ambitions and they crashed at his feet.

We can only guess the extent of the mystery that indirectly caused Archbishop Kowalski's downfall. Ultimately, it concerned the secret of the Three. The Trinity is a Marriage. The royal Prince, as Jacob Frank said, comes from the womb of the Mother and he is also the Lord. The Mother holds them both in the embrace of eternity. In his teaching after 1935 the Archbishop pushed the Trinitarian idea as far as his mind would let him. The marriage in this case is a triple union, wholly incestuous if we apply the human terms of kinship, and also androgynous by implication. To dismiss it as a bourgeois concept of respectability tacked on to mysticism would be a facetious way out. Kowalski had a genius for undercutting the respectable with the inappropriate—a quality that should endear him to the young. As for theology, everything in it seems inappropriate. The devil's advocate might well argue that it is highly disrespectful to provide the Creator with a theological context.

The Trinity is a Marriage then, the mystery of a triple union in a non-dimensional and timeless continuum. The completeness of the Kingdom of God on earth will reflect this union.[1] In the Mariavite breviary there is a dialogue between the Little Mother and the disciple, from which I quote this significant passage:

> LITTLE MOTHER: Because of my Passion you will be joined to my Divine Beloved and Husband with the bond of married love, a love similar to that which exists between the Persons of the Most Holy Trinity and between myself and my Divine Husband.
> DISCIPLE: O dearest Little Mother, it was your most holy Passion which gained for us nearly as much as the Passion of the Lord Jesus. It opened to us the Third Heaven which Holy Scriptures foretold.

There is a corollary here between the secret of the Third Heaven and the secret of a dead person. For what the Little Mother says is spoken out of time. In a sense all revelations do intervene from outside and are cast widely like a net; that's why it is often difficult to pin them down to a particular time sequence. They have to remain elusive in meaning. This is true even of such specific orders from outside as those delivered at La Salette and Fatima. The intervention of the Little Mother in the affairs of the Mariavites came, as it were, through Kowalski's 'understandings' during his great

[1] Archbishop Raphael (whose name means 'God heals'), the present leader of the Kowalski group, spoke to me of this act of completion (*zupełność Królestwa Bożego*) in a conversation on 28 August 1971.

crisis after her death. One might say that his parapsychic receiver intercepted the messages from the Third Heaven, and they startled him at first, causing a mental storm.

An English visitor saw madness in his blue eyes ten years later. Was it perhaps a glazed memory of that storm? Face to face with the half-comprehended secrets of the incestuous marriage of the Three, Kowalski reacted as a Siberian shaman would have done: he plunged into the whirlpool of contradictory emotions, he became mentally sick so that the darkest cells of his brain could provide clues. The cure of madness goes through madness. The glass man in Cervantes' *El licenciado Vidriera* has to go through the experience of being made of glass. But abnormality and the so-called norm are relative terms. Kowalski the mad Mariavite shaman would have found a sympathetic listener in R. D. Laing or I. M. Lewis. Disorder against social order, mystery against meaning. What matters is the shaman's triumph over the experience of chaos. Shabbetai Zevi fought the dark with darkness.

'Out of the agony of affliction and the dark night of the soul comes literally the ecstasy of spiritual victory.' Without ecstasy there is no way of glimpsing the mystery of the unknown God in a flash which blinds reason. 'Certainly religions which employ ecstasy seem much more sensitive to the impact of changing circumstances than those which do not,' writes I. M. Lewis in his analysis of the ecstatic phenomena. Possession 'represents an assertion in the most direct, dramatic, and conclusive form that the spirits are mastered by man. What is proclaimed is not merely that God is *with* us, but that He is *in* us. Shamanism is thus the religion *par excellence* of the spirit made flesh.'[1]

Kowalski's mysteries are always incarnated mysteries. He sees the whole Trinity in the Eucharist which is a body triumphant. '*Le Verbe, cet amour des trois personnes divines*,' said Vintras. And this triple love was made flesh.

I have used two terms in this book to denote the directions of growth in religion: one is 'horizontal', the other 'vertical'. The explorers of the unknown, whether they are possessed prophets, shamans, or contemplative mystics, make the vertical growth possible. Like the shaman climbing the Cosmic Tree on his ascent to heaven, each of them chooses the upward direction. The vertical line of the tree is a paradisiac example,[2] a longing for the sun god, the god in the sky.

The horizontal religion, on the other hand, clings to the surface and is

---

[1] I. M. Lewis, *Ecstatic Religion* (1971), ch. 7.
[2] '. . . *In illo tempore*, in the mythic time of Paradise, a Mountain, a Tree or a Pillar or a Liana connected Earth with Heaven, so that primordial man could easily go up into Heaven by climbing it.' Mircea Eliade, *Myths, Dreams and Mysteries* (1960), ch. 3.

usually well adjusted to its environment. When it grows, it grows into an organization. One sees it, for instance, in the development of the Franciscan order after the death of its founder. Brother Elias who modified the austere Rule was accused of betraying St. Francis. But what he did, in fact, was to alter the vertical direction which reached its highest point on Mount La Verna.[1] He wilfully made the Order grow horizontally into a multi-national organization. This was inevitable, and he had to sacrifice his early reputation to achieve this purpose.

Archbishop Kowalski chose a shaman-like climb towards the paradisiac Third Heaven. But somewhere on the way up he managed to snatch a vision of it and thought he could bring it down, so impatient was he to begin God's Kingdom on earth which would embody in the literal sense the secret of the Three. His priestesses and his polygamy were the consequences of his shamanistic madness. To use St. Paul's words from the Second Epistle to the Corinthians, he saw things 'which a man may not utter', but unlike Paul, he uttered them in acts which offended public morality. The third Adam in him wanted the deification of the body within the restored paradisiac pattern, if only for the duration of a sexual ecstasy.

Let's assume for the sake of argument that such a deification is necessary before the nuptials in the Third Heaven. The Trinity is an unknown dimension of love, '*cet amour des trois personnes divines*'. Unless you go through the unknown in yourself, you cannot enter the unimaginable dimension. Your own secret must be absorbed by the mystery. In Sufism, to take a parallel example, 'the secret protects itself'.[2] And Sartre argues in his apotheosis of Genet that the Eternal (i.e. the unknown) can order a man to commit a crime. True, God told Abraham to kill his son, and Abraham did not question the order.

The ecstatic passion in the vertical growth of religion often acts contrary to the morals on the surface. The prophet Hosea married a whore, for such was God's command: Léon Bloy must have felt a similar inspiration when he found a mediatrix in a prostitute. What do we know of the hidden motives behind each holy outrage? The law-giver breaks the tablets with God's commandments. Is a true believer then a man of contradictions always ready for the unexpected? In search of the divine secrets he 'should go through all religious rites and established orders so that he might annihilate every one of them from within'.[3] A violent iconoclast destroys what is

---

[1] The mount where St. Francis received the stigmata corresponds to the symbol of the Cosmic Tree and also to the mystical mounts like Tabor.
[2] According to Idries Shah, *The Sufis* (1969), p. 331.
[3] I quote from G. Scholem's essay on Shabbetai Zevi, cited above.

merely on the surface. Only through a process of spiritual annihilation can a transfigured pattern emerge, ablaze with mystery.

If Christ did claim that he could destroy the Temple and build it up again in three days, his words were meant to shock the people out of their complacency. His cross is an intersection of the vertical with the horizontal.

4

We are all priests. This was the final message of Archbishop Kowalski. He instituted the People's Mass in 1935 after his downfall. Any Mariavite could in theory celebrate Mass and give himself communion.[1] This solved the problem of small communities with no priest in residence and of isolated Mariavites who lived miles apart from one another. But the deeper implications of Kowalski's reform were not apparent before the Second World War. All churches, however small, seemed then confident about their future. Today the situation is totally different. Not only is the number of those with a vocation steadily declining but the priests themselves feel at odds with the world around them.

Many priests don't know how to respond to the pressures of a rapidly changing society, some give up either in despair or in anger, and leave the Church altogether. Is the priest then becoming a redundant figure, a relic of the old system of professions, uncertain of his spiritual role and ignored only too often by those who should need him? The question: 'What to do with priests' is changing into 'Why priests at all?' It is this latter query that recalls Kowalski's bold attack on the institution, and is also the title of Father Küng's recent essay, *Why Priests?*[2]

Hans Küng who is a Catholic and a theologian sees the future priest as a leader in a Christian community 'who directs the Church by means of the sacraments', but he is highly critical of the whole hierarchical organization of the clergy, which is set above and apart from the communities of laymen. When he talks about the general priesthood of all believers he is, in fact, very close to Kowalski's formulation concerning the universal priesthood. Küng reminds us that 'in principle all Christians are empowered to administer

[1] In the Mariavite breviary the text of the People's Mass occupies only three pages. The act of contrition has a prayer addressed to the Virgin Mary, the Little Mother, and St. Michael. There is also a shorter version of the same Mass which is consecration alone, and it can be performed on the palm of the hand in lieu of a chalice or a glass. 'This way the Mariavites celebrate Mass in secret whenever they are among the ungodly and the sneerers. . . .'
[2] Hans Küng, *Wozu Priester* (1971); I quote from the translation by John Cumming (1972). Unfortunately, this little book is turgid to read.

baptism and the eucharist'. He raises serious objections to the sacramental view of priesthood, a relatively late concept which was the cause of much abuse within the organization of the Church. Historical evidence supports Küng's argument.[1]

In his criticism of the religious establishment Kowalski again and again invoked the names of the apostles who, according to him, never tried to impose their superiority on the early communities of Christians. He derided the papal claims to the throne of Peter as much as the throne itself. But since he himself was deposed from high office, he had good enough reasons for distrusting the priestly charisma. We are all priests, he said. Celebrate Christ's mystery in your homes, and lay the foundations of the new Temple in your hearts. The dispersed groups of Kowalski's followers saw the guiding beam of his apostolic lighthouse. But soon came the blackout of the war and the Mariavites faced the possibility of being left without any leaders. Should a believer fend for himself in extreme situations such as deportation, imprisonment in a concentration camp, or while hiding from persecution? Is he to be deprived of the sacrament because there is no priest to give it to him?

The individual right to priesthood, however justified, poses a sacramental dilemma: is the sacred in man strong enough to sustain his communion with the mystery? If it isn't, then the sacrament has no validity and the celebration of it becomes a ritual, nothing more. Ritual is like dressing up; it may look mysterious, but the true mystery touches the limits of perception. Our physical existence can, of course, do without it. For better or for worse, the will to live reasserts at every moment the primordial condition from which no human being is exempt. It is the condition of the first Adam.

In a remote village in central Poland I was allowed to attend the People's Mass celebrated by a peasant woman. On entering her house I said the Mariavite greeting, 'Let us praise the Most Holy Sacrament.' It startled her, but it was also a sign, after which I explained the purpose of my visit and we began talking. Finally she agreed to say Mass in a cottage nearby, belonging to her sister, and went out to wash herself and prepare the table which was to serve as an altar. It didn't take long. I crossed the yard, walked into a bigger cottage and saw a round table between two windows, covered with a white cloth. Two candles were on it, a crucifix in the middle and the photograph of the Little Mother on her death-bed propped up against the

---

[1] 'One cannot assert,' says Küng, 'that ordination ("ordination to the priesthood") was "instituted by Christ", since everyone knows that it is neither mentioned nor implicit in any Pauline text. . . . Instead it was taken over from Judaism, as were the colleges of "elders".' *Why Priests*, op. cit.

crucifix. A middle-aged farmer, his wife, and two young boys were present with me in the room.

Visibly nervous, the peasant priestess knelt and read out the opening prayers from the Mariavite breviary. But as she spoke on in a trembling voice she forgot our presence, her face altered, became almost beautiful, and at the moment of consecration I saw tears pouring down her face. Her whole being seemed to be lifted up into another dimension. And I noticed, too, that the flame of one of the candles bowed, as if in reverence. I hadn't been prepared for a mystery that powerful and yet utterly simple, devoid of any outward signs of glory. As a Catholic I knew in my heart that Christ was present at this offering; I was even more aware of it when communion was being received by that family of five. How could this Mass be anything else but valid? Was I a heretic because I accepted its validity without any reservations?

Later I learnt that during the German occupation some Catholics deprived of their parish priests who had been taken to concentration camps, would often come to hear the Mariavite Mass and receive communion in two kinds. Would this happen again if religious worship had to go underground under persecution?

You are all priests, said Kowalski. Act on it. This was his message to our age of fear, which his apocalyptic radar predicted. So we are potential priests even if such religious self-service offends our customs. But does it mean that we are also potential mediators between the divine Will and the will which is supposed to be exclusively our own? The distinction between the two wills is difficult to draw, as Kowalski found out to his detriment. The trouble with a notion like the Will of God is that the strong-willed tend to take it up and do their best to impose it on those with weak wills. One could, of course, argue that the Almighty uses all manner of man: the weaklings, too, have to absorb his Will. But in practice they submit to a strong personality which claims to dispense divine energy.

Kowalski was such a strong-willed man, and an insufferable bully at his worst. The third Adam in him fiddled with the arithmetics of the Third Heaven and multiplied the number of brides accordingly. And his sexual appetite grew with the progress of passion. When, after initiating so many virgins, young and middle-aged, the Mariavite King David gat no heat, he used small girls to revitalize himself in the service of ecstasy. Most of his theological speculations could be subjected to a psychoanalyst's scrutiny. A Freudian looking for genitals in any dressed-up fantasy would have no problem with Kowalski. He manifested his lingam so well, vertically speaking, that it became a myth. Yet the truth of the myth is in the mystery.

What strikes me as mysterious in Kowalski's posthumous reputation is the ambivalent behaviour of his enemies and victims. As I talked about the Archbishop in Plock, every person who knew him—even the woman whom he raped brutally while she was still in the convent school—all felt the glow of his glory and admitted it. If anything, they were sorry for him that he had to let them down in the end. Maybe Bishop Philip had saved the Mariavite church from total collapse, but without Kowalski Mariavitism became a tepid affair. As one of the Old Catholic churches it is weak, because they are weak. Obviously, Philip did not wish to kill the spirit of the Little Mother, yet he nearly killed the interest in her.

In 1903 she said about Kowalski: 'I felt a new Adam in Father Michael.' The first Adam and the second, Christ, are fixed points in the paradisiac pattern, and between them a process of transfiguration goes on from age to age. The third Adam is a recurring promise, a man caught between two mirror images. They double his primordial archetypes and cancel themselves out in the space which he wants to inhabit. The third Adam is reborn into the myth of the Fall, yet his vertical vision draws him up towards the woman clothed in the sun: the Virgin, the Mother, the Eternal Feminine in the androgynous mystery of the Creation.[1]

We prayed with our bodies, a seventy-year-old nun confessed to me in a moment of paradisiac innocence. She had a photograph of Kowalski by her bed. Did she pray to him? Yes, oh yes. He was Archangel Michael, didn't I know? Yes, I said, I knew that, and my imagination was stirred. Somewhere in outer time, Kowalski and Vintras had met after all; he as the other Michael and Vintras as his prophet of Tilly.

An esoteric interpretation of the zodiac explains this with stellar clarity. Seven archangels rotate in the heavens—six are the planetary intelligences and the seventh, Michael, is the Sun.[2] They guide the cosmic evolution of man and with their rotation come the new ages. After Gabriel (the Moon Intelligence) Archangel Michael's era began in 1879, and it will last about four hundred years. Kowalski was born—or reborn as he would say—in the first decade of the Archangel (1871). According to the esoteric zodiac, cosmic Christianity is now being charged with the power of Michael who will fight the Dragon once again. The date of the battle is a secret, of course.

[1] The vulva of the female force in the creation is a central symbol of Tantric art. Women carry the cosmic energy: the great Goddess is in every one of them. The joys of heaven are erotic and polygamous.

In Salvador Dali's interpretation of the Ecumenical Council (1960) it is the female force that breaks through the pattern of conventional symbols.

[2] See John Jocelyn, *The Meditations on the Signs of the Zodiac* (New York, 1970), which is based on Rudolf Steiner's teaching. I find the link between the sun image of the Archangel and the sun image of the monstrance very interesting.

You have to wait until the seasonal four is multiplied by the sacred three, and then, behold! the twelfth chapter of the Apocalypse breaks open with a clap of thunder. And, hearing the Archangel's watchword, *Quis est Deus*, the third Adam rises from the ground.

Epilogue for Two Voices

I

The devil's advocate speaks:
There are two voices audible in this book, and one of them may sound flippant to a discerning ear. But how else should the devil's advocate address the non-religious public of today on the subject of religion? The tone apparently is what matters. I suppose that even now I could demolish the Mariavite case with a few thrusts of derision, but this is precisely what I mustn't do. The vanity of human wishes is so abundant in examples that if you place any person against his destiny, he is soon cut down to size by his unfulfilled aspirations.

Take, for instance, the folly of titles which religious worship seems to encourage. Man never tires of flattering his Maker with grand epithets. Some of this glory is reflected in the titles of the senior clergy. Splinter groups as a rule indulge in such self-promotion. Kowalski raised himself from Bishop to Archbishop, he made his first wife Archpriestess, the other elect received titles, diadems, and symbolic names according to his estimation of their worth. Once the process of titular upgrading is set in motion it tends to spread rapidly. A mitre begets a mitre.

In his apostolic zeal, Kowalski bestowed honours on foreigners, half expecting to win some small corner of England or France for the Little Mother. Mariavitism in England is a story as peculiar as the chief character who adopted Kowalski's gospel. He was Walter Wilman, born into a poor family in Bradford, who had a liking for the pious smell of incense and the pulpit but, apart from being a lay missionary in Yorkshire, could not get much satisfaction out of the Church of England. With a friend (later to be known as Brother Augustine), he visited Plock a few months before Kowalski's deposition. As soon as he saw the Mariavite pageantry he wanted to run away. The attraction of the unfamiliar proved stronger and he found himself chatting in English to a nun with a deformed back (Sister Gertrude). He returned home a Mariavite apostle and began to preach the Little Mother's message. A Mariavite parish was established in Woodstock, of all plausible places, and Wilman had a number of followers, mainly among women. The split within the mother Temple affected the work: Wilman declared himself on the side of the deposed Archbishop who, in turn, appointed him to the episcopate by post (Kowalski was fond of mailing such favours). Brother Augustine remained loyal to Plock and his position became untenable. For a short time he tried to run a Mariavite mission in a hired hall at Bournemouth, but he couldn't raise money for a church. Wilman's Woodstock parish faded away.

Over the years a strange thing was happening to Wilman: he stooped more and more until he began to look like a Mariavite Richard III, a little man with a wry smile. Was it the memory of that hunchbacked nun that affected his spine? Wilman enlarged the realm of the mitre by 'enthroning' one bishop ('Bishop Anthony of Leeds'), and after the war tried to exercise some authority over his stray lambs as Minister-Provincial of the Mariavites. He earned his living as a verger in York and also worked in a factory producing altar bread. In the end he lived in a damp hermitage until his poor health forced him to go to a home for old people in York. He died at the age of seventy-five in September 1962, twenty years after Kowalski.

The other English Mariavite was left with a divided heritage. Despite their differences in the past, Brother Augustine speaks with affection of his dead colleague, but has no bishop's title. When I visited him, he opened an old chest-of-drawers and showed me two mitres lying there in readiness for a call from Plock. Had Kowalski lived he would not have allowed them to lie in an English drawer, unused. He certainly encouraged his French apostle, Brother Marc Maria Fatôme (consecrated in September 1938), who became the *évêque mariavite* of Nantes and distributed a picture of the Little Mother with a poem in French underneath.[1] A Hungarian who stayed in Plock during the war now has his own church in Canada and is robed with this sonorous title: 'His Excellency the Most Reverend Monsignor Dr. Thomas J. Fehervary, Archbishop-Metropolitan, Montreal.' It sounds equally impressive in French.

The devil's advocate, of course, must understand the ecclesiastical lore and those who are captivated by it for life. There are indeed many bishops, archbishops, and metropolitan patriarchs at large, each perpetuating the

---

[1] The last stanza reads:

> Marie Françoise conduisez vers Jésus;
> Nous tous vos enfants, Mariavites de nom,
> Nous suivons vos pas, imitant vos vertus,
> O Sainte en renom.

On his stamp with the Mariavite emblem Marc Fatôme put the words: *Les Mariavites de Port-Royal.* The link is significant.

mitre-topped species by the act of consecration. Kowalski's myth, however, is too strong and too elusive for any such mitre to stay on. It keeps falling off. You can tread on it or pick it up with mock reverence. Talking about Kowalski is like invoking a spirit in a dark room, and his presence is soon felt. How often didn't I try to unravel his sexual secret? How often did I hear the truth muffled by the aged secret which his women felt obliged to protect.

One conversation brought me close to a medical explanation. According to the Mariavite doctor[1] who knew Kowalski's state of health, the Archbishop did suffer from partial impotence and needed stronger stimuli as his years advanced. His righteous critics labelled these as perversions, perhaps too readily, and the trial tinged everything with scandal. What shocked the contemporaries was probably the practice of *fellatio*, but this form of sexual stimulus appears to have been quite common in secret rituals over the ages. As for the alleged intercourse with girls under age, it could well have been his other remedy for his diminishing sexual prowess. Besides, as part of the ceremony of initiation it enhanced both the pleasure and the secret. In many instances, I am sure, the mere act of fondling a child was a stimulus for the Archbishop. I asked an ex-nun who had played in the mandolin orchestra whether she thought that Kowalski was sexually inadequate. In a round-about way she said no, but for obvious reasons she refused to be explicit. Another ex-Mariavite answered my queries with a rhetorical cry: 'Why, why this passion for immature bodies?'

Polygamy could have been as much a convenient arrangement as the way of controlling jealousy which flashed green lights in the Mariavite cloister. One of the priestly children described it by using a term borrowed from the west: 'wife swapping'. A recent newspaper report from America concerns a Protestant theologian, much revered by the intellectuals, whose widow has revealed him as having erotic obsessions which would have shaken the foundations of conventional morality had they been known to his admirers in his lifetime. Is hypocrisy then a timid cousin of sincerity?

The Mariavite Archbishop accepted the sexual force in religion. He discovered for himself that the intimacy between two or more human bodies could also prefigure the soul's intimacies. Is his religious experiment to be regarded as suspect just because it so obviously gave outlet to his desires? Could someone like Isabel have been filled with holiness and yet had a taste for the dark side of sex?

In Hellheaven the sins of saints hang upside down so that the moralists on earth should fall over backwards, in wonderment. The case for the canonization of John Maria Michael is dismissed because too much evidence

1 The admirable humanitarian, Dr. Kopystyński, now dead. (See p. 150.)

in his favour has recently come to light under the auspices of the Demon of Noon.

2

The witness speaks:

When I turned up at the Felicjanów commune in August 1971 I didn't know that I had chosen the right year for my visit. For it was the centenary of Kowalski's birth, the fiftieth anniversary of the Little Mother's death, and twenty-five years had passed since the death of Archpriestess Isabel. A numerical knot had tied those three together in celebration of a Mariavite trinity. I am still puzzled why I had arrived at Plock that August and why I decided to go to the Kowalski commune first. As my work developed I began to notice more such coincidences. I would suddenly act on a mere hunch, travel hundreds of miles in search of a remote chance, and at the end of my journey find an answer to a query or a pile of 'lost documents'. Characters would appear out of the blue to put me in touch with people whom I assumed to be dead or untraceable.

This type of experience, I suppose, must be familiar to writers of biographies; but it was never my intention to write a biography. Kowalski asserted his posthumous claims on my imagination in much the same way as he used to assert himself in people's lives. I began to learn his mental habits. One incident, in particular, struck me as a sort of parapsychic joke, and it doesn't matter who or what played it on me that memorable morning. I travelled in Spain with my portable library of photocopies and notes, writing in odd places, a week here, a week there. One evening I realized that I would need the novel of Barrès, *La colline inspirée*. The next day I was on the move again, between two towns, and stopped at a supermarket by the road to buy mineral water. A stand with paperbacks was outside, most of them soaking in the sun. Among the Spanish titles I noticed a couple of Simenons in French and then like a secret message *La colline inspirée* leapt towards my eyes. I got it for half price because the cover was so bleached. I couldn't possibly work out the odds of this coincidence, but it taught me a useful lesson: that the witness should be open to the evidence of chance and never interfere with the time of his inner clock.

Moreover, the witness is a movable link in a crowd of other witnesses. The documents, however accurate, are one-sided; the people, however biased, are many-sided. Those who trust the printed evidence more than the oral record give the past an unfair advantage over the evidence in the making. Again and again I was reminded of the vulnerable nature of all data. Had I for some reason delayed my research on the Mariavites, I would have allowed a good deal of oral material to vanish without a trace. Within two years five of my older witnesses, those who provided me with invaluable comments on the early years of Mariavitism, have died. And the shadow of death, whether true or invoked by anxiety, accompanied my travels and my work. Moreover, I was told that some of my potential witnesses were lost or mislaid like files in the library of human existence. I soon learnt to distrust such information.

One person who played a big part in Kowalski's trial proved hard to find. I chased her from address to address until I reached a bleak tenement building and entered a big room with washing hanging from wall to wall on barely visible lines. I was too late; the woman had died at a tram stop a few months earlier. I listened to the story of her old age, and nothing in it suggested her Mariavite past, so I began to doubt whether it was the same person. My witness mentioned the visit of the police soon after the woman's death, the room being thoroughly searched, and I had an uneasy feeling of having stepped into a sinister thriller. As I was about to leave, something prompted me to ask: 'Did she keep any picture by her bedside?'

'Oh, yes,' said my interlocutor, 'a small picture of the Virgin. Our Lady of Perpetual Succour, you know. And she often cried while praying to her.'

I needed no further proof.

Archbishop Kowalski knew that sexual ties were the best means of reinforcing the vows and oaths of secrecy, and he relied on their endurance. I was often touched by the erotic memory that informed the reminiscences of old women who had agreed to talk to me about their Most Reverend Father, Husband, and Lover. I trusted their evidence, though it was often veiled, because I received it in a glow of love at the sunset of their lives.

The places connected with the Archbishop's career had, on the whole, less to offer. On my first visit to the Plock Temple I thought it felt like an empty tomb deprived of the mystery. It was a cold winter day and my hospitable hosts took me round. We walked through long corridors past the cells, into the Little Mother's rooms, into the choir, then below into the cellars where her remains are immured but inspire no mystical aura. Perhaps she wished it to be so: the Little Mother disliked the cult of relics. No plaque to Kowalski in the Mariavite Temple; his presence there is anonymous.

Did I feel him more in the chapel room at the Felicjanów commune? I heard his name invoked in the liturgy of the Mass: 'Saint Michael pray for us.' And I saw his successor, a tall, handsome man who was once a pilot, bending low to kiss the altar, his whole body transformed and sweat pouring down his face. Yes, I could sense the concentration of a body, all nerves in it attuned to the expectation of the mystical presence. And I believed then in the meaning of the bodily succession, the mystery that can only be passed on in tangible form through sexual union. From the Little Mother down the ladder of initiation, each rung serving a purpose in the system of the elect. They were all a family once, a multiple marriage in the likeness of the Marriage whose other name is the Trinity. If so, Archpriestess Isabel, who is buried under the statue of the Virgin in the front of the house, must have been instrumental in passing on the angelic succession which she received from the body of Michael, her Husband and the Son-Lover of the eternal Mother. Without secrets there is no mystery.

I was shown a medallion worn by a married nun, in which the layers of these relationships on the model of the Third Heaven were clearly exemplified. At the bottom there lay a wisp of the Little Mother's hair and a tiny bit of her habit. It was covered with the photograph of Kowalski. Only his head. Above this layer there were the photographs of the nun's husband and their four children with wisps of their hair. Visible on top of the medallion was a picture of Our Lady of Perpetual Succour, the Mother of the Mariavites. The person who allowed me to examine this family relic was not aware of its full significance, that is of Kowalski's role as mediator. But why should a child born of a mystical union know that much?

Kowalski repeated often enough that the only Rule of the Mariavite congregation was Love. And he had Sister Love in the Temple who in the end rejected the offerings of his heart, left Plock, and married.

Obstacle after obstacle was put in my way when I tried to trace Sister Love. And I couldn't get any photograph of her. Some Mariavites obviously didn't want me to meet her, others appeared to imply that she was already in her grave, silenced for ever. At last, after nearly a year, I discovered her married name, and then someone suggested that I should look for her in Lodz, a big industrial city. I boarded the plane on a hunch, hoping that I would find her at home a week before Christmas. Finally, after a few false attempts, I heard her voice on the telephone. What could I say but pretend that I had an urgent message from London? The trick worked and she invited me to come round the same evening. A lined face with a nose wide at the nostrils greeted me in the doorway. She was a small woman over seventy, her movements agile and precise, and when she switched off the television and sat down, I said very quietly: 'The message is from the past. I've come to talk about Archbishop Kowalski.'

Her whole face contracted, she lit a cigarette, inhaled twice, peering at me through the smoke, and for a moment I thought she would ask me to leave. But her feminine curiosity was stirred; how did I find her? Then she glanced at the door.

'My two grandchildren will be back any minute. They know nothing. We'll talk tomorrow. Could you come to my place at ten in the morning?'

She gave me an address and soon after I heard the door open.

It was snowing hard when I entered her small flat on the tenth floor of a gloomy functional building. The glow of whiteness seemed to soften her features and her mood. Yes, she was willing to answer my questions but I soon realized that she was not going to tell me everything.

Yes, she was a proud, independent girl of noble birth when chance brought them together—it so happened that she took a seat next to him at a social gathering in Lublin. For Kowalski it was love at first sight, and a surprise in view of his elaborate system of mystical unions. Perhaps he wanted to conquer a spirit as strong as his own. He persuaded her to come to Plock and she became a Mariavite at eighteen partly to assert herself against her family and public opinion. But it wasn't an act of faith in the Little Mother. 'You don't allow yourself to believe in her wholly,' the Archbishop would repeat when Sister Love became restless in the convent. The name, of course, was his choice—later he added Sister Faith and Sister Hope but the other two were merely complementary.

Sister Love's rise to the pinnacle of the Mariavite hierarchy caused envy among other nuns. Her novitiate was a speedy affair though difficult emotionally. She had to humble herself before Sister Celestina, her spiritual adviser, who found it very hard to love the Archbishop's darling. When later it was Celestina's turn to humble herself by kissing Sister Love's foot, she feigned illness or was really sick because she couldn't face the ordeal.

'What did you feel during that ceremony when nun after nun was paying homage to you the new symbol of Love?'

'I hated it all,' she said. 'I was red in the face seeing them bend and kneel. And I think I cried.'

At this point she showed me her visiting card printed at the cloister:

SISTER MARIA LOVE [followed by her surname]
Superior of the Mariavite Sisters

This puzzled me. 'What about Isabel, the Mother Superior?' I asked.

'Well, how should I explain it?—there were to be two Superiors over the nuns, spiritual and—'she hesitated—'and administrative. Yes, that's it. As there were two vicarial Sisters.'

It seemed to me a clear enough explanation of how the inner church was structured into the outer. On Sister Love at the centre rested the invisible edifice with Isabel and Philip at either side. The Archbishop stood above them all, and he also loved her in a special way. Our discussion became awkward. I understood the system while she was trying to convince me there was no inner church, or that it wasn't really active during her three years in Plock. Later she told me that Kowalski never abused any of the girls from the boarding school. How did she know? I had evidence to the contrary from those who participated in Kowalski's initiations.

Why did she herself run away? Simple, she didn't want to be (remain?) one of Kowalski's wives. And she loved Philip. He wrote poems for her, and two of them she has kept, also a couple of letters from Isabel, protesting sisterly love. Yes, Kowalski tried every stratagem to win her back, after her first escape[1] and later, when she left for good, married, and had children. Mariavite priests and nuns in secular disguise were sent with his ardent letters to the country estate where Love was staying with her own sister.

'Wherever I went to hide from them he knew how to find me. Just like you,' she said with a mischievous smile. 'By the way, how did you trace me here?'

'If I told you, would you think I was capable of discretion?'

'Maybe you're right.' She lit her fifth cigarette that morning. It was still snowing outside.

I wanted to know how she remembered her triumphant return to the Temple. I had heard about the big banquet of welcome from a number of people, including her former pupil. Sister Love, like Isabel, taught at the cloister school. She had a firm hand with the children, unlike Isabel; this she admitted with some pride. Archbishop Kowalski resembled an eager adolescent on that occasion but his generosity and joy impressed everyone. There was music and dancing, and kisses of homage, even the children were invited to witness the return of the prodigal Sister-Goddess to her palace of Love. Only the doves of Venus were missing, and a chariot decked with garlands of roses.

'It is true, isn't it, that he grabbed your hand and held it out so that everyone could kiss it as he walked with you?'

'Oh, I don't remember. I was too confused.' But a twinkle in her eye betrayed her. At the banquet, she had winked at one of her pupils who

---

[1] In 1926. One of the immediate reasons was the planned visit to the Holy Land. Although he had taken her to the Bern conference in 1924, to humble Love's pride (love mustn't be proud), the Archbishop decided not to include her this time in his group. But he had second thoughts on the day of departure and sent Sister Celestina to her when they were already sitting in the car. Celestina as a messenger was the last straw. Her again! When they were gone, Love went too. Back to her family.

stared at her as they approached the children. The boy, now a bishop, never forgot the incident:

'Sister Love—oh, she knew what was funny. We shared a joke then with our eyes, at the Archbishop's expense. He would have done anything for her to keep her in the cloister.'

And Sister Love told me that he had been prepared to accept her back with her children. He went on writing letters.

'Have you got any of those letters?'

'No, I burnt them all.'

'They were probably the best things he wrote.'

'Maybe they were.'

Sister Love displayed her Mariavite relics on the table. I could have some photographs to reproduce. I chose two of her. The wide nostrils looked different then—gay, almost quivering with excitement, and the lips were the lips of a woman conscious of her power over men.

'Three men loved me at the same time. It was too much.'

'And you loved him alone,' I said pointing to Philip's photograph.

'He said be patient, wait, wait, trust me. That was during my second stay in Plock. I think he was already then planning Kowalski's deposition.'

'But you left.'

Sister Love looked away, towards the window and the sky a-dance with the white butterflies of winter. She was crying for Love, the goddess of the Temple of Mercy.

.

St. Anton
Grasse
Assisi
La Mancha
London
1972–4

Principal Mariavite Sources

Works by Archbishop Kowalski:

PUBLISHED

The place of publication is Plock unless otherwise indicated. Titles are given in the spelling used before 1936.

Dzieło Wielkiego Miłosierdzia (The Work of Great Mercy), 1922 (published 1924). The second edition of 1929 incorporates 426 additional pages of the so-called *Świadectwa* (Testimonies), and is altogether over 1,000 pages.

Psalterz do Ducha Świętego (A Psalter to the Holy Spirit), 1922; 2nd ed. 1930. Translation of an anonymous work used as a prayer book by the Mariavites.

Nowy Testament po polsku (New Testament in Polish), 1923. Translation with commentary. A second edition was published in 1928, under the title *Pismo Święte Nowego Testamentu.*

Apokalipsa (Apocalypse), 1923; rev. 2nd ed. 1929. Translation of St. John's Revelation, with 200 pages of exegesis.

Brewiarz Eucharystyczny (Eucharistic Breviary), 1923.

Pismo Święte Starego Testamentu (Old Testament), 2 vols., 1925. Translation with ample commentary.

Brewiarzyk maryawicki (Mariavite Breviary), 1925. A fifth revised edition appeared in Felicjanów, 1967.

Modlitwy codzienne (Daily Prayers), 1925.

Co to jest maryawityzm (What is Mariavitism), 1927.

Katechizm zakonny (Conventual Catechism), 1927.

Główne zasady wiary i ustrój Kościoła Maryawickiego (Chief Principles of the Creed and Structure of the Mariavite Church), 1928.

O rzeczywistej obecności Pana Jezusa w komunii świętej (On the Real Presence of Jesus Christ in the Holy Communion), 1929.

Żywot i dzieła świętego Jana Złotoustego (The Life and Works of St. John Chrysostom), 1929.

Korespondencya między biskupami maryawickimi a biskupami rz.-katolickimi (Correspondence between the Mariavite Bishops and the Roman Catholic Bishops), 1930.

Boska Komedja, 1932 (published 1933). Verse translation of Dante's *Divina Commedia* with copious notes and Doré's illustrations. This most ambitious of Kowalski's publications, containing 748 pages, bears the name of M. I. Wiłucka-Kowalska as publisher on the title-page. The printing of the whole text was completed in July 1933.

Mój ideał (My Ideal), 1932. A novel, serialized in *Głos Prawdy* (without the author's name), 7 Jan. to 11 Aug. 1932 (nos. 1–32).

Błąd papiestwa (The Error of Papacy), n.d. Refutation of the bull on papal infallibility.

W ważnej sprawie Mesjanizmu polskiego (On the Important Matter of Polish Messianism), n.d.

Nowenna, n.d. To the Virgin of Perpetual Succour.

UNPUBLISHED
In the Felicjanów archive

J. K. Huysmans, *En route*. Manuscript of 10 chapters translated in the years 1896–1900.

Pamiętnik (Memoir). Manuscript. Dictated to his wife Isabel, probably in 1928.

Beatrycze. 455 pages of typescript. Poem about the Little Mother in 3 parts, 1933.

Syn Człowieczy (The Son of Man). Unfinished poem, 1933–4.

Psałterz Ducha Przenajświętszego (A Psalter to the Most Holy Spirit). Verse paraphrase of an anonymous psalter, 1934.

Psałterz Dawidowy (David's Psalter). Paraphrase in verse, 1934–6.

Naśladowanie Pana Jezusa według Ewangelii św (The Imitation of Jesus Christ according to the Holy Scriptures). 93 pages of manuscript. Unfinished, 1936–7.

Przypowieści Salomonowe (Solomon's Parables). Verse paraphrase of the Book of Proverbs, 1936.

Księga Eklezjastesa (The Book of Ecclesiastes). Paraphrase in verse, 1936.

Św. Jan Chrzciciel (John the Baptist). Two scenes of an unfinished drama, 1936–7.

Męka Pana Jezusa (The Passion of Jesus). Two dramatic scenes, a fragment, 1936–7.

Raj Przywrócony (Paradise Restored). A long poem included in letters from the Rawicz prison, 1937.

Among Kowalski's minor verse compositions 33 have survived, including *Pieśń do Mateczki* (Song to the Little Mother), a few poems addressed to his wife Isabel, and *Zdrada Feldmana*, a piece on 'Feldman's Treachery'.

Mariavite publications edited by Kowalski or to which he contributed:

Maryawita (The Mariavite), weekly, Lodz, 1907–10.

Kalendarz maryawicki (Mariavite Calendars), Lodz, 1908–14.

Maryawicka Myśl Narodowa (Mariavite National Thought), Plock, 1924–5.

Królestwo Boże na ziemi (The Kingdom of God on Earth), weekly (published with the supplement *Głos Prawdy* (The Voice of Truth), Plock, 1927–35; monthly, then fortnightly, Felicjanów, 1936–9.

Wiadomości Maryawickie (*Jednodniówka*) (Mariavite News—Occasional), Felicjanów, 1935.

A quite separate source on which I have drawn occasionally is *Mariawita*, the organ of the group now known as the Old Catholic Church of the Mariavites. This periodical was revived in January 1959 and is still published monthly from Plock.

J.P.

Reference Notes

Titles of Kowalski's works and of Mariavite periodicals are given in full in the list of sources at p. 233.

PROLOGUE

Page 1 'Suddenly he pulled me . . .': *Rok pobytu w klasztorze marjawickim* (A Year's Stay at the Mariavite Convent). Wynurzenia Pani Janiny Zygmuntowej Tołpyhowej, in *Mazowsze Płockie i Kujawy* (Plock), Aug.–Dec. 1926.

I. THE LITTLE MOTHER

Page 8n. So Kozlowska told . . .: Philip Feldman's sketch of her life, *Mariawita* (Plock), no. 3, 1962.   10 'In the year 1893 . . .': *Objawienia Mateczki* (Revelations), in *Dzieło Wielkiego Miłosierdzia*, 5–6.   11 'And you too must not kill . . .': ibid. 7.   12 'Again in a clear light . . .': ibid. 14.   13n. *visio intellectualis*: see Kowalski's pamphlet, *Co to jest maryawityzm*.   14 the ceremony of acceptance: described in *Tygodnik Illustrowany* (Illustrated Weekly) (Warsaw), 3 March 1906.   14n. Father John's memoirs: in *Królestwo Boże na ziemi*, 17 Oct.–24 Dec. 1929.   16 'I felt abandoned . . .': *Objawienia Mateczki*, op. cit., 23–4.   16 'Of all the graces . . .': ibid. 26.   17n. 'Your pride was in this . . .': ibid. 27.

II. BORN ON THE DAY OF CHRIST-ADAM

Page 18 'The desire left me . . .': *Dzieło Miłosierdzia*, 89.   19 '. . . with her little hand . . .': ibid. 94.   20n. 'Brief Life of the Little Mother': *Krótki życiorys Mateczki*, in ibid. 81–316.   21n. Feldman's unpublished memoir: TS. in the possession of his family.   22 'On the sweet night . . .': 'Któż jako Bóg', in *Królestwo Boże*, 8 Dec. 1936.   24 'Everybody was amazed . . .': *Dzieło Miłosierdzia*, 143.   24 'soon, without any reason . . .': ibid. 82.   26 'I didn't know what I had asked for . . .': ibid. 84.   26 'True enough, I thought . . .': ibid. 94.   29 'It was then that the Little Mother saw me . . .': ibid. 161–2.   29 when she pronounced . . . felt at peace: ibid. 166.   29 'In January 1902 when I was . . .': ibid. 167–8.   30 'Whenever the Little Mother noticed . . .': ibid. 168.   31 'At that time, too . . .': ibid. 168–9.   31 'At last on the eighth day . . .': ibid. 170.   33 Father Honorat's pamphlet: *Prawda o maryawitach* (The Truth about the Mariavites), (1906).   34 'An artist by nature . . .': *Tygodnik Illustrowany*, 10 March 1906.

III. THE TEMPLE OF LOVE

Page 35 'As the Israelites in the desert . . .': *Dzieło Miłosierdzia*, 218.   36 report on education: *Przyczyny braku oświaty . . .* (Reasons for the Lack of Education), *Tygodnik Illustrowany*, 17 March 1906.   37 'It is not yet known . . .': 'Maryawici', ibid. 3 March

1906.   39n. pamphlets printed in Russia: e.g. Nikolay Reynke, *Mariavity* (St. Petersburg, 1910); K. Rovinsky, *Mariavity v Tsarstve Pol'skom* (St. Petersburg, 1910).   40 '. . . the state of his own soul': *Dzieło Miłosierdzia*, 228.   41 '. . . This search was not evil . . .': ibid. 227.   42 the entry into the New Jerusalem: ibid. 230.   43 Van Thiel's letter: printed in full in the jubilee number of *Mariawita* (Plock), May–June 1962.   43 'So often, spurred by pride . . .': *Dzieło Miłosierdzia*, 231.   43n. Kozlowska's 'understanding' about the new priesthood: ibid. 219.   45 the building of the Temple: ibid. 236–9.   49 'The others still walked . . .': Feldman's unpublished memoir.   49 'The Mariavites differ from other churches . . .': *Co to jest maryawityzm*, 79.   51 'The Last Moments of the Little Mother's Life . . .': *Ostatnie chwile życia Mateczki i Najświętsza Jej Ofiara*, in *Dzieło Miłosierdzia*, 275–316.   51n. Philip Feldman recorded . . .: in his unpublished memoir.   55 All this happened . . .: *Dzieło Miłosierdzia*, 308.

IV. THE DIVINERS OF THE THREE:

Page 57n. Kowalski's translation of *Tayna Tryokh: Królestwo Boże*, 31 Mar.–15 Aug. 1938. 60n. his commentary on Isaiah: see *Pismo Święte Starego Testamentu*, vol. II.   63n. 'Towianski's Work of Mercy . . .': *Królestwo Boże*, 20 July 1937.   65n. mention of *Le secret de la Salette: Królestwo Boże*, 15 Feb. 1937.   67n. 'The Sons of the Kingdom': on Towianski, ibid. 17 Oct.–24 Dec. 1929.   71 'The whole earth will be consumed by fire': from the announcement signed by Kowalski and printed in *Maryawicka Myśl Narodowa*, 6 Aug. 1924.   74 Lermontov's 'The Demon': translated in *Królestwo Boże*, 1 Sept. 1939.

V. THE MYSTICAL MARRIAGES

Page 77 'what the human eye hasn't yet seen . . .'; 'the wedlock that took place . . .'; 'And what is conceived . . .'; 'From this wedlock . . .': *Początki Królestwa Bożego na ziemi*, Kowalski's introduction to *Świadectwa*, p. 5 in *Dzieło Wielkiego Miłosierdzia* (1929 ed.).   78 'We print them . . .': ibid. 6–7.   80 'I didn't at first understand . . .': Mother Isabel's Testimony, ibid. 40.   87 'the soiled clothes . . .': footnote to Sister Honorata's Testimony, ibid. 84.   87 'All things that God creates . . .': Kozlowska's letter, quoted in Sister Gertrude's Testimony, ibid. 185.   88 'The Lord Jesus united me . . .': Sister Boguslawa's Testimony, ibid. 330.   89 'It was on 13 December . . .': Sister Melania's Testimony, ibid. 210.   90 I understood what it is to be denied . . .: ibid. 95.   90 Kowalski's birth and the Nativity: footnote to Sister Honorata's Testimony, ibid. 82.   91 'On the 22/23 of October 1923 . . .': ibid. 339–40.   92 'the Little Mother continues to unite body-souls . . .': footnote 1 to the Song of Songs, *Pismo Święte Starego Testamentu*, vol. II.   95 'In these marriages the Holy Spirit itself . . .': Bishop Andrew's Testimony, *Świadectwa*, op. cit. 194.   95 'This union lifted me out of . . .': Sister Gertrude's Testimony, ibid. 189.   95 'With a child's simplicity . . .': Sister Dilecta's Testimony, ibid. 291.   96n. the Bern conference of Old Catholics: see *Maryawicka Myśl Narodowa*, 16 Oct. 1924, for a detailed Mariavite report.   97 Sister Celestina describes . . .: *Świadectwa*, op. cit. 340–1.   98 'They all looked so incredibly young': conversation with Brother Augustine, somewhere in East Anglia, 21 March 1973.

VI. EROTIC RITUAL ON TRIAL

Page 99 'A Year's Stay at the Mariavite Convent': *Rok pobytu w klasztorze marjawickim* (Tołpyhowa), op cit.   101 *The Crimes of the Mariavites* . . .: M. Skrudlik, *Zbrodnie marjawitów w świetle dokumentów*: Part I (Warsaw, 1927); Part II, *Z tajemnic 'klasztoru' płockiego* (Warsaw, 1928).   101 the 'open letter': *Epoka* (Warsaw), 18 Aug. 1927.   102n. the so-called *Mysterium: Wieczory mesyaniczne. Misteryum* (Plock, 1928).   102n. another Jan Kowalski: *Kurjer Warszawski* (Warsaw Courier), 19 Sept. 1928.   103 trial expected to take a fortnight: ibid. 13 Sept. 1928.   103 people in the corridor could catch . . .: *Dziennik Płocki* (Plock Daily), 24 Sept. 1928.   103n. some only seven years old: ibid.

27 Sept. 1928. 104 One of the girls complained . . . .: see *Rok pobytu* (Tołpyhowa), op. cit. 104n. 'he seated her on his knees . . .': *Dziennik Płocki*, 21 Sept. 1928. 105 'One was horrified to listen to the details . . .': ibid. 24 Sept. 1928. 106 'Each of us went up to Kowalski . . .': as reported by Skrudlik, *Zbrodnie marjawitów*: Part II, 54–6. 106 Banasiak's morals questioned by the defence: see *Kurjer Warszawski*, 27 Sept., and *Dziennik Płocki*, 3 Oct. 1928. 107 '. . . kept calling them his royal daughters': *Kurjer Warszawski*, 30 Sept. 1928. 107 the *Warsaw Courier* lost its temper: ibid. 21 Sept. 1928. 107 'After that, convinced they already had . . .': *Dziennik Płocki*, 29 Sept. 1928. 108n. 'Why then did you make all those purchases?': ibid. 1 Oct. 1928. 109 'here they look white': ibid. 3 Oct. 1928. 109 Kowalski's round of embraces to dispel shyness: ibid. 6 Oct. 1928. 109 the Holy Ghost Junior: ibid. 110 Rogowski's speech: *Kurjer Warszawski*, 10 Oct. 1928. 110n. 'He can do what he likes . . .': reported to the author in a conversation with an ex-priestess. 111n. Zarębski's admission at the trial: *Dziennik Płocki*, 8 Oct. 1928. 112 Kowalski's speech: ibid. 12 Oct. 1928. 113 *Warsaw Courier* leader: *Po procesie marjawickim* (signed B.K.), *Kurjer Warszawski*, 12 Oct. 1928. 114 'The trial was not free from the tendency . . .': K. Askanas, in a letter to the author, dated 1 Sept. 1972. 114 'How can a nun still wearing a habit . . .'; 'He loved this dog more than his mystical wife': both testimonies in *Dziennik Płocki*, 3 Oct. 1928. 116 'We have to omit the most hideous moments . . .': Skrudlik, *Zbrodnie marjawitów*: Part II, 43. 117 'The Little Mother said to me . . .': printed at the end of *Brewiarzyk mariawicki* (1967 ed.).

VII. SUBTERRANEAN CHANNELS

Page 122n. 'Duchy ludzkie to duchy wcielone . . .': *Nowy Hexahemeron*, in *Królestwo Boże*, 10 Oct. 1929. 126n. 'The Third Heaven, which was prefigured . . .': *Pismo Święte Starego Testamentu*.

VIII. THE PRIESTESSES

Page 138 'an extraordinary light' in his cell: the happening of 12 Aug. 1937, reported in *Królestwo Boże*, 15 May 1938. 139 'The world is going to destruction . . .': Merezhkovsky, *Tayna Tryokh*, in *Królestwo Boże*, 31 Mar. 1938. 142 the ceremony of ordination: ibid. 4 Apr. 1929. 143 'On the New Priesthood of the Holy Virgins': *O Nowem Świętych Dziewic Kapłaństwie*, the pastoral letter of 14 Mar. 1929, in *Dzieło Miłosierdzia* (1929 ed.). 143 'the first Mass celebrated by a woman': *Królestwo Boże*, 4 Apr. 1929. 144ff. the tour of the Mariavite centres: reported in ibid. 13 June 1929. 145 Bishop Bartholomew's sermon: ibid. 1 Aug. 1929. 147 'On the Love of Our Beloved Little Mother': ibid. 18 July 1929. 148 'In the past it was the time of the male . . .': reported to the author by Brother Augustine, conversation of March 1973. 152 'When God was about to throw . . .': *Królestwo Boże*, 7 Nov. 1929.

IX. ADAM AFTER THE FALL

Page 159 The whole sequence . . .: The People's Mass is printed in full in *Brewiarzyk mariawicki* (1967 ed.). 159 there were no new parishes: *U Maryawitów* (Plock, 1934). 160 'the apostles had wives . . .': letter to Archbishop Ropp, 8 Dec. 1929, *Korespondencya między biskupami*. 160n. 'If the evidence of my immorality was written . . .': ibid. 162 Two Englishmen . . . had no doubt: conversation with Brother Augustine, March 1973. 162 the jubilee number of *The Kingdom of God on Earth*: *Królestwo Boże*, 5 Oct. 1934. 163 'Even though the whole world abandon you . . .': address of the Sisters novices, ibid. 163 Philip Feldman's background: from his unpublished memoir. 165 a personal account . . . of the deposition: TS. in the Feldman family's possession. 167 pastoral letter of 30 Jan. 1935: TS. copy in the author's possession. 168 'Dearest Brother': letter of 26 Feb. 1935, in Feldman's papers. 169n. 'A good Mariavite should every day . . .': *Wiadomości Maryawickie*, 15 Sept. 1935.   171–6 Kowalski's letters to Isabel from Rawicz: unpublished MSS. at Felicjanów.   171 'It seems to me that I have come . . .': letter of 10 July 1936.   172 So 'let our Temple be founded in human hearts': letter of 28 Dec. 1936.   172 'głoście że dla wszystkich . . .': letter of 6 Oct. 1936.   172 advice on the juice from grapes: letter of 21 Oct. 1936.   173n. Peasants saw Christ holding the host: see *Królestwo Boże*, 20 July 1937.   173n. He objected to Milton . . .: see letter of 9 May 1937.   173n. 'Cieszcie się tedy wszystkie . . .': *Stolica Boża i Baran-kowa*, in letter of 24 Nov. 1936.   174 'The Treachery of Feldman': *Zdrada Feldmana* (unpublished), dated 17 Apr. 1937.   174 'Don't praise me too much . . .': letter of 21 Mar. 1937.   175 'What Sister Celestina has . . .': letter of 26 Nov. 1937.   175 'here in the Poznan district they take us for Masons too': letter of 1 Aug. 1937.   175n. the Demon of Noon 'who removed the Little Mother . . .': letter of 15 May 1937.   176 'Our beloved Leader . . .': *Królestwo Boże*, 31 Jan. 1938.   176 The prison doctor had . . . placed a card . . .: letter of 15 July 1936.   177 'I apologize for writing in pencil . . .': *Królestwo Boże*, 30 June 1939.   177n. 'the reformed priest Skrzypiciel hanged himself . . .': ibid. 31 May 1939.   178n. 'Danzig and East Prussia should be returned . . .': ibid., 15 June 1939.   180 'She radiated that delicate angelic beauty . . .': *Wspom-nienia w wysiedlenia*, written in Nov. 1947, unpublished.   182 'Yes, the strength was there . . .': details from a conversation with Prelate A. Murat, Leicester, 2 March 1973. 183n. 'I had the impression that he knew . . .': letter from W. Gastpary to the author, 22 Mar. 1974.

X. THE SURVIVORS

Page 187 Kowalski sneered . . . 'retained the younger': *Królestwo Boże*, 24 May 1939. 203 'Because we would have had to make our position clear . . .': letter to the author from Chief Bishop Innocenty (Gołębiowski), 15 Nov. 1971.

XI. WITHOUT SECRETS THERE IS NO MYSTERY

Page 210 'Spouse of the Very God . . .': from *Brewiarzyk mariawicki* (1967 ed.).   211 'O Heavenly Prince, Saint Michael . . .': ibid. 423.   211 Litany to St. Michael: *Litania do św. Michała Archanioła*, ibid. 327.   211n. 'Redeemer of the Eternal Church . . .': ibid. 219–20.   215 'LITTLE MOTHER: Because of my Passion you will be joined . . .': *Adoracja z Objawień Mateczki*, ibid. 173.   218n. 'This way the Mariavites celebrate Mass . . .': ibid. 43.

EPILOGUE FOR TWO VOICES

Page 223 As soon as he saw the Mariavite pageantry . . .: conversation with Brother Augustine, March 1973.

Index of Names